ROUTLEDGE LIBRARY EDITIONS: COLD WAR SECURITY STUDIES

Volume 30

NATO'S CHANGING STRATEGIC AGENDA

NATO'S CHANGING STRATEGIC AGENDA
The Conventional Defence of Central Europe

COLIN McINNES

LONDON AND NEW YORK

First published in 1990 by Unwin Hyman Ltd

This edition first published in 2021
by Routledge
2 Park Square, Milton Park, Abingdon, Oxon OX14 4RN

and by Routledge
52 Vanderbilt Avenue, New York, NY 10017

Routledge is an imprint of the Taylor & Francis Group, an informa business

© 1990 Colin McInnes

All rights reserved. No part of this book may be reprinted or reproduced or utilised in any form or by any electronic, mechanical, or other means, now known or hereafter invented, including photocopying and recording, or in any information storage or retrieval system, without permission in writing from the publishers.

Trademark notice: Product or corporate names may be trademarks or registered trademarks, and are used only for identification and explanation without intent to infringe.

British Library Cataloguing in Publication Data
A catalogue record for this book is available from the British Library

ISBN: 978-0-367-56630-2 (Set)
ISBN: 978-1-00-312438-2 (Set) (ebk)
ISBN: 978-0-367-61240-5 (Volume 30) (hbk)
ISBN: 978-1-00-310481-0 (Volume 30) (ebk)

Publisher's Note
The publisher has gone to great lengths to ensure the quality of this reprint but points out that some imperfections in the original copies may be apparent.

Disclaimer
The publisher has made every effort to trace copyright holders and would welcome correspondence from those they have been unable to trace.

NATO's Changing Strategic Agenda

THE CONVENTIONAL DEFENCE OF CENTRAL EUROPE

Colin McInnes

London
UNWIN HYMAN
Boston Sydney Wellington

© Colin McInnes 1990

This book is copyright under the Berne Convention. No reproduction without permission. All rights reserved.

Published by the Academic Division of
Unwin Hyman Ltd
15/17 Broadwick Street, London W1V 1FP, UK

Unwin Hyman Inc.
955 Massachusetts Avenue, Cambridge, MA 02139, USA

Allen & Unwin (Australia) Ltd
8 Napier Street, North Sydney, NSW 2060, Australia

Allen & Unwin (New Zealand) Ltd in association with the
Port Nicholson Press Ltd
Compusales Building, 75 Ghuznee Street, Wellington 1, New Zealand

First published in 1990

British Library Cataloguing in Publication Data

McInnes, Colin, *1960–*
 NATO's changing strategic agenda: the conventional defence of Central Europe.
 1. North Atlantic Treaty Organisation. Strategy
 I. Title
 355.031091821

ISBN 0-04-445211-X

Library of Congress Cataloging in Publication Data

Applied for

Typeset in 10/11 point Bembo
Printed by Billing and Sons Ltd, London and Worcester

For Sally

'From now on I'm thinking only of me.'

Major Danby replied indulgently with a superior smile: 'But, Yossarian, suppose everyone felt that way.'

'Then,' said Yossarian, 'I'd certainly be a damned fool to feel any other way, wouldn't I?'

Joseph Heller, *Catch 22*

Contents

		Page	
	Acknowledgements		xi
	Abbreviations		xii
	List of tables		xiv
	List of figures		xv
	Introduction: changing strategic agendas		xvii
1	NATO, nuclear weapons and conventional defence		1
	Flexible response		1
	Problems with nuclear reliance		6
	Raising the nuclear threshold		8
	Minimum deterrence		13
	Common security		21
	Conclusion		29
2	The central front		31
	The political context		33
	The geography of the central front		39
	NATO: organization and deployment		44
	The WTO: organization and deployment		48
	Conclusion		57
3	The balance of forces		59
	Bean counting		60
	Measuring force effectiveness		72
	Analysing combat dynamics		79
	Conclusion		82
4	Soviet military doctrine		85
	The Great Patriotic War		86
	Stalin and the nuclear age		91
	The 'revolution in military affairs'		92

	Developing a conventional variant	95
	The Ogarkov revolution	103
	Gorbachev and 'new thinking'	104
	Conclusion	113
5	NATO operational doctrine	116
	AirLand Battle and US army doctrine	116
	Defending northern Germany: the British-NORTHAG concept of operations	134
	Follow-on forces attack (FOFA)	149
	Conclusion	161
6	Non-offensive defence	163
	The development of non-offensive defence	167
	The spider and the web: the SAS model	171
	Characteristics of non-offensive defence	174
	Criticisms of non-offensive defence	177
	Conclusion	183
	Conclusion	185
	Bibliography	187
	Index	198

Acknowledgements

Special thanks are due to the officers and officials of the UK Ministry of Defence, NATO and SHAPE who spared the time to talk to me but who cannot be mentioned by name, and to Lt. Col. Roger Smith and the staff of the Tactical Doctrine Retrieval Centre, Army Staff College, Camberley, for their willing help in tracking down source material. I would also like to thank Ken Booth and David Gates for their advice at various stages, and to Gary Sheffield who prompted the research in the first place. Finally I would like to tnank Susan Davies and Marian Davies for their word processing skills, and Pete Wright for his help and advice with computers.

Abbreviations

ADE	Armoured Division Equivalent
AFNORTH	Allied Forces Northern Europe (NATO)
AFSOUTH	Allied Forces South (NATO)
ATACMS	Army Tactical Missile System (NATO)
ATAF	Allied Tactical Air Force (NATO)
ATGM	Anti-tank Guided Munition
CENTAG	Central Army Group (NATO)
C3	Command, Control and Communications
C3I	Command, Control, Communications and Intelligence
CAS	Close Air Support
CFE	Conventional Forces in Europe
CGF	Central Group of Forces (WTO)
DIVAD	Divisonal Army Defence Gun (US)
ERA	Explosive Reactive Armour
ET	Emerging Technology
FEBA	Forward Edge of the Battle Area
FIBUA	Fighting In Built Up Areas
FLET	Forward Line of Enemy Troops
FLOT	Forward Line of Own Troops
FOFA	Follow-on Forces Attack
FPU	Firepower Unit
GSFG	Group of Soviet Forces in Germany
HDE	Heavy Division Equivalent
IDS	Interdiction-Strike
IGB	Inner German Border
INF	Intermediate-range Nuclear Forces
M+	Mobilisation plus (figures in days after mobilization)
MBT	Main Battle Tank
MD	Military District (WTO)
MLRS	Multiple Launch Rocket System (NATO)

MRD	Motor Rifle Division (WTO)
NATO	North Atlantic Treaty Organisation
NGF	Northern Group of Forces (WTO)
NOD	Non-Offensive Defence
NORTHAG	Northern Army Group (NATO)
NSWP	Non-Soviet Warsaw Pact
OCA	Offensive Counter-Air
OMG	Operational Manoeuvre Group (WTO)
OTA	(US Congress) Office of Technology Assessment
PGM	Precision Guided Munition
PLO	Palestine Liberation Organisation
POMCUS	Pre-positioning Of Material Configured in Unit Sets (US)
REFORGER	Reinforcement of Forces in Germany (US)
SACEUR	Supreme Allied Commander Europe (NATO)
SALT	Strategic Arms Limitation Talks
SAM	Surface to Air Missile
SAS	Study Group on Alternative Security
SHAPE	Supreme Headquarters, Allied Powers Europe (NATO)
STOL	Short Take-Off and Landing
STO(V)L	Short Take-Off and (Vertical) Landing
TRADOC	Training and Doctrine Command (US)
TVD	Theatre of Military Operations (Soviet)
V/STOL	Vertical/Short Take-Off and Landing
WEI	Weighted Effectiveness Indices
WGF	Western Group of Forces (Soviet)
WTO	Warsaw Treaty Organisation (Warsaw Pact)
WUV	Weighted Unit Value

List of tables

2.1	Frequency of water obstacles in West Germany	40
2.2	Divisional strength of Western TVD	51
2.3	Schematic illustration of Western TVD fronts and echelons	52
2.4	WTO readiness categories	55
2.5	WTO divisional readiness status	55
3.1	NATO estimates of the conventional balance of forces	62
3.2	WTO estimates of the conventional balance of forces	64
3.3	Battle outcome vs. force ratio	73
3.4	Hamilton estimates of NATO reserve manpower	77
5.1	Categories of FOFA operations	152
5.2	Technological deficiencies for FOFA tasks	155
6.1	A non-offensive air defence	170

List of figures

2.1	NATO Higher Military Command	31
2.2	Schematic illustration of NATO and WTO deployments on the central front	45
2.3	NATO central front commanders	46
2.4	Schematic illustration of Soviet command structure	50
2.5	NORTHAG–WGF order of battle	53
3.1	Atlantic to the Urals: NATO proposed sub-limits	66
3.2	(a) CFE: Warsaw Pact zoning proposal	67
	(b) Warsaw Pact alternative regional proposals	68
5.1	Schematic illustration of Soviet/Warsaw Pact concept of echeloning	151

Introduction: Changing strategic agendas

We live in interesting times. The truisms which have dominated the first four decades of the nuclear age are no longer insurmountable bastions of political or strategic reality. The extent and nature of the Soviet threat is under review. The days of a competitive relationship between the two blocs – which existed even in the headiest days of détente – may be numbered. There has already been some nuclear disarmament, unilateral and bilateral, and there is a further likelihood of deep cuts in the numbers of strategic nuclear weapons, the weapons which have figured most prominently in postwar strategic thinking. The very centrality of nuclear weapons to security policy, for so long the shibboleth of Western strategy, is being challenged not merely by peace activists and ivory tower academics, but by military officers and government officials (many of whom are retired and thus freed from the obsequies of office), and by major political parties. The debate between 'orthodox' and 'alternative' defence may be one which has yet to be won in the pages of learned books and articles, but the pace of political and military change is now such that this debate is being conducted against the background of a changing strategic agenda.

The strategic agenda of the early 1980s was set by hawks and super-hawks in the US. Responding to a perceived Soviet build-up of conventional and nuclear weapons, critical of détente and its strategic centrepiece SALT, and advocating a countervailing American build-up and strategic assertiveness, these critics achieved political influence in the first years of the Reagan administration. Thus the strategic agenda in the early 1980s was dominated by confrontation, arms racing and military posturing. Arms control became a forum for confrontation rather than negotiation. Diplomacy was replaced by rhetoric and wars of words, often conducted via the mass media. And defence spending, particularly in the US, was increased.

By the end of the decade this had changed. Just as the strategic agenda of the early 1980s was set by the hawks in Washington, so that of the late 1980s was set by the 'new thinking' in Gorbachev's Moscow. This new strategic agenda was dominated by the concerns of cost cutting and threat reduction. Unilateral troop reductions, unilateral cuts in short-range nuclear missiles, and the attempt to restructure conventional forces for defensive operations were all key Soviet developments as the prevailing mood of strategic dialogue began to shift from confrontation to cooperation. In this process, arms control emerged to a position of prominence. The possibility of major reductions in conventional and nuclear forces acquired more than a touch of reality. And a stability which relied less on the balance of terror and more on the removal of threatening weapons systems, force postures and military doctrines began to force its way into negotiations between the two blocs.

Where this will lead is uncertain. It may result in a new 'legitimate' international order; or it may be curtailed by new tensions and uncertainties, just as détente was reversed at the turn of the 1980s by the onset of the 'second cold war'. But for the present the strategic paradigm which has governed NATO strategy for the past 40 years — one of an unambiguous Soviet military threat and the centrality of nuclear deterrence — is beginning to look dated. That the perception of a Soviet threat is not yet obsolete may be in part due to old mindsets unable to react to the changing international security system. But it is also a product of the continuing presence of a massive WTO military machine in Eastern Europe still capable of offensive operations, of a cautious (if not necessarily pragmatic) approach to change, and of uncertainties over the political future of Gorbachev and the Soviet Union, over the political future and stability of Eastern Europe, and over the acceptance and implementation of a defensively oriented military structure and doctrine. Thus the Soviet threat remains for the present, though its nature and extent is under review.

Similarly, the dependence on nuclear weapons remains despite growing doubts over the wisdom and credibility of such a policy. With the Soviet achievement of strategic nuclear parity in particular, the credibility of the American nuclear guarantee was questioned (would the Americans use nuclear weapons and thus risk the possibility of uncontrolled escalation leading to their own destruction?). More, in what sense was a strategy which threatened to use nuclear weapons on NATO soil a strategy for the *defence* of NATO? Nuclear artillery shells and short-range missiles, from both NATO and the WTO, would destroy and/or irradiate the very territory NATO is committed to defending. Finally, the long-term prospects of a system based on the balance of terror were unsatisfactory. If the system worked indefinitely, then the confrontational bloc system developed in the cold war might continue indefinitely. Europe would remain a divided continent,

INTRODUCTION

dominated by the two superpowers, and a hostage to nuclear fortune. If the system failed the consequences would be too awful to contemplate. The nuclear component in NATO strategy has therefore been a major source of debate throughout the 1980s. Although this was accentuated by the INF deployment controversy, the debate was broader than the issues of cruise and Pershing II, and has remained after the signing of the INF treaty.

At the end of the 1980s NATO was faced with two major problems. The first was how to respond to developments in the Soviet Union and Eastern Europe; the second was the debate over NATO strategy and the criticisms of nuclear reliance. These two problems coincided in the debate over conventional defence. By reducing nuclear reliance, conventional defence could improve the credibility of NATO strategy. But was conventional defence feasible? And was it affordable within financial and manpower constraints? Was the conventional defence advocated by 'orthodox' strategists, involving large armoured formations and attacks by aircraft and missiles deep into WTO territory, compatible with the changing strategic agenda which emphasized threat reduction and cooperation? Would area defence concepts advocated by 'alternative' strategists be better suited to the evolving strategic relationship? Or were such concepts unrealistic for the modern high-technology armies on the central front?

This book was written at a time of change. It is not intended to be prescriptive, but is rather intended as an examination of one of the crucial issues facing NATO at present: the defence of its central front. The central front has lain at the very heart of NATO since its formation. Politically it marked the postwar division of Europe into two competing blocs, and militarily it represented the most important of NATO's three fronts, the area of greatest force concentration, and arguably the area of greatest threat. As the strategic agenda changes, the question of the defence of the central front will still remain critical. Questions of force reduction, conventional stability and defensive doctrines are likely to replace the traditional questions of nuclear use and perceived conventional inadequacies. This book examines the roles of conventional and nuclear weapons in NATO strategy, what constitutes the central front, its military structure, geography and the forces stationed there, the Soviet threat, and NATO's conventional doctrine. It concludes by examining one of the most important alternatives offered to current NATO doctrinal thinking, that of non-offensive defence. The focus is on doctrine rather than strategy, and on military rather than political problems. But the two cannot be divorced; rather they exist in a synergistic relationship, each feeding off the other. This is a point of considerable importance, since as the political relationship changes, so the doctrinal questions raised here will be considered in a new light. If doctrine fails to match politics, then tension will emerge not merely between these two levels of strategy, but possibly between East and West as well.

C. J. McI.
Aberystwyth
December 1989

1

NATO, nuclear weapons and conventional defence[1]

NATO strategy has been dominated by nuclear weapons, despite the fact that the vast majority of resources, human and financial, have been devoted to conventional forces. The reason for this is not difficult to identify: NATO has consistently relied upon the nuclear threat to deter war, rather than upon conventional forces to defend in the event of war. But this is beginning to change. Dissatisfaction with nuclear reliance is not new for NATO, but for the past decade the pressure has been unremitting. This dissatisfaction has received public prominence in the debates over INF and Lance modernization. But the question of nuclear reliance is broader than these two issues and concerns the entire thrust of NATO security policy. Although there is no critical mass of support within the Alliance for the abandonment of nuclear deterrence, the consensus has clearly shifted in favour of raising the nuclear threshold – in one commentator's words to place nuclear weapons on the 'back burner' of NATO strategy (Baylis 1988, p. 50). The direct corollary of this has been an increased interest in conventional defence, and the extent to which NATO can successfully defend its central front. The debate over the role of nuclear weapons in NATO strategy is the subject of this chapter; the subsequent question of whether NATO can successfully defend its central front is the subject of the rest of the book.

Flexible response

The NATO strategy of flexible response involves meeting an attack with direct defence at the same level of aggression, while retaining the option to escalate should NATO forces be unable to hold at that level. Flexible response thus balances defence and deterrence: NATO would begin by attempting to defend its territory, but its willingness to escalate and use nuclear weapons would hopefully deter attack. As Morton Halperin has scathingly commented:

'NATO doctrine is that we will fight with conventional weapons until we are losing, then we will fight with tactical [nuclear] weapons until we are losing, and then we will blow up the world' (Baylis 1988, p. 45). Flexible response was devised in the 1960s as a compromise between the various interests in the Alliance, particularly between the Americans who favoured a strategy which emphasized defence rather more than the previous NATO doctrine of massive retaliation, and the Europeans with their emphasis on deterrence. The result was more satisfactory as a political solution to these different requirements than as a military strategy. Flexible response did not provide a guide for military action, nor list the objectives which would contribute to a satisfactory military outcome. Rather it made a virtue of the uncertainty and vagueness which stemmed from the underlying compromise between defence and deterrence, by asserting that Soviet inability to determine when NATO would escalate would induce caution in decision-making. Flexible response was therefore a political strategy in that it attempted to influence Soviet decision-making, rather than a military strategy in attempting to influence the outcome of battle (Freedman 1986, pp. 130 and 158).

The compromise between defence and deterrence is the essence of flexible response. As Lawrence Freedman has pointed out it is a convenient form of words, or 'myth', which helps to promote unity amongst diverse factions (Freedman 1986, pp. 59). The vagueness of the strategy means that NATO officials can endorse it wholeheartedly while retaining different views over what that strategy actually consists of. In particular two broad interpretations of flexible response can be identified as coexisting, namely those of uncontrolled escalation and warfighting. These are described in detail below. The problem with this situation for NATO in the 1980s was not merely that flexible response was increasingly recognized as being little more than a 'myth', but that a number of issues emerged (particularly those of INF and Lance modernization) which threw the two interpretations into direct conflict. More than this, both interpretations became increasingly ragged in the face of concerted criticism.

Uncontrolled escalation

The uncontrolled-escalation approach to flexible response rests upon the premise that the central purpose of NATO strategy is to deter war. Even a conventional war would cause physical destruction, social upheaval and human suffering on a scale such that the priority is to deter war from ever happening. The means by which war is to be deterred is by threatening uncontrolled nuclear escalation: the initiation of hostilities would risk the destruction of both superpower heartlands so that it would be in neither's interest to start a war.

Not surprisingly it is largely the European members of NATO who derive comfort from this approach (Flanagan 1988a, p. 100). Europe would be in the forefront of any conventional war between NATO and the WTO and would thus suffer the greatest loss if war was contained at that level. Similarly, if nuclear weapons were used on a small scale at the tactical or theatre level, Europe would be devastated while the superpowers might remain relatively unaffected. If the superpowers believed that they might be able to avoid direct attack, and could limit the conflict, then they might risk starting a war or escalating to a low-level tactical nuclear use. But by threatening the security of the superpower heartlands through uncontrolled escalation war might be deterred (Blackaby 1984, p. 13; Kaiser et al. 1982, p. 1116). Thus this approach to NATO strategy attempts to couple conventional attack to strategic nuclear retaliation through the risk of uncontrolled escalation.

The essence of this approach is that uncertainty over the ability to control war produces caution and therefore deters. The fear that once a war began it would soon pass beyond the ability of either side to manage it would override any benefit an aggressor might identify. Quite simply the risks would be so great that any potential benefits would be obscured. Tactical and theatre nuclear weapons are important in providing links on the slippery slope to strategic nuclear war. Rather than providing identifiable thresholds, they serve to blur the process of escalation (Bundy et al. 1982, p. 755; Freedman 1986, pp. 64–5).[2] The inherent ambiguity of such weapons makes war uncontrollable, and therefore unthinkable. Similarly the failure to create either a workable command and control system for these weapons, or a detailed war plan for their use, assists deterrence in creating uncertainty for both the WTO and NATO (Bracken 1983; Bundy et al. 1982, p. 756; Sigal 1983, p. 116).

In this uncontrolled escalation approach conventional forces have a limited role in defending against 'smash and grab' raids, but their main role is to pose a sufficient obstacle that any Soviet attack would have to be massive and unambiguous. This clear, large-scale assault, coupled to the loss of substantial numbers of service personnel, would make nuclear use credible (especially the loss of American service personnel from the two US corps stationed on the central front, since the US has the decisive say in the use of nuclear weapons). NATO's conventional forces would act as a tripwire for the use of nuclear weapons. Security is guaranteed not by the ability to defend NATO territory but by the surety of escalation, and the danger that it cannot be controlled.

This is clearly not a strategy for war – indeed it has been described as 'the abandonment of strategy' (Freedman 1986, p. 140). Nor does it seem particularly satisfactory in dealing with the risk of accidental war. Finally it is unlikely to deter a gambler prepared to call NATO's bluff and chance that NATO, rather than risk losing control of the war, will impose such restrictions on nuclear weapons that they will be effectively removed from the conflict.

Warfighting

In contrast the second interpretation of flexible response emphasizes controlled responses and the ability to fight a war even after the first use of nuclear weapons. Nuclear weapons would be used against targets identified as important to the conduct of the war. They would thus have a military role as well as the political ones of warning and demonstrating resolve. Escalation would be controlled by the use of identifiable thresholds which, once crossed, would indicate that the war was being conducted at a new level. For flexible response three main thresholds have been identified: the war/peace threshold, marking the initiation of a major conventional war; the nuclear threshold; and the strategic threshold. Within this rather broad framework a number of other thresholds may be used. At the strategic level for example distinctions may be drawn between strikes against strategic nuclear forces and against cities.

The warfighting approach offers three major advantages over uncontrolled escalation. Firstly it is more obviously a strategy for the use of nuclear weapons, providing clear goals for war plans and force structures (Freedman 1986, p. 136). Secondly, in offering controlled responses it improves the credibility of extended deterrence. The Soviet possession of a strategic nuclear retaliatory capability, and particularly the achievement of parity, was seen as threatening the credibility of extended deterrence. That the United States should risk its own destruction to save Western Europe appeared to some incredible. But by threatening a limited, controlled response, and therefore by limiting the risk of strategic retaliation, credibility might be restored (Blackaby 1984 p. 17; Kaiser *et al.* 1982, p. 1160). And finally it allowed the United States to reduce the risk to its territory in the event of war. As Lawrence Freedman commented:

The logic of geography gives the United States an interest in defining the escalation process in terms of a succession of firebreaks, with the presumption that at each stage it might be possible to impose dominance. The West European interest lies in stressing the difficulty of establishing firebreaks and the consequent uncertainty as a source of deterrence. (Freedman 1986, p. 145)

This raises an important point. For the United States, warfighting represented a rational attempt to bolster credibility and limit risks to its own security. But for the Europeans it appeared to erode deterrence by reducing the risks for the *Soviet Union*. Some even suspected a US conspiracy to fight a limited war in Europe at the expense of the Europeans (Kaiser *et al.* 1982, p. 1160). As American strategists began to devise warfighting strategies in the 1970s and 1980s, so the Europeans became anxious over American intentions and reliability (Freedman 1986, pp. 67 and 142; Herken 1985, pp. 318–19). The desirability of a strategy which made war 'thinkable' – especially nuclear war – was less than apparent to the European members of NATO. The neutron bomb debate in the mid-1970s, in particular, highlighted these different concerns, with the Americans pressing for a more 'usable' tactical nuclear weapon, and the Europeans hesitant not merely over a weapon which killed people and left buildings intact, but over the clear American preference for warfighting (Bundy *et al.* 1982, p. 756).

In addition to these doubts over the desirability of warfighting, questions were raised over its practicability. A number of studies highlighted the difficulties involved in the command and control of nuclear weapons (Ball 1981; Bracken 1983). Distinguishing between the various levels of escalation also appeared less than straightforward: would the use of chemical or biological weapons signal an escalation? Would a strike by *theatre* weapons against targets in the Soviet Union be considered a *strategic* attack? And the impact of a nuclear war in Europe upon the environment, the world economy and global society would be such that to describe it as limited would appear something of an understatement.

A final concern was that warfighting was becoming not merely a means of improving the credibility of nuclear use, but something which could assist in the implementation of US foreign policy. This concern appeared particularly in the early years of the Reagan administration. For those Europeans who placed deterrence at the centre of NATO security policy, this was an alarming and dangerous reversal of accepted wisdom concerning nuclear weapons (Gray

1980a, pp. 24–46; Herken 1985, pp. 317–18). Nuclear weapons were no longer viewed exclusively as a means to deter war, but as tools to be used to gain political advantage.

Within the warfighting approach conventional forces remain a secondary consideration. Nuclear not conventional forces are used to offset Soviet military strength. Although attention is shifted towards a more recognizably military strategy, this derives from the changed role of nuclear weapons, not from any increased emphasis on conventional forces. Nuclear weapons therefore perform a dual function in warfighting strategies. They assist in the defence of NATO by destroying WTO forces, a task conventional forces would be incapable of achieving in such a cost-effective manner. And the inevitability of nuclear use (given conventional weaknesses) would create a deterrent effect.

Problems with nuclear reliance

The nuclear reliance made explicit in both of the approaches to flexible response outlined above has been criticized on a number of grounds. The first and most obvious criticism is that the stategy is only satisfactory for so long as the 'balance of terror' works and war is succesfully deterred. Should deterrence break down, then the best that could be hoped for would be a nuclear war limited to Europe. This alone would be sufficiently cataclysmic as to cast doubts over the worth of such a strategy. But if war could not be limited to Europe, then the result might be the destruction of the world as we know it. The penalty for the strategy's failure, then, is sufficiently grave as to cause concern over its value.

But the strategy has not failed, at least not according to the advocates of nuclear reliance. Nuclear advocates (or, to use Ken Booth's description, 'nuclear addicts') argue that NATO's reliance on nuclear weapons has produced an unprecedented period of peace in Europe, despite the considerable strains and pressures of the cold war. Nuclear deterrence has worked, and will continue to work *because* the penalties of failure are so high (Booth 1989, pp. 72–3; *Statement on the Defence Estimates* 1987, p. 13).

This defence of the *status quo* is not particularly satisfactory. Europe has had similar periods of peace in the past, the period between Waterloo and the Crimean War being one such example. Interestingly this period of peace was a product not so much of the costs of aggression, but of the stability of the European states system. One may similarly argue that the postwar peace has been a product of a stable European system. Peace has occurred not because of the nuclear threat, but because both blocs have been satisfied with the division of Europe at the end of the Second World War and have not been inclined to upset the *status quo* (Booth 1989, p. 72). Moreover, from the inception of flexible response in 1967, and probably even before, nuclear deterrence has not been sufficiently tested as to demonstrate whether it can keep the peace. The case that flexible response has worked is not proven; the best that can be said is that it has not failed.

More worrying is the fact that, even if nuclear deterrence could be shown to have worked in the period since 1945, that is no guarantee of its future success. No strategy, and no international system, can be guaranteed against failure. The European system may evolve or break down under pressure from political change, while nuclear deterrence may fail by accident, miscalculation or from a deliberate gamble. When this is coupled to a strategy of early nuclear use the situation is dangerous and potentially disastrous (Baylis 1988, pp. 44–5).

The second problem for flexible reponse was that by the 1980s it was a strategy which was becoming increasingly incredible. Early nuclear use, and particularly warfighting, required that nuclear weapons be closely integrated and responsive to developments in the land war. But NATO's short-range nuclear weapons were ill-suited for this: the decision-making process for their use was cumbersome and insensitive to the requirements of a fast moving war; many of the weapons were obsolete and of limited military use, while their location near the inner German border (IGB) made them tempting targets for pre-emptive attack (either by nuclear or conventional forces); and the dual capability of many nuclear delivery systems (particularly aircraft and artillery) created uncertainty over their availability (Barnaby 1978; Sigal 1983, pp. 109–17) This situation was exacerbated by the INF treaty which removed some of NATO's newer, more reliable, more controllable and less vulnerable systems. The use of short-range nuclear weapons by NATO would also cause radiation and even blast damage to NATO territory. And even if this collateral damage was minimized, the Soviets would be likely to respond by using their nuclear weapons against NATO territory. Thus NATO strategy would involve the nuclear destruction of the territory the Alliance was created to defend. For some this was not only incredible but highly unsatisfactory (Blackaby 1984, p. 12; Bundy *et al.* 1982, pp. 756–7; Freedman 1986, p. 63). Finally, with the advent of strategic parity doubts were cast over the credibility of extended deterrence (Flanagan 1988a, pp. 100–1; Pierre 1986, pp. 10–11).

Two final problems have been identified with the strategy of nuclear reliance. Firstly, the requirement for an early decision to use nuclear weapons would place considerable strain upon the Alliance's political structure. At what would almost certainly be a time of great tension and uncertainty anyway, this requirement could prove to be a major source of division. Alliances formed in peacetime do not always survive the transition to war, and the necessity for an early decision on an issue which might spell thee destruction of a number of the member states in a quite literal sense could create strains which the Alliance might not be able to bear. The disintegration of NATO would be a real possibility (Freedman 1986, p. 149). Secondly, it is difficult to see how troops could be motivated to fight if they faced the prospect of early nuclear escalation (Flanagan 1988a, p. 102). The build-up to battle is an anxious time for troops (Holmes 1986). If they are placed in a situation where the chances of military success are negligible, and where the battlefield is likely to become a nuclear holocaust with little chance of survival, then the strain may become too great for them.

Raising the nuclear threshold

The growing dissatisfaction with this strategy of nuclear reliance, and particularly with the planned early use of nuclear weapons, culminated in the 1980s with a variety of proposals to raise the nuclear threshold (Beach 1986; ESECS 1983; Pierre 1986). Many of the supporters of this reform were associated with the defence establishment. Indeed one of the most prominent advocates of reducing nuclear reliance was the senior NATO military commander, SACEUR General Bernard Rogers (Rogers 1982) and by the mid-1980s raising the nuclear threshold had achieved broad élite support (Baylis 1988, p. 55; Flanagan 1988a, p. 102).

Raising the nuclear threshold was far from a radical response to the problems posed by nuclear weapons. It was a modification *within* the strategy of flexible response rather than a reform of that strategy. In particular it did not remove the reliance on nuclear weapons. Rather it advocated postponing nuclear use until a later stage in the conflict – though quite at what stage nuclear weapons would be used was usually left vague. Raising the nuclear threshold acted as a compromise. It eased concerns over nuclear reliance without offering anything sufficiently radical as to alarm defence establishments and upset the balance of interests within the Alliance. It was a palliative rather than a solution.

NATO, NUCLEAR WEAPONS AND CONVENTIONAL DEFENCE

Despite the moderate nature of the proposal, raising the nuclear threshold encountered a number of objections, two of which were particularly familiar. The policy of nuclear reliance had been, in part at least, a response to the perception that NATO forces were decisively outnumbered. Although a number of recent analyses have challenged this perception (see Ch. 3), the defence establishment and advocates of raising the nuclear threshold tended to adopt a comparatively pessimistic assessment of the military balance. In particular they tended to assume that NATO would be hard pressed to defend successfully with conventional weapons alone over a protracted period of time (Beach 1986, p. 155). Thus if the nuclear threshold was to be raised, the conventional balance had to be shifted in NATO's favour. In the mid-1980s, with conventional arms control showing no signs of progress, this could only be achieved by unilateral NATO efforts. Thus raising the nuclear threshold became associated with strengthening conventional forces (Blackaby 1984, p. 14; Flanagan 1988a, pp. 100 and 102). A number of priorities were identified for this: improving sustainability so that NATO had the fuel and ammunition to fight for weeks rather than days (in particular attempting to reach the NATO target of 30 days of war stocks); better training of reserves to give NATO the forces to cope with a fully mobilized WTO assault (especially the large numbers of Soviet second strategic echelon divisions which might arrive in the second or third weeks of an assault); and modernization of conventional forces, particularly the exploitation of a new generation of force multipliers, collectively termed 'emerging technologies' or ETs (Flanagan 1988a, p. 102).

This all cost money; as Lawrence Freedman has commented, NATO leaders tend to see conventional forces and strategies largely as a resource problem (Freedman 1986, p. 74). Although defence budgets were growing in the early 1980s, by the late 1980s they had stalled or were in reverse, with the future looking not at all promising. The prospects of major and continuing funding for new weapons and forces to raise the nuclear threshold therefore had begun to appear bleak.

This pessimism is mitigated by three important factors. Firstly, by the late 1980s conventional arms control had developed a momentum which, when coupled to unilateral WTO troop reductions (particularly the cuts in Soviet forces announced by Mikhail Gorbachev at the UN in December 1988) offered the prospect of a more favourable conventional balance. Secondly, a number of analyses using sophisticated means of assessment began to appear which questioned the degree of WTO conventional superiority. In particular the generally higher standard of NATO equipment and training, the weight of NATO tactical air power, the constraints on WTO mobilization and problems in concentrating sufficient force given the force to space ratios offset to varying degrees WTO numerical superiority (see Ch. 3). And finally, although defence budgets began to stand still or even fall back in real terms, the increases of the early 1980s had borne important dividends in improving equipment and training levels, and in raising some NATO members' defence budgets to a higher level so that falling expenditure had somewhat less than catastrophic effects. Therefore the tendency to equate raising the nuclear threshold with increasing defence budgets now looks questionable.

The second familiar objection to attempts at reducing nuclear reliance is the possibility of an adverse impact on deterrence. Since the immediate risks from aggression would be less, particularly for limited acts of aggression, deterrence might be weakened by raising the nuclear threshold and war made more likely. The prospect of annihilation would recede sufficiently for war once more to be considered as a policy option. For Europe such a war would be a disaster, but for the superpowers it might not be (Flanagan 1988a, pp. 100–1; Freedman 1986, p. 76). There is also the possibility of signalling weakness: by reducing reliance on nuclear weapons NATO might be seen as weak and unwilling to use these weapons when necessary, undermining deterrence.

These fears appear exaggerated. Aside from the point that the policy of early nuclear use lacks deterrent value through its incredibility, there are two major reasons why raising the nuclear threshold does not undermine deterrence. Firstly, the nuclear component is not removed from NATO strategy, nor is it even placed on the 'back burner'. The threat of nuclear escalation remains. Stronger conventional forces would be used to create time to negotiate a diplomatic settlement to the war before nuclear annihilation occurs. They are not intended to create the capability for a protracted defence of NATO territory. The threat of Armageddon would remain the central component of NATO strategy. Raising the nuclear threshold is used to ease concerns over the credibility and wisdom of this threat, not to replace it. Defence has not replaced deterrence.

Secondly, the belief that deterrence would be undermined by raising the nuclear threshold underestimates the deterrent value of conventional forces. Modern, high technology war is an extremely costly as well as risky venture. A major conventional war, even if limited to Europe, would not leave the superpowers unaffected. The superpowers' wars in Vietnam and Afghanistan have indicated the domestic costs of comparatively small-scale, low risk ventures.

A European war would create vastly greater strains, economically, politically and socially. Although the economic disruption and human suffering might not be as protracted as the first two world wars, it would make up for that in its intensity. But even if the Soviet Union ignored or was willing to accept these costs, the probable consequences of aggression would still act as a deterrent to war: if the invasion began successfully, NATO would in all probability escalate and use nuclear weapons; if it failed, then an orderly retreat would be unlikely and the future of the Soviet political system would be in jeopardy (Freedman 1986, pp. 138 and 156).

Thus the two familiar problems encountered when moving away from a strategy of nuclear reliance – of finding sufficient resources and of the impact on deterrence – do not pose major obstacles to raising the nuclear threshold. Rather the major problem with this approach is that it does not do enough to solve the problems produced by a strategy which ultimately relies on the threat of mutual annihilation for security. Raising the nuclear threshold does not change the security paradigm based on nuclear threats. Rather it attempts to create an opportunity for a diplomatic solution to a conflict before nuclear weapons are used. Thus the central problems of a strategy of nuclear reliance are not solved, merely delayed in terms of the conduct of a war. Neither the credibility of nuclear responses in an age of parity, nor the illogic of a strategy of escalation (which if ever enacted would mean at best the nuclear devastation of Europe, East and West, and at worst global annihilation) are resolved by raising the nuclear threshold. Security is still inextricably linked to a threatened nuclear response, and whether this response comes at an early or late stage in the conflict these fundamental problems still remain.

The major advantage in raising the nuclear threshold lies in the creation of a gap between the outbreak of war and the use of nuclear weapons. In this gap efforts at a diplomatic resolution of the conflict may be undertaken. But the value in this is not as clear as might at first be imagined. If the Soviets are ever sufficiently motivated as to launch a large-scale attack against NATO (a venture not to be undertaken lightly), it is unlikely that they would stop merely because NATO threatened to use nuclear weapons. After all, that threat would have existed when the Soviets were contemplating aggression in the first instance. It failed to deter then, and nothing would have altered to make that threat more of a deterrent since. Nor does it seem likely that, having committed themselves to a large and costly invasion, Soviet leaders would suddenly 'come to their senses' and withdraw. Too much political and military capital would have been invested, and the momentum of war would be too great for the war to stop simply on account of cold feet or second thoughts. Rather something has to be done to change the minds of Soviet leaders. Since that something cannot (by definition) be a nuclear response – not even a demonstration shot – then it must be some event at the conventional level. By increasing the emphasis on conventional forces, advocates of raising the nuclear threshold hope to deny the Soviets a quick victory (i.e. one won within a few days by forces stationed in Eastern Europe) and through this force them to negotiate. But again the question must be asked: why would the Soviets stop and negotiate at this stage in a conflict? Having committed themselves to invasion, having incurred substantial political, military, human and economic costs, having weakened NATO (perhaps critically), and with second-echelon forces about to be committed to the attack, why would the Soviets stop and talk?

It is of course conceivable that, having been denied a quick victory, the Soviet Union would realize that it had miscalculated and would therefore sue for peace. But this would seem to rely on two further factors: firstly that NATO demonstrates a *continuing* ability to defend conventionally, removing the possibility that the Soviets might believe NATO's defensive position would crumble if the war was continued for a few days more; and secondly that the Soviet leadership is sufficiently shocked into stopping and reversing the momentum of war. Merely slowing a Soviet advance would seem unlikely to provide the sort of shock necessary to reverse the momentum of war. Rather what is required is a conventional defeat sufficient to shock the Soviet leadership into suing for peace.

But if the logic of the position is such that NATO must defeat the Soviet first echelon and demonstrate an ability to continue to defend successfully, then why retain a reliance on nuclear escalation? If to have the desired effect conventional forces must be more than an extended tripwire, why continue to rely on nuclear escalation, particularly given the problems of nuclear reliance identified above? This led to the position of minimum deterrence outlined below. Raising the nuclear threshold is a halfway house which is most appealing to those seeking an acceptable political compromise to the dilemma of unease over nuclear reliance and the priority of deterring war. Raising the nuclear threshold eases concerns over nuclear reliance, but does not remove the nuclear guarantee. Politically this was an attractive compromise for NATO in the 1980s. But the strategic logic of this position was rather less apparent.

Minimum deterrence

One alternative to flexible response which was offered in the 1980s was that of minimum deterrence. Whereas the two approaches outlined above viewed nuclear deterrence as the ultimate guarantor of Western security, and therefore placed escalation at the heart of NATO strategy, advocates of minimum deterrence placed much less emphasis on nuclear weapons. At the heart of minimum deterrence is the conviction that it is in no one's interest to go nuclear. Nuclear weapons are useful only in deterring nuclear threats and as weapons of the last resort. Any other use would be irrational, incredible or at the very least extremely unwise. Minimum deterrence therefore argues that nuclear weapons should be removed to the 'back burner' of NATO strategy and security policy (Baylis 1988, p. 50). This would create a safer and more stable European order. Battlefield nuclear weapons in particular should be reduced in numbers and emphasis since they have little or no convincing doctrinal use, would create enormous collateral damage to Western Europe, and create the impression of decoupling from the American strategic nuclear guarantee while offering no surety that their use would not push NATO and the WTO onto a slippery slope towards mutual annihilation (Freedman 1986, p. 77).

By reducing the emphasis on nuclear weapons NATO would also ease the serious concerns over the morality and legality of their use. Nuclear weapons, with their potential for mass destruction and enormous collateral damage – even if used on a limited scale – sit uneasily with the traditional Western concepts of the just war. Nuclear weapons seem to violate the two central just war principles of proportionality (that the weapons used should not cause harm and suffering disproportionate to the ends sought) and non-combatant immunity. The twentieth century has seen a steady erosion of these principles with the advent of total war and weapons of mass destruction. But nuclear weapons provide a qualitatively different level of destruction to contend with and justify. More, the threat of mass destruction which is central to the theory of nuclear deterrence directly contradicts these principles. It is one thing for just war principles to be violated in the course of a war; it is something else to place their violation explicitly at the centre of strategies formulated before a war. The combination of a strategy which explicitly contradicts the two principles of proportionality and non-combatant immunity, and the awesome destructive power of nuclear weapons, has therefore caused considerable moral unease (Ramsay 1968; Walzer 1977).

Although there is no specific legal restriction on the use of nuclear weapons, some concern has been expressed over the possible legality of their use. A first strike is clearly banned under the terms of the UN Charter, but escalation from conventional to nuclear war poses a more difficult legal question. It is unclear whether the first use of nuclear weapons is illegal through the provisions of the Hague Convention of 1907, which establishes the principle of limitation on the rights of a belligerent to harm an enemy; through the indiscriminate nature of these weapons which violates the principle of non-combatant immunity; and through the probability that fallout from nuclear weapons would affect non-belligerent states (Blackaby 1984, pp. 6–7). Minimum deterrence eases these strategic, moral and legal concerns by reducing the emphasis on nuclear weapons.

Two distinct approaches to minimum deterrence can be identified. The first argues that although nuclear weapons should receive less emphasis, the threat of escalation should remain to create uncertainty in the minds of Soviet planners, and as a weapon of last resort.

> The aim of the strategy would be to allow the Alliance to say to the Soviet Union, 'if you invade conventionally, we have the capability to defend conventionally for a considerable period of time. But we are not ruling out the possibility that we just might use nuclear weapons first, especially to demonstrate our resolve to resist. And if you use nuclear weapons against us, don't forget that we have a devastating retaliatory capability'. (Baylis 1988, p. 49)

Conventional attack is deterred primarily through the ability to defend NATO territory, but the retention of a minimum deterrent capability acts as a weapon of last resort should conventional deterrence fail and NATO begin to lose. It would also act as a variable to create uncertainty in the minds of Soviet planners.

The second approach is that NATO should take the more radical step of abandoning the threat of nuclear escalation. This policy of 'no first use' received considerable attention when advocated by four eminent American commentators, all of whom had held senior positions in a variety of administrations,[3] in the influential journal *Foreign Affairs* (Bundy et al. 1982). The willingness to escalate has consistently been a central theme in NATO strategy and in the Alliance's approach to security. To abandon it would not only require a radical reform of the existing strategy of flexible response, but would create something akin to a culture shock for

NATO planners. The Atlantic Alliance has been constructed upon the belief that war must be deterred and that deterrence is best achieved through the threat of nuclear retaliation. A commitment to no first use of nuclear weapons would therefore create major ramifications for the entire outlook of the Alliance. But if nuclear use is both unreasonable and unwise, then such a commitment would have advantages in its greater rationality and as a means of promoting a more stable European order (Bundy et al. 1982).

In a strategy of no first use, nuclear weapons would be retained to deter a nuclear attack by the Soviet Union, but any other role would be abandoned. Whereas the minimum deterrent approach outlined above perceives advantages in retaining the threat of first use in creating a degree of uncertainty and as a last resort against the possibility of conventional defeat, advocates of no first use reject these on political and strategic grounds. On strategic grounds the advantages offered are seen as minimal at best. If nuclear weapons are explicitly placed on the 'back burner' of NATO strategy, then the uncertainty created in Soviet minds over their possible use must be limited. Similarly even if a conventional defeat was imminent, the use of nuclear weapons would only trigger a spiral of destruction which would lead to even greater defeat. In reply, however, it may be stated that the *threat* of possible use does not mean that these weapons would actually be used. Therefore a degree of uncertainty (however small) might be created at little cost. And even if these weapons were used, if they were used in a careful and controlled manner as a warning and to demonstrate resolve, then the catastrophic nuclear retaliatory cycle might not ensue.

On political grounds it is argued that a policy of no first use would create greater crisis stability and promote allied unity. In a major study on the command and control of nuclear forces, Paul Bracken concluded that the most significant danger posed by nuclear weapons lay not so much in the inability to control the weapons in war, but in controlling the crisis before a war. Bracken identified the cycle of warnings and alert levels that would dominate a crisis as a major source of instability (Bracken 1983). In this context short-range nuclear weapons based near the inner German border would be particularly worrying as they would have to be placed on high levels of alert early in a crisis due to their particularly vulnerable situation. But placing forces on high levels of alert (albeit to guarantee their survivability) may appear threatening to the other side, and an action–reaction cycle can rapidly follow. By reducing the emphasis on nuclear weapons, and particularly on short-range nuclear weapons, minimum-deterrence advocates of both schools hope to reduce this problem. Where no first use differs here is in a matter of degree. By reducing even further the dependency on nuclear weapons this danger is further reduced. But whether this difference is sufficient to be important appears unlikely. As both approaches to minimum deterrence would remove most if not all short-range weapons, and would reduce dependency on nuclear weapons in general, and as both would need to maintain some alert system to guarantee the survivability of the minimum nuclear forces remaining, the difference appears marginal.

On promoting Allied unity however, the two approaches are fundamentally different. Writing at a time of great debate over nuclear weapons within the Alliance (in the middle of the cruise and Pershing II debate), the four Americans viewed no first use as a means of promoting Allied unity by removing nuclear weapons and the consequent question of modernization from the centre stage of NATO politics. For this 'gang of four' the problem for NATO was not one of deterring war but of keeping the Alliance together (Bundy *et al*. 1982, p. 765). The continued existence of the Alliance as a united body acted as the major deterrent to war. If it fell apart over the question of nuclear modernization then, even if some of the new weapons were deployed, deterrence would be severely undermined. Advocates of retaining first use do not necessarily disagree with this assessment of the importance of Allied unity to deterrence, but do disagree with the argument that no first use would unite the Alliance. Given the broad range of interests and opinions within NATO there is always the danger that radical reforms will generate discord rather than unity. By retaining the threat of escalation, albeit at a much lesser level of importance, a balance can be struck between those concerned with the problems of nuclear reliance, and those concerned with retaining some escalatory component in NATO strategy to reinforce deterrence. But by removing the threat of nuclear escalation, no first use would upset this balance of interests and could therefore threaten the very unity it seeks to promote.

Concern over the implications for deterrence of reducing the emphasis on nuclear weapons lay at the centre of many of the doubts expressed over minimum deterrence. Whereas raising the nuclear threshold at least retained the option of escalation, minimum deterrence relegated this to a marginal position. How then was war to be deterred? Fears were expressed that not only would minimum deterrence (and no first use in particular) greatly reduce Soviet uncertainties in calculating the effects of aggression, but that the failure to threaten Soviet territory would undermine deterrence. The risks and uncertainties involved in attacking Western Europe would be so reduced as to make war conceivable as a policy option (Freedman 1986, p. 78; Kaiser *et al.* 1982, pp. 1160–2). Minimum deterrence also raised the spectre of a war limited to Europe: the strategy's failure to couple European security directly and unequivocally to an American strategic nuclear guarantee could create the opportunity for a war fought on European soil alone (Kaiser *et al.* 1982, p. 1160). When this was linked to concerns over deterrence being undermined, the gate seemed to have been opened for a conventional war in Europe.

But this is to underestimate minimum deterrence. In this approach deterrence is not undermined but altered. War is deterred not so much by the threat of nuclear retaliation and devastation, but by the capabilities of conventional forces to deny victory to the WTO, and in particular a quick victory. The basis for this is the assumption that, if the Soviets ever did launch a large-scale attack against NATO, they would try to avoid becoming bogged down in a prolonged war of attrition. Rather they would attempt to secure a quick, *Blitzkrieg*-style victory (Donnelly 1985, pp. 23 and 27; Vigor 1983, pp. 2–9). Such a victory would be secured largely by forces already stationed on the central front and in Eastern Europe – the first strategic echelon (see Ch. 2). By demonstrating a capability to hold or even to defeat this force, and thus deny the WTO a quick victory, NATO may deter conventional attack by the use of its conventional forces alone.

The deterrent effect of conventional forces has until recently received little attention (Lebow 1987; Mearsheimer 1983; Orme 1987). Most deterrence theorizing has concentrated on nuclear weapons, and this has tended to obscure the deterrent potential of conventional weapons. Whereas elaborate, highly intellectual and often very abstract theories of nuclear deterrence have been devised, conventional deterrence has suffered from a lack of detailed analysis. To complicate matters further, until recently comparatively little attention was paid to military doctrine outside the professional military services. Academics and policy analysts were generally well versed in the elaborations of nuclear deterrence, but had little detailed knowledge or understanding of conventional doctrine.

Although deterrence theorizing has concentrated almost exclusively on the nuclear dimension (for which it was, by and large, devised) the underlying theoretical structure identified for nuclear deterrence can also be loosely applied to conventional arms. Deterrence is based upon a cost/gains analysis whereby the likely costs of aggression are judged to outweigh the potential gains. In this context two types of deterrent threat have been identified: deterrence by punishment (the threat of unacceptable damage to the state in reply to aggression), and deterrence by denial (the ability to deny aggression the gains it seeks) (Snyder 1961). As conventional weapons lack the potential to deliver massive societal punishment quickly and cheaply (especially when compared to nuclear weapons) their ability to deter by punishment is limited. Much more promising is their ability to deter by their capability to defend successfully against attack, and thus deny victory to an enemy.

The problem with conventional deterrence by denial is in ensuring that a potential aggressor does not perceive the chance of victory as a risk worth taking. For example it may be argued that the risks for the Soviet Union in attacking Western Europe would be minimal if NATO relaxed its nuclear threat, while the potential gains would be enormous. Put starkly, if the Soviets attacked conventionally the worst that might happen from Moscow's perspective would be that these forces are defeated and have to retreat ignominiously; the best would be that NATO collapses as a united bloc, and large chunks of Western Europe fall under Soviet control.

To deter conventionally NATO must therefore convince the Soviets that (a) the worst-case scenario is the most likely; and (b) that the consequences of defeat are real and substantial. The first of these is a function of military strength and political unity in crises. Efforts must be made to demonstrate not only that NATO has the military strength to *defeat* the Pact's first strategic echelon, but that the Alliance would not dissolve under the various pressures of an East–West crisis. Judging these two factors involves a substantial subjective element. Perceptions are therefore important, and consequently sending the right signals to Moscow. But a number of substantive measures can also be undertaken to reinforce these two factors. Although assessing military strength may be difficult and may incorporate subjective judgements, assessments are based on the objective fact of numbers of men and weapons, and on the quality of manpower and equipment. Through arms control and force modernization, NATO can affect these measures and consequently revise assessments of its military strength. Similarly political unity can be improved by minimizing those areas of likely disagreement in a crisis. The most obvious area of disagreement is the question of nuclear release. By adopting a policy of minimum deterrence and therefore removing the necessity for a quick decision on nuclear release, NATO would reduce this potential source of disagreement. Reducing the emphasis on nuclear weapons would also mean that Alliance members would have less to fear (the prospect of nuclear devastation being considerably reduced) and might therefore be less likely to waver in a crisis. By minimizing potential areas of friction such as these, NATO may affect Soviet calculations on Alliance unity and so reinforce deterrence.

The second requirement for conventional deterrence to work is that the costs of a defeat for the Soviet Union be substantial. The simple human and economic costs of a war − appalling though these would probably be − may not be sufficient for this. Military and political leaders can misjudge these costs, or may even be willing to incur them in an effort to obtain some political, military or economic goal. Thus although these costs may be an important component in deterring attack, they may not in themselves be sufficient − particularly in a crisis situation where different concerns may assume pre-eminence.

But these would not be the only costs of a Soviet conventional defeat. Such a defeat would have repercussions for the Soviet Union internationally, in Eastern Europe, and domestically. Internationally its reputation would be dealt a severe blow both by its aggressive actions, and by its failure to exploit its military strength − the one area in which it is undoubtedly a superpower. The ramifications of this would be considerable. At the very least the Soviet Union would fall from its position of parity with the United States, and it may well fall from superpower status. This would be particularly so if its economy, weakened by war, is unable to rebuild its military strength. Its position as the pre-eminent communist power would also be threatened, and its ability to influence events worldwide would be severely undermined through the consequent lack of power and prestige.

Possibly even more importantly, Eastern Europe may be plunged into turmoil which a weakened Soviet Union might be unable to control. Here a variety of factors may come into play. It is likely that some East European governments would not be wholehearted in their support of a war against NATO, even if they did eventually acquiesce to Soviet pressure. This is particularly so with the non-communist governments beginning to emerge at the end of the 1980s. Defeat might then lead them to question even further their loyalty to the Soviet Union and the WTO: historically alliances have tended to suffer under the strains of defeat. Even if the WTO governments did support such a war, there is no guarantee that the people of Eastern Europe would be enthusiastic about this. Defeat may lead to an undermining of those governments which supported the war. In this situation the disintegration of the WTO and defections from the Soviet bloc would be very possible.

Finally, in the Soviet Union itself defeat may threaten the established power structure. At the very least the position of those leaders who advocated aggression would be under severe pressure while, at the other end of the scale, defeat (possibly compounded by an intensification of the nationalities problem) may threaten the dismemberment of the Soviet Union, or place at risk the entire system of communist rule.

The costs of defeat for the Soviet Union may therefore be considerably more than simply the human and economic costs. If NATO can convince the Soviets that defeat is possible, and that these are the probable costs of such a defeat, then conventional deterrence may work. Persuading the Soviets of this may not be easy given the highly judgemental nature of the necessary assessments. But nuclear deterrence also includes a substantial subjective element, while the credibility of this threat may be somewhat more realistic than that of the irrational threat of nuclear escalation.

In reply to this advocacy of a greater emphasis on the deterrent power of conventional forces, critics of minimum deterrence focused upon the inadequacies of NATO's conventional forces (Kaiser *et al.* 1982, p. 1163). For these critics, NATO's conventional inferiority would fatally undermine the credibility of conventional deterrence. Conventional forces would be outnumbered and unable to inflict a defeat upon an invading force. More, given NATO's inability and unwillingness to improve force levels dramatically, this position of inferiority could not be easily corrected. The familiar problem of resource constraints which had helped to rationalize NATO's strategy of nuclear reliance, and had been used against advocates of raising the nuclear threshold, was once more deployed against advocates of minimum deterrence. As with the debate over raising the nuclear threshold, though, so with minimum deterrence this criticism can be countered with arguments that it is too simplistic in its assessment of the military balance, and that it is rapidly becoming obsolete with WTO unilateral actions to cut force levels, and with the movement in conventional arms control. The problem of resource constraints is one whose day, if not quite yet passed, certainly appears to be slipping away.

Two further criticisms have been raised specifically in connection with no first use, namely that such a policy would increase the chance of nuclear blackmail, and of what to do if conventional forces began to lose (or even lost) the war (Kaiser *et al.* 1982, pp. 1160-5). Neither of these are relevant to the first use school of minimum deterrence: nuclear blackmail would be deterred by the retention of a NATO nuclear deterrent; and if conventional forces did begin to lose, NATO would escalate as a last resort. Nor is it clear that no first use particularly increased the chance of, or NATO's vulnerability to, nuclear blackmail. No first use does not advocate abandoning all nuclear weapons, and the retention of minimum deterrent arsenals would therefore act as a deterrent to nuclear blackmail (Booth 1988, p. 12; Herring 1988).

The problem of what to do if conventional forces began to lose has been less easily dealt with. Aside from arguing that the military balance should be improved to prevent this from happening, the answer has seemed to lie either in a protracted war of attrition akin to the Second World War (which would exploit the West's superior economic strength over an extended period of time) or in the argument that it would be better to live under communist rule than to die in a nuclear Armageddon – that it is 'better to be red than dead'. Although neither of these is particularly reassuring, neither is the strategy of nuclear reliance which, if NATO began to lose, could lead to global devastation. Defeat is an unpalatable situation and no strategy can offer a satisfactory solution to this. But at the very least no first use offered a somewhat less cataclysmic end point than nuclear reliance.

Common security

A second alternative to the NATO strategy of flexible response is that of common security. This simple but radical idea is based upon the belief that long-term security can only be attained through policies which promote the common good, thus reducing tension and defusing potentially provocative actions. Common security first achieved prominence when advocated by the independent Palme Commission (Palme 1982). It has since been advocated by a number of thinkers on 'alternative' defence, and provides an important new way of thinking about security (Booth 1989; Vayrynan 1985; Windass 1985).

Postwar Realist international relations theory has portrayed the international system as an arena dominated by the competition for power. States are trapped in a Hobbesian world of perpetual conflict. The international system is characterized by anarchy and the 'state of war', whereby states are either preparing for war (by building and maintaining armed forces, creating alliances, etc.), or fighting wars. Security in such a world is guaranteed principally by unilateral means (the maintenance of armed forces and preparation of defences), but also by alliances. These alliances can range from formal treaty commitments, such as the 1949 Atlantic Treaty which founded NATO, to more fluid and informal arrangements such as the nineteenth-century balance of power system. Security is centred upon the state (hence the common use of the term 'national security'), whose principal function is the promotion of its own security at the expense of its enemies (Waltz 1979). In the Realist interpretation of the international system, we live in an age of 'armed peace': security, and hence peace, is guaranteed by military strength. NATO's military strength – in particular its nuclear weapons – maintains the peace by threatening the Soviet Union and its allies. But according to critics of Realism this is unsatisfactory on three counts. It is an inaccurate picture of the international system; its advocacy of nuclear deterrence as the means for promoting peace is dangerous and short-termed; and the 'national security' approach is flawed and prone to backfire.

To deal with each of these problems in turn, the Realist interpretation of the international system is inaccurate because not all relations are dominated by conflict. The Scandinavian countries for example live in a state of mutual cooperation. Nor does war, or the threat of war, dominate all conflicts – what conflict there is in the EEC does not assume a military dimension. Indeed peace is the norm in the modern international system, and war the exception. Therefore not all states live in a 'state of war', nor are all conflicts irredeemable (situations which can at best be managed, and can only be resolved by victory or defeat in war). Britain and France, enemies for much of the last millennium and belligerents on several notable occasions, now exist in a relationship in which war is unthinkable. The international system is not necessarily a 'war system'. Rather there are indications that relationships can be formed in which the military dimension is of little or even no importance (Booth 1989).

Secondly, the centrality of nuclear deterrence to the current system of armed peace is dangerous and a short-term expedient only. It is dangerous because it has become increasingly difficult to believe that nuclear weapons will continue to maintain peace given the irrationality (and hence incredibility) of the threat of mutual destruction. Nuclear deterrence also assumes a degree of technological stability. It assumes that technological breakthroughs will not create a first-strike capability. But in an age of technological dynamism this appears somewhat optimistic. The experience of SDI alone tends to suggest that such faith is misplaced. It is partly through this fear of technological instability that nuclear deterrence has promoted rather than restrained arms races. Both sides pursue technological advances through fear of the other side achieving a breakthrough. The resulting arms race inherently contains the potential for destabilizing the 'delicate balance of terror' and is therefore dangerous as well as expensive. Finally the system of nuclear deterrence is short-termed because it contains no concept of system change. Deterrence works best when operating in a system of clearly defined opposing blocs. It is less satisfactory when these blocs relax and the lines dividing them are less clearly drawn.[4] Preferring this clearly divided world, nuclear deterrence encourages policies which will further such a world, and which accordingly hinder the development of a more cooperative system. When change does occur, nuclear deterrence is not well equipped to meet the demands of a system in flux. It can not only be a brake on change, but can become obsolescent (Buzan 1987b, p. 269; Hellstrom and Rothschild 1985, p. 219; Hoffman 1985, pp. 57–8; Vayrynam 1985, p. 4).

For some advocates of common security, the problems involved with nuclear deterrence are such as to require a move away from deterrence and towards nuclear disarmament (Palme 1982; Krass 1985; Vayrynam 1985). For others nuclear disarmament is an unrealistic goal (at least for the foreseeable future), and therefore a strategy of minimum deterrence is advocated within a common security framework (Buzan 1987b; Hoffman 1985). But both are agreed that a new approach is required in which nuclear deterrence is removed from its position of centrality in security policy, and is replaced by a more satisfactory and long-term solution to security (Hellstrom and Rothschild 1985, p. 219; Hoffman 1985, p. 59).

Finally, the national security approach is unsatisfactory on two counts. Firstly unilateral attempts at security – the basis of the national security approach – are undermined in the nuclear age by the existence of assured nuclear retaliatory capabilities and the widespread environmental consequences of nuclear use. Since the risks of deterrent failure (mutual destruction and worldwide environmental catastrophe) are shared to an unprecedented extent, viewing security as a 'national' problem is quite inappropriate (Buzan 1987b, p. 266). And, secondly, the national security approach is prone to backfire through the workings of the security dilemma. The security dilemma identifies a relationship whereby attempts to improve one state's security by increasing its level of armaments may lead to a perception of increased threat by other states, prompting a countervailing reaction. An action–reaction spiral then begins, the result of which is that security and stability are improved for neither side. Rather, the reverse may occur as both sides are left in a position of heightened mistrust and at a higher level of armaments (Jervis 1978, pp. 169–70).

According to Jervis, the operation of the security dilemma is affected by two variables. The first of these is the ability to distinguish between defensive and offensive weapons and policies. If some weapons are purely defensively oriented, then an increase in such weapons would not accelerate the security dilemma as they would pose little or no additional threat. Conversely if weapons or policies were offensively oriented, then they would appear threatening and could therefore stimulate the security dilemma (Jervis 1978, pp. 186 and 199). The difficulty however lies in distinguishing between what is offensive and what is defensive. Most modern weapons systems can be used for either purpose. And even ostensibly defensive weapons can be used for tactical defence when on the strategic offensive. (In 1973 the Egyptians used surface to air missiles – weapons with a defensive role - to provide air cover for their offensive across the Suez Canal.) Therefore even weapons which are procured for defensive purposes can be seen as possessing some benefit for offensive operations, and can appear threatening.

Jervis's second variable concerns whether it is easier to conduct defensive or offensive operations. If the defence is superior then an increase in armed forces would pose less of a threat. This defensive superiority would have a dampening effect on the security dilemma. Conversely if the offence holds the advantage then the security dilemma would be highly sensitive to increases in military power.

The balance between offence and defence is determined by the geography of the states involved and the level of technology (Jervis 1978, pp. 187–98). If borders are protected by major geographical obstacles such as mountains, seas or large rivers, then the defence will have an advantage, while the absence of such barriers would ease offensive operations. But the effect of this ought not to be overestimated: such barriers are no more than a hindrance whose value may vary according to circumstance. The American island-hopping campaign in the Pacific, the Allied invasion of Normandy, and the Egyptian attack across the Suez Canal all demonstrate that 'secure' borders do not prevent attack. Geographical conditions can therefore only dampen the workings of the security dilemma.

The second factor determining the balance between offence and defence is that of technology. Some care needs to be taken here. There is a danger of adopting too simplistic a view of the role of technology in the offence/defence balance. For example the deadlock of the First World War is often attributed to the increased power of artillery, and the success of the *Blitzkrieg* in the Second World War to the internal combustion engine used by tanks and motorised transport. Thus technology is said to have determined the character of the two world wars and the balance between offence and defence in them. But in the First World War both 1914 and 1918 were characterized by major and highly mobile offensives, and many of the decisive battles of the Second World War were won by fixed defences (Kursk, Leningrad, Alam Halfa). In both of these cases there was little change in technology to account for a seeming reversal in the balance between offence and defence. Attributing success in battle to technology alone also tends to ignore many of the human and circumstantial factors which might be equally or more important (the particular battle scenario, the degree of surprise achieved, the abilities of the respective commanders and men). Thus even if the technological balance can be determined – a point Jervis concedes as being far from easy – its effect on success in war is not decisive, and therefore its impact on the security dilemma may be limited (Jervis 1978, pp. 187–98; Wheeler and Booth 1987, p. 326).

Although the security dilemma is a useful analytical tool, as Wheeler and Booth note its importance can be overestimated. Clearly the security dilemma does not operate in situations where there is a stable expectation of peace ('security communities' such as the EEC). In contrast when there is no expectation of stable peace the security dilemma is tautologous: it merely states a proposition which is, logically, always true. But the most important point is that these two positions represent extremes which do not often occur: states rarely exist in conditions of pure hostility, or in security communities. Rather they tend to exist in what Wheeler and Booth term the 'insecurity trap':

> many states are unable to be 'friends' with others because of real or imagined incompatibilities, but they are unwilling to fight because of the limited benefits and excessive costs of such an outcome . . . States cannot live in positive peace with others, but they do not see any profit in war. (Wheeler and Booth 1987, p. 317)

States must therefore manage their insecurity. The level of insecurity and the degree of management required may vary, but it will rarely reach the extremes of either the security dilemma or the security community. Thus the relationship between the United States and the Soviet Union (and between NATO and the WTO) falls short of total enmity. It is a limited adversarial relationship.

The two superpowers exist not in the security dilemma, but in an insecurity trap. For states in the insecurity trap, war remains a possible but unlikely instrument of policy (Wheeler and Booth 1987, p. 320).

Common security attempts to meet these concerns by offering a new approach to thinking about and to conducting security policy.

> 'Common security' describes a reformed international system beyond the present one, which is characterized by political tensions, strategic instabilities, continued technological sophistication of weaponry and fears of nuclear warfare . . . To this end, 'positive' and even 'irreversible' processes contributing to common security must be created. This means, furthermore, that 'nations must come to understand that the maintenance of world order must be given a higher priority than the assertion of their own ideological or political positions'. (Vayrynan 1985, p. 1; quotation from Palme 1982)

Common security attempts to move away from an international system focused on the threat or use of force by encouraging trends which reduce fears and vulnerabilities. In particular it asserts the centrality of interdependence. Stable long-term security can only be attained if states feel neither threatened nor vulnerable. Thus there is a mutuality of interests in reducing those factors which contribute to such fears and vulnerabilities. Common security therefore provides an image to which policy can be directed (Hoffman 1985, pp. 54–6; Buzan 1987b, pp. 265–6 and 278; Booth 1988, pp. 9–10) but it is as a process that it is most important, not an end.[5] Common security is as much about encouraging positive trends as providing an end-point solution to the problem of European security. A number of policies have been identified as contributing to this process. These are not mutually exclusive, nor is the list below comprehensive. Rather they indicate some of the trends which a common security approach might include.

1 *Arms control* figures prominently in much of the literature on common security. It is advocated as a means of controlling the technological arms race and therefore preventing the deployment of threatening or destabilizing military systems (Hellstrom and Rothschild 1985, p. 220; Vayrynam 1985, pp. 6–9).

2 *Confidence-building measures* have similarly been emphasized as a means for reducing fears. These may consist of verbal reassurances (for example a declaration of no first use of nuclear

weapons), or linked to specific actions such as the creation of a nuclear-weapons-free zone (Hellstrom and Rothschild 1985, p. 221; Vayrynam 1985, p. 9).

3 *Non-provocative defence/non-offensive defence* is widely accepted as a necessary precondition to common security. By reducing or eliminating offensive weapons systems and moving towards a structurally defensive force posture, offensive capabilities would be dramatically reduced to the point where military threats were no longer credible (see Ch. 6).

4 *Nuclear disarmament.* Common security identifies nuclear weapons as a major source of insecurity, so it is not surprising that most advocates of common security support some degree of nuclear disarmament. Two schools of thought can be identified. The first considers nuclear weapons to be so threatening and destabilizing that nothing short of total nuclear disarmament will suffice. The second views total nuclear disarmament as unrealistic. Problems of verification, policing and third-party agreement (especially China, but also near-nuclear and newly nuclear states) would dog any such attempt. Minimum-deterrent arsenals should therefore be retained, though without any potentially destabilizing counterforce potential (Buzan 1987b, pp. 268–70).

5 *Non-military dimensions.* The debate over common security involves more than the 'hardware' questions of weapons and force structure. Since security concerns more than purely military considerations, other issues (such as economics, schisms within society and the relationship between poverty and security) have been raised in an attempt to widen the understanding of what constitutes security. Certain commentators have argued that, as security is a culture-bound concept, advancing common security requires an understanding and accommodation of cultural variables (Hellstrom and Rothschild 1985, p. 221; Vayrynam 1985, p. 1).

6 *International security regimes.* Stanley Hoffman has identified the general lack of international security regimes as a major factor in limiting the perception of commonality in security. Whereas states have identified unilateral economic and financial actions as having potential boomerang effects through the independent nature of the international economic and financial system, and have therefore established a variety of international regimes to manage this interrelationship, few such regimes operate in the realm of force. The creation of a variety of regional and global security regimes would assist in raising the perception of common interest and could provide the mechanisms for peaceful change, peacekeeping,

verification and possibly international policing (Hoffman 1985, pp. 55–6). As a result of the establishment of such regimes, a legitimate international order may be encouraged. Such an order would be characterized by states agreeing on what is permissible in foreign policy as regards both aims and methods. In a legitimate international order

> states would have a justifiably high expectation that there will not be a major war, and that in the peace which prevails, their core values will not be under threat. If each major power is basically satisfied, this will ensure that none need express its dissatisfaction against the prevailing international order by a revolutionary foreign policy. (Booth 1989, p. 89)

Common security offers a radical alternative for NATO defence not merely in terms of policy and strategy, but in the manner in which security is considered. The way in which it thinks about security is fundamentally different from the more traditional approaches outlined above. Although a critical mass has yet to develop in favour of common security, and it notably lacks broad élite support in the West, the idea is beginning to gain in popularity and significance. But common security is no panacea, and problems can be identified with it. Its approach tends to be Utopian, particularly in assuming a common conception of what would assist in promoting security, and what a legitimate international order would constitute. Although it is unclear to what extent common security has to be a shared approach, the implication is that the degree of cooperation must be substantial. But the possibility for disagreement over the substantive issues, as opposed to principles, might be considerable. Similarly the possibility of misinterpretation over the parameters of cooperation also exists – i.e. what is and what is not to be included. The essence of this problem is that ideas of what constitutes common security may diverge and may therefore produce friction which might undermine the essential basis of trust, much as divergent views over what constituted détente in the 1970s assisted in its downfall. Finally the strategy of non-provocative/non-offensive defence has been subjected to substantial criticism over its viability (see Ch. 6) and has arguably yet to gain the necessary degree of military credibility.

But these problems are no greater than the problems afflicting other strategies, and to some extent are considerably less. Much of the fear of 'Utopianism' and incredible strategies stems from the fact that common security consists of unfamiliar concepts and new thinking. The shibboleths of the past 40 years have acquired a degree of comfort through their familiarity, regardless of their contemporary feasibility or credibility. Alternative thinking by its very nature is unsettling and offers unfamiliar paradigms. Thus, although there are some 'hard' problems of credibility and feasibility with common security, these can be exaggerated by its radical nature.

Conclusion

The four approaches to NATO strategy outlined above each envisages a difference role for conventional forces. In the uncontrolled-escalation approach they act as little more than a tripwire; in raising the nuclear threshold they provide a pause before nuclear release; in minimum deterrence they are required to defeat an attack; and in common security they are to be structured in such a way as to provide defensive capabilities alone. As the credibility of nuclear use has declined so attention has begun to focus on the latter two strategies.

Notes

1 Some of these ideas first appeared in my 'NATO strategy and conventional defence', in Ken Booth (ed.), *New Thinking about Strategy and International Security* (London: Unwin Hyman, 1990).
2 An example of this was the Pershing II which was perceived by the Americans as a theatre weapon because of its range limitations, but which the Soviets considered to have strategic possibilities through its ability to hit targets in the Soviet Union. Its use in war could therefore lead to inadvertent escalation.
3 The so-called 'gang of four' were McGeorge Bundy, Special Assistant to the President for National Security Affairs from 1961 to 1966, George F. Kennan, former Ambassador to the Soviet Union, Robert S. McNamara, Secretary of Defense from 1961 to 1968, and Gerard Smith, head of the US delegation to the SALT talks from 1969 to 1972.
4 The US failure to deter the North Korean invasion of South Korea, for example, has been attributed in part to its failure clearly to identify its commitment to the South. The line of containment had not been clearly drawn.
5 Booth uses Joseph Nye's distinction between 'process Utopians' and 'end-point Utopians':

> Most utopian visions . . . point to what are considered to be a better set of future conditions. Ideas about general comprehensive

disarmament or world government are of this type . . . In a sense history comes to an end when end point utopias are reached . . . 'process utopias' [are] benign or pacific trends with the end point being uncertain. The process utopian takes modest, reformist steps in order to make a better world somewhat more probable for future generations. What exactly that better world would look like must be settled by future generations, when the possibilities and new problems become clearer. We cannot now see far enough ahead. (Booth, 1988, p. 9).

2

The central front

The defence of NATO's central front involves a number of considerations, including technology, weapons, doctrine and forces. One factor which is often ignored, however, is the structure of the central front, and its relationship with and implications for its defence. As Steven Canby has noted, there is a stark contrast between the fascination of today's strategists with technology and the attention paid to military organization by classical strategists (Canby 1989, p. 26). This chapter therefore attempts to outline the 'strategic geography' of the central front. Its principal concern is the structure of forces and the impact of geography. The following chapter examines the balance of forces, and subsequent chapters consider doctrine and the related question of technology.

The central front is one of five main commands under NATO's Supreme Allied Commander Europe (SACEUR), who is in turn one of the three main military commanders in NATO (see Fig. 2.1). Running south of Schleswig-Holstein (part of Allied Forces

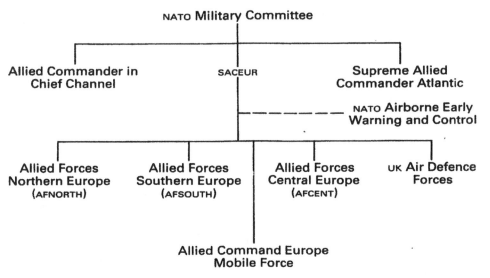

Figure 2.1 NATO Higher Military Command

Northern Europe) along the entire length of the West German border with East Germany and Czechoslovakia (what will for convenience be collectively termed the inner German border, or IGB), the front is central to NATO geographically, politically and militarily.

Geographically the central front sits between Allied Forces Northern Europe and Allied Forces South (AFNORTH and AFSOUTH respectively), is supported by Allied Command Channel and Allied Command Atlantic, and forms the keystone to NATO's defences. Politically, running along the IGB, it is the symbol of the postwar division of Europe. Militarily it contains an unparalleled peacetime concentration of force. In terms of numbers of units, firepower and levels of sophistication the forces deployed by NATO and the WTO either side of the IGB represent an awesome accumulation of military power. The most sophisticated weapons and support equipment available to both alliances are deployed there; many of the most advanced high technology systems are designed with the requirements of the central front in mind; and units deployed there are often amongst the most capable available maintained at high states of readiness. Almost all the forces are mechanized: aside from a high proportion of tanks, infantry ride into battle in tracked armoured vehicles deploying cannons or missiles of their own, and much of the artillery is also on tracked armoured vehicles; command posts are mobile, as are anti-aircraft guns and missiles and many radar systems. The firepower of these units is staggering. Heavier, more destructive shells are fired over longer ranges and at faster rates of fire than ever before, while guided missiles of unprecedented accuracy are carried by aircraft, helicopters, armoured vehicles, or even by the solitary infantryman. In the air large numbers of aircraft and helicopters pose complex and disparate threats to each other and to forces on the ground, while the airwaves are saturated by communications equipment allowing commanders far removed from the battlefield to talk to (and, with the advent of TV cameras on remotely piloted vehicles, see) small-unit commanders involved in tactical engagements and firefights – provided communications are not jammed by the ever more complex electronic warfare equipment.

The central front is the pivotal arena for any East–West conventional conflict. Whereas other theatres might be important the central front has assumed a pre-eminence which is only partly a product of its political and geographical centrality. Whereas NATO might suffer reverses in other theatres, defeat on the central front would be an unparalleled disaster. A wedge would be driven through NATO, exposing the two flanks and the whole of Western

Europe. Whether NATO could survive this crisis is debatable. That nuclear weapons would be used seems probable under the current strategy of flexible response. Whatever, if NATO wishes to offer a credible conventional defence, it is on the central front that it must do it.

The political context

No military assessment of the central front can afford to ignore the political background of modern-day Europe and of the two alliances. To a greater or lesser extent the forces on the central front, their size, structure, roles, doctrines and problems are all determined by the political context of the past 40 years. Although this context is complex and ever-changing in its details, it is possible to identify some of the broad themes and patterns which have underpinned politics within and between the two blocs.

At the most basic inter-bloc level, central Europe is divided into two powerful alliances with two neutral but pro-Western states to the south (Austria and Switzerland). The two alliances are often portrayed as being in an overtly competitive relationship, the degree of hostility varying over the past 40 years. It is also common to view the relationship as a zero-sum game – that which is to the advantage of one will be to the detriment of the other. From this have arisen the concepts of the 'security dilemma' and 'common security' outlined in the previous chapter.

The politics of NATO are dominated by the fact that the bloc leader and military superpower – the United States – is removed from the focus of confrontation – Europe – by several thousand miles of the Atlantic Ocean. This is not merely a substantial logistical problem, but a major political feature. The Atlantic Treaty establishing NATO was signed in 1949 with the specific purpose of tying the United States into the defence of Western Europe. That such a formal commitment was necessary, and remains so, is indicative of a perception that American and West European interests may not and sometimes do not coincide. In the 1980s this difference was seen to arise in a number of areas. West European security is dominated by events in Europe. The United States however is a world power with worldwide interests, of which Europe is only one. Some commentators have perceived a shift of emphasis in the 1980s away from the predominately European focus of the 1970s towards a greater emphasis on the Pacific basin. Similarly the United States has identified interests in Central America, the Middle East and the Persian Gulf which have led to various degrees of military commitment. In contrast, European commitments in these areas range from the marginal to none at all. Thus there is an important difference in perspective between Europe and the United States, and one which has grown rather than diminished in the 1980s.

Following from this is the question of the nature and extent of the American commitment to Europe. Although few would question that the Americans remain committed to Europe, two sets of concerns have arisen based on the realization that the United States is a world power, physically removed from Europe. The first set of concerns questions the *degree* of American commitment. In the 1960s de Gaulle publicly questioned whether the United States would expose itself to nuclear devastation by using nuclear weapons in the defence of Western Europe. With the growth of the Soviet nuclear arsenal in the 1970s, and the arrival of strategic parity (or even nuclear inferiority), this danger has increased. Thus the threat of nuclear retaliation has posed questions over the American nuclear commitment to Europe.

This is not a problem new to the 1980s; the only difference is that some of the more extreme estimates of the nuclear balance have strengthened the hand of the doubters. What is new, or is perhaps more accurately described as the re-emergence of an old problem, is the question of the strength of the American *conventional* commitment to Europe. To some extent this is a product of the perception which emerged during the Reagan Presidency of the United States being a power with world interests, not one whose security concerns were dominated by the single theatre of Europe. Thus, although Europe remained important to American national security perceptions, its position of pre-eminence was to some extent undermined. More publicly, though, this is a product of concerns over burden-sharing: the argument that the United States contributes disproportionately to the defence of Western Europe, and that the European members of NATO should do more for their own security – an argument which boils down to spending more on defence. In particular, critics of European defence spending point to the fact that NATO agreed to a 3 per cent annual increase in spending during the early 1980s, a figure only met by the United States (and arguably by Great Britain). For American critics, the Europeans are getting a free ride, and if they are not willing to pay for their own defence then why should the United States? This climaxed in the Nunn Amendment of 1984 which threatened to pull large numbers of troops out of Europe unless the Europeans spent more on defence.[1]

The arguments over burden-sharing are complex (the Europeans for example pointed out that American increases in the 1980s barely cancelled out reduced spending in the Carter years). Although some of the pressure has been reduced there is still a strong feeling in certain American circles that the United States is contributing a disproportionate amount to the defence of Western Europe, and that its burden should be reduced – if necessary by unilateral measures.

The second set of concerns addresses not the degree but the nature of the American commitment. They range from leftwing criticisms of excess American political influence in Europe, influence which for some verges on a form of imperialism, to concerns over different American/European conceptions of security. American initiatives on nuclear warfighting, arms control, strategic defence and out-of-area operations in the 1980s indicated that a gap had emerged between mainstream European and North American thinking. Although a free alliance will always encounter differences of opinion between members, the combination of American pre-eminence in NATO and a perceived insensitivity to European concerns made the appearance of any such gap an important Alliance issue.

In addition to these problems of American–European relations, there are a number of other strands to NATO's political backcloth. One important factor is the European concern over nuclear policy (to some extent present in the United States as well in the form of the freeze movement), which has led to various calls for unilateral nuclear disarmament, deep cuts in nuclear arsenals, raising the nuclear threshold, and no first use of nuclear weapons. This movement reached a popular peak in the early 1980s, focusing on the stationing of cruise and Pershing II missiles in Europe. Although a powerful political force, the movement failed to achieve a decisive political breakthrough in any of the more important NATO states. The movement's popular appeal now appears to be on the decline, but its intellectual basis remains a testing critique of the 'regressive mindset' of nuclear deterrence.

Another important factor in NATO politics has been the question of resource constraints, particularly financial but also in manpower. As equipment costs continue to rise above the level of inflation, so the cost of defence rises. Although NATO states on the central front are clearly amongst the wealthiest on earth, defence expenditure is constrained by opportunity costs in other areas of government budgets (more money spent on defence might mean less on health, housing or social security). Thus NATO states periodically face defence reviews which cut back on either the money available for forces, or on the number of forces. In particular, after the boom early years of the Reagan administration, the United States' defence budget of the late 1980s–early 1990s is facing substantial cutbacks, British defence policy appears to have embarked on a review 'by stealth', while the Netherlands and Belgium encounter continuing problems over force levels. For West Germany, however, the problem is more one of declining manpower: as those born in the baby boom end their national service, so the numbers replacing them are substantially reduced. The West German government have gone some way to rectifying these manpower problems by extending the length of conscription and increasing the number of reservists, but further increases may be difficult due to their political unpopularity (Hubatshek 1988, p. 574; Schulte 1988, p. 1327). So it is that, despite the comparative wealth of NATO, pressures on force levels appear omnipresent (Cordesman 1988).

The peculiar position of West Germany creates an additional political dimension. As any war fought on the central front would be fought in the Federal Republic, West Germans are understandably none too keen on war breaking out. This has helped produce two sets of ideas. In one the danger of a conventional war being almost as destructive as a nuclear war has led some West Germans to call for a low nuclear threshold to increase deterrence, rather than raising the nuclear threshold and increasing the chance of conventional war (Kaiser et al. 1982). The other set of ideas is a reaction to the large numbers of short-range nuclear weapons in Europe, which if used would devastate German territory. The emphasis here is to reduce and even remove reliance on nuclear weapons, and to adopt a non-provocative force posture based on purely defensive conventional forces (von Bulow 1986; Gates 1987; Saperstein 1988).

Associated with this, a major West German preoccupation over the last three decades has been that any war be fought as far to the east as possible, limiting damage to West German territory and civilians. Although this strategy of forward defence has the added advantage of displaying NATO's determination to defend all of its territory, it has been criticized by many as limiting operational freedom of manoeuvre, and even by some as creating a Maginot Line mentality (Bagnall 1984; Isby and Kamps 1985, pp. 14–15). Although there does now seem to be a willingness to allow greater flexibility in defence, the concern over forward defence is still present.

A final problem concerning West Germany is that of the likely reunification with East Germany. The state of Germany was artificially divided after the Second World War into zones of occupation by the victorious Allies. Although the Western Allies amalgamated their zone into the Federal Republic, the Soviet zone remained separate. With the fall of the Honecker government in East Germany, and the profound changes which followed in late 1989, the prospect of a unified Germany emerged as a realistic ambition for the first time in 40 years. The reunification of Germany remains a NATO goal, and a deepseated desire on the part of the Germans themselves. But the division has been seen by a number of European states and the Soviet Union as a useful means of restraining German strength and influence. In NATO West Germany is one of the three most important states (with the United States and Great Britain). It is economically, politically and militarily strong. Similarly East Germany, formerly considered one of the most loyal of the WTO northern tier states, is also economically and militarily the strongest. The reunification of Germany would therefore produce a singularly powerful European state – perhaps a European superpower – dominating other European powers in terms of its strength and influence.

In addition to these distinctive West German concerns, some consideration must be paid to the position of France. In 1966 de Gaulle withdrew France from NATO's integrated military structure. This was partly through his perception of alliances as being incredible in the nuclear age (would an American President risk the destruction of New York by using nuclear weapons to save a European city?). It was also a reaction to what he saw as the domination of NATO by the British and Americans. NATO forces and headquarters (including the top military headquarters in Europe, SHAPE) were required to leave French territory, and France withdrew its forces from NATO's order of battle (though one corps remained in southern Germany in what was the postwar French zone of occupation). The French also began to pay greater attention to their own nuclear deterrent, and emphasized a low nuclear threshold. But France remained a part of NATO and a signatory to the Atlantic Treaty. It is thus committed to coming to the aid of the central front if attacked. Moreover there have been moves to place the French position in a more coherent Alliance framework, including the revival of the Western European Union (of which France is a member). France balances between membership and independence. Talk of reintegration into NATO is largely absent, but France does play a leading role in West European military circles, and is an important member of the Atlantic Alliance.

The WTO was formed in May 1955 on the back of a series of existing bilateral defence treaties, and was renewed in April 1988 for a further 30 years. The signing of the Warsaw Treaty six years after the formation of NATO was occasioned by the West's decision to allow the rearmament of the Federal Republic of Germany. It was probably also used to place the Soviet military presence in Eastern Europe on a longer and more coherently organized basis. The stereotype of an alliance almost totally dominated by the Soviet Union had some basis in fact before the reforms of the late 1980s, but also obscured a significant amount of diversity. Soviet domination was secured by its pre-eminent military strength (the bulk of WTO forces, and the best-equipped are all Soviet), and by its control of the WTO command structure (all of the top military positions are held by Soviet officers). This position of pre-eminence is reflected by the substantial (though not universal) standardization of equipment, doctrine and tactics along Soviet lines. However all of this guaranteed neither loyalty to Moscow, nor reliability in a crisis. On three occasions (Hungary in 1956, Czechoslovakia in 1968, and Poland in 1981) Soviet forces either intervened militarily, or were on the brink of intervention to maintain acceptable governments in Eastern Europe. In the wake of the 1968 intervention in Czechoslovakia, Moscow outlined the Brezhnev Doctrine whereby the Soviet Union claimed the right of military intervention in a socialist state if the 'gains of socialism' were under threat. The implication of the Brezhnev Doctrine was that loyalty to Moscow could only be guaranteed if the threat of military force was present as an instrument of persuasion. But if loyalty could only be secured in this way, then the reliability of non-Soviet forces could be questioned. Their willingness to fight would almost certainly have been scenario sensitive, and at the very least the degree of commitment may vary significantly, although it seems unlikely that any WTO member would have refused outright to fight (Korbonski 1982).

But this mould of limited diversity and communist orthodoxy imposed by the threat of military intervention was shattered in the late 1980s, perhaps irrevocably, by the reforms sweeping Eastern Europe. By the turn of the decade communist power had collapsed or was collapsing in all non-Soviet Warsaw Pact (NSWP) states. In particular the crucial northern tier states of East Germany, Poland and Czechoslovakia were beginning to break their links with any form of communist orthodoxy. The Brezhnev Doctrine was being replaced with what Gennady Gerasimov termed the Sinatra Doctrine: WTO states were doing it their own way, not Moscow's way.

The implications of these changes for the WTO are profound. Loyalty to the Soviet Union in a crisis can no longer be guaranteed.

In a war, the integrity of the alliance may collapse. Wholesale defections are possible, with organized, active resistance conceivable. Even in peace the integrity of the WTO can no longer be guaranteed. In short, the process of reform may render the WTO impotent as an offensive military alliance.

The geography of the central front

Despite the technological advances of the last four decades, geography remains an important factor in any military assessment of the central front. Although mechanized vehicles are more powerful and faster than those of the Second World War, their mobility is still constrained by poor ground or extensive urbanization. Although remote sensors are now used extensively for targeting and weapon guidance, line of sight is still the most reliable (and often the most favoured) form of targeting, a method highly dependent upon extensive vistas and favourable weather. Although some aircraft and helicopters can fly low level at night and in poor weather, this is far from universally the case. Mountainous and hilly terrain still offers plenty of opportunity for aircraft to hide from enemy radars, and proves a major handicap for fast-moving armoured offensives of the kind the Soviet Union is generally considered to favour. Any assessment of the defence of the central front must therefore examine the terrain and the weather in central Europe, and its implications for military operations.

The modern state of West Germany is some 850 km long, with a 1381 km border with East Germany (roughly 400 km in a straight line) and a 356 km border with Czechoslovakia. Depth is limited to under 300 km, and as low as 225 km in the centre. In the north, Belgium and the Netherlands provide some operational depth, but with the withdrawal of France from NATO's military structure the south and centre lacks depth. Moreover, roughly 30 per cent of West Germany's population and 25 per cent of its industry is located within 100 km of the border. NATO must therefore defend a relatively long border with little room for operational manoeuvre (i.e. at corps or army group level) and with a major political incentive to hold any attack as far to the east as possible.

The West German state consists of a patchwork of villages, rivers and canals, woodland and pasture, hills and mountains, and a surprisingly small number of heavily industrialized urban areas. Roughly 30 per cent of West Germany is covered by woodland, and the amount of forestation is increasing by just under 1 per cent each year (Faringdon 1986, p. 278). Despite the obvious success of the Germans in moving panzers through the Ardennes in May 1940 and December 1944, it remains the case that woods are generally difficult areas for armoured offensives to pass through, reducing mobility and offering considerable cover for light infantry armed with anti-tank weapons. Although woods can offer some protection from aerial attack, and it is difficult for anti-tank teams to find long lines of fire (forcing them to approach their targets uncomfortably close), wooded land severely constrains the speed and manoeuvrabilty of today's highly mechanized forces.

Although many of West Germany's forests are in hilly terrain which perhaps would not be chosen anyway as likely axes of advance, the high level of forestation does offer some defensive advantages. Faringdon however cautions that there might be psychological factors inhibiting the extensive use of woodland for defensive purposes: 'Nobody who proposes to employ woods for military purposes can afford to ignore the place which this greenery occupies in the German imagination as a symbol of peace, freedom and unspoilt nature' (Faringdon 1986, p. 278). In addition to forest and woodland, much of Germany is covered by a latticework of waterways, principally rivers and manmade canals. Table 2.1 indicates the frequency at which such obstacles would be encountered along a given axis of advance. Although some mechanized units are capable of fording water obstacles, it is more generally the case that large armoured forces will be dependent upon bridges to cross all possibly bar minor water obstacles. Bridges are vulnerable not only to pre-placed demolition charges, but to modern highly accurate guided weapons, especially air-delivered bombs. To counter this, WTO forces have considerable bridging equipment integral to combat units. Although some remarkable statistics have appeared concerning WTO bridging capability,[2] many of these are for forces as they approach West Germany, which may be using pre-positioned replacements. WTO bridging capabilities in West Germany, when they would probably be under attack from NATO ground and air forces, are much less certain. This, though, is something of a two-edged sword: the WTO

Table 2.1 Frequency of water obstacles in West Germany

Type	Size (m wide)	Frequency (km)
Minor	*c.* 10	5–10
Medium	10–100	30–60
Major	100–300	100–150

Source: Faringdon 1986, p. 279.

can equally destroy bridges in NATO's rear to hinder the movement of reserves and supplies, and could even destroy bridges at a tactical level to prevent counter-attacks. As a result, NATO forces also have bridging capabilities (the Americans for example practice bridging the Rhine every year). The crucial distinction, though, is that whereas NATO would be bridging water obstacles in its rear and in friendly country, the WTO would be forced to bridge obstacles on or near the battlefield under the constant threat of attack.

Although northern Germany is relatively flat, there is some high ground in the British and Belgian sectors. Straddling the IGB the Harz mountains constitute a steep and heavily wooded range of peaks generally 6–700 m in height, while the Weiser-Leine heights provide a series of low ridges and ranges dividing the North German Plain from the Rhineland. Southern Germany is considerably more mountainous with higher peaks, but also a number of deep corridors providing natural axes of advance. Particularly important are the Gottingen Gap south-west of the Harz Mountains (on the border of NORTHAG and CENTAG areas of responsibility), the Fulda Gap running from the border near Eisenach to Frankfurt, the Grabfeld on the eastern side of the Rhône, which opens up a flanking attack against NATO forces defending the Fulda Gap, the Hof corridor bordered by the Frankewald and Fichtelgebirge, and the less frequently referred to Weiden Gap and Coburg entry (Faringdon 1986, pp. 297–309). Mountains and high ground have historically been seen as of advantage to defensive forces. Again technology has done little to alter this. Although the radar shadow cast by hills and mountains might assist WTO aircraft attempting to penetrate NATO airspace, mobility on the ground can be severely restricted (particularly in bad weather) while effective defensive positions are readily available. The exception would appear to be when surprise is achieved. Of particular interest is the fact that German success in the Ardennes in 1940 and 1944 was in part due to an Allied belief that attack would not come through such difficult terrain, particularly in the winter of 1944. Although these gaps sometimes appear more figments of military planners' nightmares than geographical features (the Fulda Gap, for example, is scarcely a highway), suitable avenues of advance clearly do exist from the east. Equally clear is that the number of avenues are limited (particularly those with good road networks). That WTO forces cannot choose from an unlimited number of attack options but must conform to some geographic restrictions is well understood by NATO planners, and may be seen as an advantage. But as one commentator has put it, 'the history of armoured warfare is . . . the story of tanks going where they are not supposed to be able to go' (Rosen, in Cohen 1988, p. 64).

The crosscountry mobility of large armoured formations such as the WTO would use in any major attack against NATO is also dependent upon the condition of the ground being crossed, and hence the soil types. Isby and Kamps identify three zones of soil types along the IGB. Along the Baltic coast there is a narrow sandy strip which offers excellent crosscountry trafficability. Further south and west (from Kiel and Hamburg south to Celle and Hanover, across to the Elbe, the Netherlands and Flanders) the water table is high and the ground quite marshy. Large numbers of heavy vehicles could quickly churn this up into a mud bath, considerably limiting crosscountry mobility. Still further south the ground is much firmer but also more hilly and mountainous. Forces could travel off roads without too much difficulty here, but might be forced into valleys or around hills along easily predicted lines of advance. Such lines might have been surveyed and prepared in advance by NATO forces for defensive operations (Isby and Kamps 1985, p. 43).

Although modern MBTs and mechanized vehicles have considerable crosscountry agility, and WTO manoeuvres have emphasized movement across open terrain, the easiest and quickest way to move mechanized formations remains by road.[3] Thus the West German road network is of considerable military importance, both for a WTO advance and for NATO's movement of reinforcements and supplies. Since 1945 the road network in West Germany has been considerably expanded, but unfortunately for military planners this expansion has been directed by economic rather than military considerations. Many of the newer main roads bypass towns which might otherwise prove difficult obstacles for a high-speed armoured advance, and a number of excellent new autobahns have been built running on an east–west axis. These main trunk roads are designed for heavy articulated lorries, and should be capable of carrying modern 50–60 ton MBTs with little difficulty.

When considering these roads as a possible asset for a WTO advance, there are a number of factors which need to be taken into consideration. The West German road network is less dense than those of other West European countries, and is inadequate for today's peacetime traffic. Many of the older trunk roads have just two lanes, and the newer generally have just four. The autobahns constructed during the Third Reich are in a poor state of repair. Many of the roads have soft verges making it difficult to bypass obstacles on the road surface. Roads are also such obvious routes that they can be mined, making their use hazardous, or cratered by demolition charges to slow an enemy advance. Road bridges in particular may make tempting targets. On the NATO side, though, there are also problems. The road network would have to carry large numbers of civilian refugees (15 million civilians live within 100 km of the border with the east), and although contingency plans do exist for an orderly evacuation they are untested on any large scale. The likelihood is that NATO would find many of the roads it would like to use clogged by civilian traffic. In addition lateral movement is clogged by the existence of only one major trunk road east of Fankfurt running north–south. Movement of tactical and operational reserves by road could therefore be severely restricted. Thus roads provide problems and opportunities for both NATO and the WTO (Griffith and Dinter 1983, p. 31; Faringdon 1986, pp. 179–80; Isby and Kamps 1985, p. 41).

Another important consideration is the extent of urban sprawl in West Germany. Fighting in built-up areas (FIBUA) is slow and time-consuming, generally favouring the defender (Donnelly 1977; Dzirkals 1976). With the advent of long-range precision-guided anti-armour weapons, urban areas and villages may offer potential strong points which light infantry can fight from (Gates 1987, p. 303). Given the lack of permanent field defences on the central front (for political and environmental reasons as well as their vulnerability to prewar enemy reconnaissance), urban areas and villages may offer not just concealment but important infantry protection from artillery bombardment - especially given the deep cellars found in many older West German buildings. Thus urbanization might be a problem for the WTO not only in slowing any advance, but in offering NATO positions to fight from. Although less than 10 per cent of West German territory is heavily urbanized much of the land is dotted with villages of varying size, and the pattern sseems set for considerable urban spread in the 1990s (Faringdon 1986, p. 279).

A further important consideration is the weather. Bad weather is far from unusual in Germany. Poor weather conditions restrict visibility aiding tactical surprise, but can also slow down the movement of forces and add complexity to military ooperations. Although generally temperate, winters in Germany can be severe, with sudden temperature thaws and the spring thaw making crosscountry movement difficult. Visibility may be restricted by fog (urban areas suffer 60–70 days of fog a year) and by the long winter nights when even daylight is dim. Cloud cover is similarly a near constant, falling under 2000 feet 16 per cent of the time in summer and 43 per cent in winter. Rain is fairly common, often concentrated in the summer into thunderstorms, reducing trafficability. Line of sight targeting can be considerably hampered by poor visibility, aircraft flying hourss can be limited, reconnaissance may suffer extensively, and ground movement can be slowed by rain or fog. Electronic surveillance and targeting may offer some solution to the problems of poor visibility, and in particular advanced avionics are essential for 24-hour all-weather low-level flight. This would seem to indicate that more technologically advanced equipment would hold a significant advantage. Fixed defences and the more mobile ground forces (both in terms of equipment and organization) would seem to have some advantage if the weather is bad. Poor visibility may aid tactical, even operational surprise, which generally favours offensive actiions (including counter-attacks). Again modern surveillance aids may ease this problem, favouring the side with the best electronic warfare equipment and the command structure best able to react to this.

One final point needs to be made concerning what Clausewitz termed 'friction'. It is in the nature of military operations for things to go wrong or not happen as planned. Problems mentioned above with weather, roads, bridges and so forth all contribute to friction. Friction affects both offensive and defensive operations but, all else being equal, it is the attacker who is worse affected since it is his plan which has to work and can be the more easily disrupted when things go wrong. Moreover, it is to the attacker's advantage to keep forces moving quickly, maintaining momentum and keeping the defender off balance. Thus anything which slows momentum, such as unbridged water obstacles, blocked roads, or marshy ground, although affecting both offensive and defensive fforces, will be of greater concern to the attacker.

NATO: organization and deployment

NATO's central front is divided into two Army Groups, each of which is in turn dividedd into four corps sectors (see Fig. 2.2). Colocated with each Army Group is a tactical air force (ATAF). Further British and American aircraft based in Britain would probably be available, as might French tactical aircraft and US Strategic Air Commandd bombers configured for conventional operations. The more northerly Army Group, NORTHAG (Northern Army Group) is located in the former British occupation zone and is predominately European. From north to south the corps deployed

THE CENTRAL FRONT

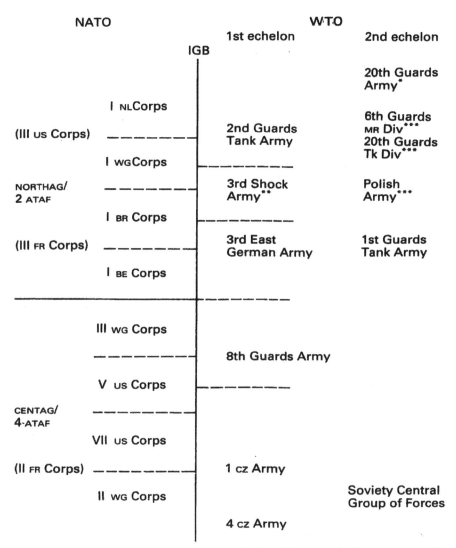

Figure 2.2 Schematic illustration of NATO and WTO deployments on the central front

are I Netherlands (NE) Corps, I West German (WG) Corps, I British (BR) Corps, and I Belgian (BE) Corps, with 2 ATAF providing air cover and ground support. The more southerly army group, CENTAG (Central Army Group) reflects its origins in the American zone of occupation with the powerful 7th US Army holding the army group's centre, deploying two corps (V and VII Corps). This Army is flanked to the north by III West German Corps, and to the south by II West German Corps.[4]

Colocated with CENTAG is 4 ATAF. This whole arrangement of corps sectors has thus been likened to a layer cake.

NATO's central front command structure is multinational. Each corps has its own national commander – thus the commander of 1 BR Corps is a British general. NORTHAG's commander is also British, while CENTAG's is American. The commander of Allied Air Forces Central Europe is American, while the commander oof 4 ATAF is West German and 2 ATAF is British. Overall command of the central front is in the hands of Commander in Chief Allied Forces Central Europe, a West German, who in turn is subordinate to Supreme Allied Commander Europe (SACEUR), an American general, with his British and West German deputies. The command chain is illustrated in Figure 2.3. The division of responsibility between American, British and West German commanders is largely a political one, reflecting the postwar occupation of West Germany by British and American forces, NATO Europe's attempt to tie American forces into the defence of Europe, and the delicate balance between on the one hand the unease felt by some Europeans over any significant West German military influence and on the other the need to reflect the major commitment made by West Germany to the central front.

The layer-cake deployment and associated command structure creates a number of problems for NATO. Firstly the peacetime command structure is not a command structure at all, in the sense that SACEUR has little control over the forces under him. Indeed

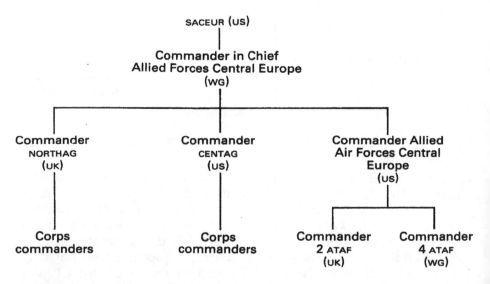

Figure 2.3 NATO central front commanders

SACEUR and the commanders immediately below him only acquire operational control of their forces in the event of war. SACEUR therefore resembles a chairman whose subordinates exercise both considerable autonomy and divided loyalties between NATO and their national commands. As with many multinational command structures, the relationship between commanders is a political affair rather than a simple command relationship. Successive commanders of NORTHAG for example have complained that attempts to impose a common operational doctrine upon the army group have been frustrated by the independence of corps commanders (Bagnall 1984). Although in theory many of these problems should disappear in the event of war as the major commanders assume operational control, peacetime habits and national interests may still hamper the command and control of conventional forces.

Secondly, peacetime barracks often bear scant relation to wartime deployment areas. I BR Corps for example is scattered throughout the former British zone of occupation, bar one brigade which is based in Britain along with the entire rear-area security division. US 3rd Infantry Division would have to march through West German 12th Armoured Division, while both the Dutch and Belgian corps are based mostly in their home countries with only a small permanent presence in West Germany (Faringdon 1986, pp. 268–71). In addition the deployment of NATO forces is largely a postwar legacy bearing little relation to the military threat. The bulk of NATO's more capable forces – the American and West German corps – are located in the more easily defended southern half of Germany, while the weaker NORTHAG corps face perhaps six WTO armies across terrain better suited for mobile offensive operations.

Finally, in-place reserves which are formally committed to NATO army groups are non-existent. Army group commanders would have to rely on hastily formed reserve units, on US forces airlifted across the Atlantic, or upon French forces reintegrating in time of war to provide substantial reserves. II French Corps is located in the CENTAG area and would probably be available as an operational reserve. In 1984 III French Corps was moved to Lille where it is in a good position to move into the NORTHAG area as an operational reserve. Under the 1989 'Forces 2000' plan, this corps is to be strengthened considerably as I Corps (based at Metz) is disbanded. The lightly armed *force d'action rapide* (FAR, rapid deployment force) would also probably be available for the central front (Cordesman 1988, p. 205; Isnard 1989, p. 240). The availability of these forces though is heavily dependent upon French willingness to reintegrate into NATO's military structure in time of war. Although some form of commitment seems likely, the extent of the commitment and the nature of the command relationship are both uncertain. Although some French forces do train with NATO, and French observers do attend NATO exercises, there is obviously a problem in that French forces do not have the same experience of operating under NATO operational control as other corps on the central front.

In addition to these French forces, the United States under its REFORGER plans intends to boost its forces in Europe from four to ten divisions within ten days of mobilization. Six divisions currently stationed in the US would be airlifted to Europe, and would be equipped by pre-positioned equipment stores (called POMCUS).[5] Three of these divisions would form US III Corps, which SACEUR identified in the early 1980s as an operational reserve for NORTHAG. The remainder would be used as reinforcements for CENTAG. To work effectively, the REFORGER/POMCUS scheme requires a period of strategic warning (8–12 days) to allow forces to be airlifted and assembled as coherent fighting units. Given the vulnerability of POMCUS to attack, coupled to the confusion of war, it is uncertain whether these forces could be deployed effectively if there was no strategic warning. As Isby and Kamps comment, 'Once a war had started it would be almost too late to start the [REFORGER] process' (Isby and Kamps 1985, p. 455). In addition there is a degree of uncertainty over how quickly REFORGER units might actually be able to arrive in Europe (Cordesman 1988, p. 235; Isby and Kamps 1985, pp. 455–6).

Operational reserves for the central front are therefore heavily reliant upon a period of strategic warning allowing full mobilization. But mobilization might be constrained by political pressure to avoid escalating a conflict, by French unwillingness to reintegrate to some degree into NATO's military structure, or by the Soviets achieving a degree of strategic surprise.

The WTO: organization and deployment

In theory the WTO is controlled by a Political Consultative Committee consisting of political and military leaders from both the Soviet Union and its East European allies. In practice however thiss body has rarely met and political control has been exercised by Moscow. The military structure is similarly Soviet-controlled, the top military organ being the Joint High Command based in Moscow and chaired by the Soviet FFFirst Deputy Minister of Defence. Further, as Laurence Martin has commented: 'The Warsaw Pact, unlike NATO, is not intended to be a structure for command in wartime. If hostilities began, the East European armies would be brought under direct Soviet control' (Martin 1985, p. 16). For this reason, and since 80 per cent of Pact forces are Soviet (Faringdon 1986, p.95) the wartime organization of the Warsaw Pact is best understood by examining the Soviet command structure and the place of the East Europeans within that.

Although there is some uncertainty over the Soviet command structure, it is generally accepted that it divides its military concerns geographically into three theatres of war (TVs): the Far East, South-West Asia, and Europe. Each TV in turn is divided into theatres of military operations (TVDs), recently renamed 'strategic directions', three of which face Europe: North-Western (Scandinavia), Western (the central front), and South-Western (the Balkans/southern Europe). According to Isby some TVDs might only be activated in wartime. However, it appears that the Western TVD facing NATO's central front is active in peacetime (Bellamy 1987, pp. 106–112; Isby 1988, pp. 17–18).

The TVD is an important level in the Soviet command structure. It is the focus of operational thinking, and integrates operations by all military services and Soviet allies. Under TVDs there may be a number of Second World War-style fronts, into which East European armies may also be integrated. Therefore the level at which NSWP armies are integrated into the Soviet command structure is not clear - it may be at either the TVD or front level. Each front has its own air support (called frontal aviation) and consists of a number of armies. These armies, usually comprising four divisions with supporting units, form the basic operational unit. A schematic command structure can therefore be devised (Fig. 2.4). Both fronts and armies can act independently of TVDs under the direct control of the Soviet General Staff. Nor is their size fixed but may vary according to task. Although corps have sometimes been used for small operations not requiring a full army, they are not usually found in Soviet-style command structures. In the mid-1980s there were some indications that the Soviets were experimenting with a corps/brigade structure rather than the existing division/regiment, but these experiments do not seem to have produced any major changes to the Soviet military structure (Isby 1988, p. 18; Office of Technology Assessment, 1987, p. 60).

Four major organizational differences are apparent between the WTO and NATO. Firstly, Pact organization is largely standardized along Soviet lines whereas the size and composition of NATO forces varies according to nationality. However, what have been up to now relatively minor instances of diversity within the WTO

Figure 2.4 Schematic illustration of Soviet command structure

may mushroom with the process of reform in Eastern Europe. Secondly, NATO is organized into corps and army groups, the Pact into armies and fronts. Thirdly, the Pact chain of command is relatively clear, and TVD commanders exercise considerable control over their formations (though again the process of reform may have some impact here). In contrast, NATO high-level commanders have much less control over the forces under them, particularly in peacetime, and often resemble chairmen rather than military commanders.

Finally, whereas NATO is organized into a front line with reserve formations, Soviet theory and practice emphasizes the echeloning of forces to create numerical superiority without massing (which would provide vulnerablee targets to attack). Thus a typical Soviet-style offensive would involve two waves of forces and a small reserve at each command level, from front down to regiment. The second echelon differs from a western reserve formation in both its strength and its allocation of objectives as part of a plan *before* operations commence. Thus the first echelon would have a series of objectives, and its success would be built on by the second echelon with its own series of objectives. The second echelon might relieve the first, but more likely would fight alongside the remains of the first echelon. The number of echelons may be increased or reduced according to the particular situation (three echelons may be used against fortified positions, a single echelon if surprise is achieved). Reserve formations are kept small (a divisional reserve might be no more than a single battalion) and used for specific tasks identified as the operation progresses (Isby 1988, p. 23; OTA 1987, pp. 62–3). Echeloning is a key feature of Soviet offensive and defensive operations, and is present at all levels of command. There is no NATO equivalent to this.

The Western TVD is under the command of the Soviet General Staff, and in war would probably consist of Soviet and NSWP forces in East Germany, Poland and Czechoslovakia, and forces from three Soviet military districts (MDs), the Baltic, Belorussian and Carpathian MDs. Table 2.2 indicates the divisional strength of these forces in the late 1980s, though the combination of arms control and political reform may reduce these numbers considerably in the 1990s.[6] The United States' Office of Technology Assessment estimated that this TVD would probably be organized into three fronts. A northern front of mainly Polish and East German forces (but probably supported by one Soviet army, 20th Guards, in the second operational echelon) would be deployed in the north of East Germany against northern West Germany, Denmark and the Netherlands. These would encounter AFNORTH forces in Denmark and Schleswig-Holstein. The main attack would fall to a central front consisting of the Western Group of Forces (WGF, previously Group of Soviet Forces in Germany, or GSFG), the Northern Groups of Forces (NGF), one East German army and probably at least one Polish army and two Soviet divisions

Table 2.2 Divisional strength of Western TVD

	Tank	Mechanized*	Airborne	Artillery	Combat aircraft (regiments)
SOVIET					
WGF	11	8		1	20
CGF (Czechoslovakia)	2	3		2	
NGF (Poland)	1	1			
Baltic MD	3	7	2	2	1
Belorussian MD	10	2	2**	1	5
Carpathian MD	4	9	1**	2	7
NSWP					
Czechoslovakia	5***	5		3	9
East Germany	2	4			8
Poland	5	6			16

*   Motor rifle.
** Includes one air assault division.
*** Includes two training divisions (category C).
Note: Does not include East European reserve divisions.
Source: IISS 1989, pp. 38–40 and 46–9.

based in Poland. These would attack across West Germany into Belgium, the southern Netherlands and Luxembourg. In the south a Czech front would attack along the West German-Swiss-Austrian border with two Czech armies and the Soviet and Central Group of Forces (CGF) divisions. In addition a Danube front consisting of the Hungarian army and the Soviet Southern Group of Forces might attack through Austria into southern West Germany, linking up with the Czech front. The second strategic echelon would follow up with forces from the Carpathian and Belorussian MDs, while forcces in the Baltic MMD might act as theatre reseerve (Lok 1989, p. 1220; OTA 1987, p. 65). This is depicted in Figure 2.5 and Table 2.3.

Of these forces the Soviet divisions are generally considered the best. These are concentrated in the WGF: the NGF consists

Table 2.3 Schematic illustration of Western and TVD fronts and echelons

First Strategic Echelon	Second Strategic Echelon	Reserves(?)
Northern and central fronts (NGF, WGF, East German and Polish armies) 19 tank divisions 19 mechanized divisions* 1 artillery division	Belorussian military district 10 tank divisions 2 mechanized divisions 2 airborne divisions 1 artillery division	Baltic military district 3 tank divisions 7 mech divisions* 2 airborne divisions 2 artillery divisions
Southern† Czech front (CGF, Czech army) 7 tank divisions 8 mech. divisions* 3 artillery divisions	Carpathian military district 4 tank divisions 9 mech. divisions* 2 artillery divisions	
Total 26 tank divisions 27 mech. divisions* 4 artillery divisions	14 tank divisions 11 mech. divisions 3 airborne divisions 3 artillery divisions	3 tank divisions 7 mech. divisions* 2 airborne divisions 2 artillery divisions

* i.e Motor rifle division.
† Five tank divisions are to be withdrawn from the first strategic echelon under the unilateral reductions announced by President Gorbachev in the UN, December 1988. Illustration does not include possible Danube front, consisting of Soviet Southern Group of Forces and Hungarian Army.

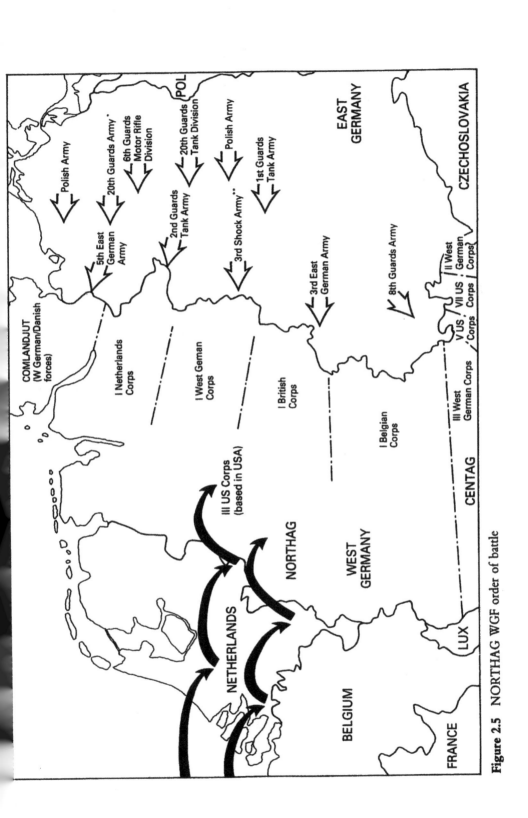

Figure 2.5 NORTHAG WGF order of battle

of just two divisions, while the CGF, although slightly stronger with five divisions, is unusual in being placed behind the Czech army as either a second operational echelon or possibly a general operationall reserve. The implication of this concentration of forces in East Germany is that the main blow will fall across the IGB, and that the Northern and Czech fronts are of secondary importance.

In addition to the Soviet divisions on the central front of the Western TVD there are three powerful East German divisions (the other three being positioned on the northern front). These are all currently under direct Soviet military control, totally integrated into both peacetime and wartime commands and would fight alongside Soviet forces (though this may change with the process of reform). Although formally organized into separate armies, Faringdon claims that the two armies are in fact deployed 'almost as far apart as is physically possible' presumably for similar reasons to NATO's dispersal of the three West German corps along the length of the IGB (Faringdon 1986, p. 69).

The largest of the NSWP armies is that of Poland. But much of its equipment is outdated, and substantial doubts exist over the commitment of Polish forces. The Czech army is similarly less well equipped than its Soviet counterparts, despite being a first echelon force. Faringdon claims that five Czech divisions form a front line with two in reserve. The remaining three divisions are kept in a low state of readiness and would require a long period of mobilization (Faringdon 1986, p. 108). WTO divisions are kept at varying degrees of readiness and in a short-warning scenario fewer divisions would be available than if extensive warning had allowed full mobilization. The Soviet Union experienced considerable difficulties in mobilizing for the invasion of Czechoslovakia in 1968, and despite attempting to improve procedures still encountered difficulties in the invasion of Afghanistan in 1979 and during the Polish crisis in 1981–2. Procedures are being improved, but this remains a problem area (Isby 1988, p. 37).

WTO forces are divided into three readiness categories, identified in Table 2.4. All Soviet divisions in Eastern Europe are Category 1 or better. However, East European divisions and Soviet divisions in western military districts of the USSR vary considerably in their readiness (see Table 2.5). Soviet second strategic echelon forces would only be available after a period of mobilization and would consist at least in part of reservists hastily called up and given a minimum of refresher training. At the same time NATO will be mobilizing its own forces. In particular the West German territorial army and other European reinforcements will

Table 2.4 WTO readiness categories

	Personnel strength (%)	Equipment strength	Full manning	Mobilization period
Cat 1	75–110	75–110%	–	24 hours
Cat 2	50–70	90%+*	3 days	30 days
Cat 3	10–33	33–50%*	1 week	90–120 days**

* Mostly in storage.
** Category 3 divisions are planned to be ready in 60 days and were used for the invasion of Afghanistan after a 60-day mobilization period. However a more realistic estimate is 90–120 days. Composite divisions consisting of two Category 3 divisions merged into one might be available after 60 days.

Sources: IISS 1989, pp. 37–8; Isby 1988, p. 38.

Table 2.5 WTO divisional readiness status (tank and mechanized divisions only)

	Cat. 1	Cat. 2	Cat. 3
SOVIET			
WGF	19	–	–
NGF	2	–	–
CGF	2	–	–
Belorussian MD	2	6–8	2
Carpathian MD	2	6	3
Baltic MD	–	4	6
NSWP			
Czechoslovakia	4	3	3
East Germany	6	–	–
Poland	8*	–	5

* Two tank divisions to become Category 3.

Sources: IISS 1989; Isby 1988, p. 35. Note: There is some discrepancy between the IISS and Isby over the number of divisions in Soviet military districts.

be quickly available. John Pay has therefore estimated that in the second week after mobilization the Soviets would have an extra 20–25 category 1 and 2 divisions available in addition to those category 1 divisions already in Eastern Europe, but that NATO would have boosted its forces on the central front from a pre-mobilization total of 678,000 to 1,788,000 within ten days of mobilization (Martin 1985, pp. 53–4).

In addition to mobilizing, forces from Soviet military districts must transit across Eastern Europe to reach the battle area. The most obvious route to East Germany lies through Poland, which has good lines of communication (especially by rail). However, following the disturbances of the early 1980s Soviet planners appeared concerned over the safety of this route, and in the summer of 1984 tested a new route bypassing Poland. It now appears that most Soviet lines of communication have been rerouted south of Poland. Communications with Czechoslovakia are reasonable, with a direct road running from Lvov (headquarters of the Carpathian military district). Good rail links exist between Czechoslovakia and East Germany and Poland, but road links are not so good, and the terrain on the Polish frontier in particular is difficult (Faringdon 1986, pp. 107–8 and 110).

Three points emerge from this. Firstly, that although the distances between the Soviet Union and the IGB are much smaller than those which separate Europe from the United States, the Soviets do have problems in moving large numbers of men quickly to the battle area. If troops have to be moved around Poland, in particular, there is a danger of overcrowding and confusion. A modern mechanized or armoured division is an unwieldy instrument to transport, occupying miles of road or dozens of trains. Moving such large units creates considerable potential for delay. When railways first emerged as factors in the mobilization of armies, rigid and highly complex plans were required for their efficient use, plans which could easily go awry. There is therefore a dilemma between firm planning for efficient use of lines of communication, and flexibility for when plans go wrong. In this context there is some debate over just how rigid Soviet mobilization plans are, some commentators believing that they are highly inflexible, others arguing that a good deal of slack has been built into plans (OTA 1987, pp. 66 and 68–71)). Whatever the case, moving more than 20 armoured and mechanized divisions quickly and efficiently over several hundred miles is no easy task. It should also be noted that not all NATO reserves have to cross the Atlantic, and that the large nummbers of European reserves have to travel considerably smaller distances than Soviet divisions in the Western military districts of the USSR.

Secondly, no matter how good the road or rail linnks between the Soviet Union and the battle area, the fact remains that their number is limited. Long columns of troops and large numbers of trains moving along a limited number of easily identified routes offer tempting targets for attack. Attacking these forces has been identified as a major NATO mission (see Ch. 5). If NATO is successful in this then the problems for the Soviets will be considerable. Not only fresh divisions but reserve stocks of fuel and ammunition transiting Eastern Europe will be subject to delay, disruption or even destruction.

Finally, transiting large numbers of troops and military supplies requires the cooperation, or at least the acquiescence, of the governments of those states the troops and supplies are passing through. By the late 1980s this had begun to appear unlikely. A secure rear area is not a luxury but a battle necessity, but with the process of reform in the late 1980s this could no longer be guaranteed.

Conclusion

The combination of geography and the structure of forces on the central front creates a mixed bag of problems for both alliances. For NATO the critical weaknesses appear to be an unbalanced force structure, with the weaker NORTHAG corps facing the greater threat, the lack of in-place operational reserves, and the extended lines of communication across the Atlantic. The major problem for the Soviet Union now appears to be the loyalty of its alliance partners. The process of reform has placed the status of the WTO as a military alliance into considerable doubt. Soviet control of individual alliance members has gone through periods of doubt in the past, but nothing to compare with the changes of 1988–9. Whether the WTO could function as an offensive military alliance currently appears extremely unlikely. It would require some extraordinary event to create the circumstances whereby WTO cohesion could be assured.

Notes

1. The Nunn Amendment was not passed (Towell 1984, pp. 1480–1). Speeches in the Senate debate over burden-sharing by Sam Nunn and Richard Lugar are reprinted in Carlton and Levine (1988). A similar ploy had been attempted in the 1970s by Senator Mike Mansfield.
2. Jon Connell estimates that if the 60 bridges across the Oder, Vistula and Elbe were destroyed by NATO, the WTO could repair most of them within two hours (Connell 1986, p. 100).
3. Though for very long distances (e.g. from the Western military districts of the USSR) rail remains the most efficient meanns of transportation.
4. Faringdon makes the point that, unlike the two American corps which have the benefit of fighting alongside each other, the three West German corps are spread throughout NATO's central front. Faringdon claims this is to avoid the unstated but deeply felt unease if too many German forces are concentrated together. An alternative explanation might be that the development is to ensure that, if NATO

NATO'S CHANGING STRATEGIC AGENDA

is attacked along its central front, the probability would be that a number of national corps would be involved, not just one nation's, and that at least one corps would almost certainly be a West German corps (Faringddon 1986, p. 270).

5 By the mid-1980s six POMCUS sets had been established, roughly one set per airfield division.. Three of these sets would be used for CENTAG reserves, three for NORTHAG. The US has also developed support facilities to increase its air strength to 60 squadrons (Cordesman 1988, p. 235).

6 According to the Soviet Chief of the General Staff, General Mikhail Moiseev, the following Soviet units had been unilaterally withdrawn from Eastern Europe by October 1989:

   3 tank divisions
   3 tank training regiments
   2 SAM training regiments
   1 air regiment
   1 helicopter regiment
   1 signals training regiment
   2 SAM brigades
   4 assault battalions
   2 assault river crossing battalions
   + unspecified 'special troop units'

The following were to be withdrawn in 1990:

   3 tank divisions
   2 assault brigades
   2 tank training regiments
   1 motor rifle training regiment
   1 assault battalion
   1 chemical defence battalion

Six tank divisions, one SAM brigade, two tank training regiments and a helicopter training regiment were amongst the forces to be deactivated from the overall Soviet force structure (i.e. not necessarily from forces withdrawn from Eastern Europe). (*Jane's Defence Weekly*, 11 November 1989, p. 1050.)

3

The balance of forces

A key question when considering the conventional defence of the central front has traditionally been whether or not NATO is decisively outnumbered. Is the balance of forces such that any attempt at defending the front is doomed to failure, or does NATO possess sufficient forces to have a realistic chance of success? Answering this question has been extremely difficult. The problem can be divided into two parts: is there an imbalance, and if so is it sufficient to be decisive? The problem is that not only is an objective assessment of either question extremely complex, but that the whole appears highly dependent upon the nature of the particular crisis scenario. For example, the cohesion of both alliances is of obvious importance to any calculation, but equally is highly unpredictable and scenario-sensitive. As the two alliances work towards a conventional arms control (CFE) treaty, some of the traditional areas of uncertainty are likely to disappear. Strict counting, monitoring and verification rules will reduce any uncertainties which may exist over numbers; NATO's numerical inferiority may eventually disappear; and the potential for surprise attack will be restricted by clauses concerning mobilization and notification of exercises. But a word of caution is necessary for the near term. A CFE treaty has yet to be signed, and even when signed is likely to take some years to implement fully. In the near term changes in the military balance may be substantial, but are unlikely to be as revolutionary as those promised by CFE.

The conventional balance is sufficiently important to the whole question of conventional defence that some attention must be paid to it. The approach adopted here is not that of creating a model which will produce a result or series of results concerning the likely outcome of a war; rather the approach is one of examining various methods of assessment and their associated caveats in an attempt to *understand* the conventional balance. Given that the balance is likely to be scenario-sensitive, that any assessment is limited by the assumptions it is forced to make, and that substantial (even revolutionary) changess are likely in the 1990s, the conventional balance is perhaps best approached not as something to be measured, but as something to be understood.

Bean counting

The most straightforward measure of the conventional balance is a simple comparison of the numbers of men and major weapons systems on each side. Factors which are difficult to quantify - such as quality of men and weapons, terrain, doctrine and organization - are excluded. This 'bean counting' approach is generally presented as a static measure of pre-battle inputs, with little attention being paid to mobilization schedules, reinforcements and rates of attrition. Although lacking in sophistication, these bean counts provide the raw data for most of the more complicated models. Tables 3.1 and 3.2 display the official NATO and WTO figures for the military balance at the end of the 1980s, and Figures 3.1 and 3.2 the 1989 proposals from the two alliances for CFE limits.

The accuracy of such figures has usually been dependent upon the quality of intelligence estimates, certainly as regards WTO strength. Past experience suggests that such estimates can be highly inaccurate.[1] Given the monitoring and verification regimes of a conventional arms control treaty, however, figures are likely to become very accurate in the future, and there is a strong probability that the figures currently available are accurate. But bean counts may still differ markedly because of different counting rules. In particular there are problems over which forces to count and what to include in the various categories (for example, should carrier-based aircraft be included in aircraft totals since they may be used on the central front though they are not necessarily deployed there? Similarly should marines be included in ground force totals, even though they might be deployed elsewhere?). Thus even given accurate raw data, decisions have to be made which can substantially affect the end result. Indeed one analyst has concluded that by using modest variables bean counts can vary between NATO being outnumbered by 4:1, to NATO outnumbering the WTO by 2:1 (Biddle 1988, pp. 102 and 104). A CFE treaty will probably reach some compromise concerning counting rules, but this will only reflect one method of counting forces on the central front, and will be neither the only, nor probably the definitive means.

Bean counts have the seductive appeal of offering a ready, easily understood comparison between forces: if NATO has 16 000 tanks and the WTO over 50 000, then NATO is clearly in an inferior position. However, the very simplicity of this method ignores a number of ffactors which are of importance to the fighting effectiveness of these forces, which is what really matters. These factors include the following.

Quality of equipment

The quality of equipment has an obvious bearing upon force effectiveness: an advanced tank or aircraft may be able to impose highly favourable kill ratios against less sophisticated opposition. In this respect the West's higher technological base is usually considered a major advantage. Nevertheless the Soviets do appear to be closing the technological gap, and in certain areas have a lead in deployed systems (such as artillery). Soviet design reflects a philosophy which eschews the leading edge of technology in favour of larger numbers of rugged, relatively uncomplicated systems (*Statement on the Defence Estimates* 1988, p. 56). In contrast the West tends to emphasize complex, highly innovative systems, an approach which some have criticized as counterproductive. Critics claim that the West's high technology weapons systems are too complex to be reliable or easily used in the heat of battle. Such critics have also noticed that this design philosophy encourages 'gold plating', whereby 'nice to have' features proliferate at substantial cost increases, but for little improvement in the weapons' combat effectiveness (Connell, 1986). Against this the WTO's evolutionary approach to weapons modernization and the high degree of standardization amongst WTO forces are often cited as advantages the West fails to fully exploit. Although some of these arguments can be overstated[2] it is apparent that the West's technological lead may be neither as all-encompassing nor as decisive as some may wish. Besides, to quote a Soviet proverb, quantity has a quality of its own.

Manpower, training. leadership and morale

In addition to the quality of weapons, the quality of manpower is an important ingredient in the effectiveness of any force. Training, leadership and morale can all act as force multipliers or dividers: large armies with low morale may quickly disintegrate in the face of concerted attack, while poor leadership may lead to disastrous defeat. None of these factors are accounted for in a simple bean count, and again NATO is commonly seen as having advantages in these areas. Soviet and WTO armies are characterized as inefficient, lacking in initiative and beset by social problems which undermine cohesion and force effectiveness. Alcoholism

Table 3.1 NATO estimates of the conventional balance of forces

	MBTs	AIFVs	OAVs	Artillery	ATWs	Combat helicopters	Ground* personnel ('000s)	Combat aircraft
A. NATO								
Belgium	320	208	1,378	248	518	–	68	144
Canada	60	–	400	35	45	–	5	40
Denmark	228	–	878	542	330	–	20.5	87
France	1,250	750	3,100	787	1,460	270	267	450
W. Germany	4,330	1,960	5,480	2,220	1,710	554	351.8	547
Greece	1,420	100	1,753	1,752	2,267	64	117	319
Iceland	–	–	–	–	–	–	–	–
Italy	1,500	–	4,900	2,100	2,200	170	297	250
Luxembourg	–	–	5	–	6	–	0.7	–
Netherlands	750	585	1,435	667	674	54	68	162
Norway	117	–	356	527	550	–	25	78
Portugal	66	–	269	260	362	–	47	99
Spain	866	–	2,740	1,038	1,222	160	210	186
Turkey	3,000	–	1,700	2,800	2,400	160	380	370
UK	717	–	5,048	394	1,196	287	140.5	445
USA	1,800	550	6,000	1,100	3,300	700	216	800
TOTAL	16,426	4,153	35,351	14,463	18,240	2,419	2,213.5	3,977

Table 3.1 NATO estimates of the conventional balance of forces

	MBTs	AIFVs	OAVs	Artillery	ATWs	Combat helicopters	Ground* personnel ('000s)	Combat aircraft
B. WTO								
Bulgaria	1,800	100	4,300	2,000	500	100	135	250
Czecho.	3,800	1,100	5,000	2,100	2,000	200	145	400
E. Germany	3,000	800	5,700	1,700	1,700	150	120	350
Hungary	1,300	300	1,700	800	800	100	80	150
Poland	3,400	1,100	5,100	2,500	2,000	200	230	700
Rumania	1,200	–	4,200	1,300	700	100	180	350
USSR	37,000	19,000	45,000	33,000	36,500	2,850	2,200	6,060
TOTAL	51,500	22,400	71,000	43,400	44,200	3,650	3,090	8,250

Figures for January 1988.
Note: MBT Main battle tank
AIFV Armoured infantry fighting vehicle
OAV Other armoured vehicle
ATW Anti-tank weapon (launcher)

Source: NATO 1988.

Table 3.2 WTO estimates of the conventional balance of forces

	Personnel ('000s)	Combat aircraft	Combat helicopters	MBTs	IFVs and APCs	ATGMs	Artillery
A. NATO							
Britain	311.2	835	700	2,000	5,480	1,480	3,320
W. Germany	495	850	450	4,900	6,840	2,760	3,190
France	442.5	880	700	3,190	4,520	2,000	8,510
Norway	41.08	100	–	370	190	150	2,320
Denmark	30.96	100	–	350	1,090	310	1,750
Belgium	92.0	170	70	530	2,020	560	1,620
Netherlands	101.85	200	20	1,250	3,240	764	1,410
Luxembourg	1.04	–	–	–	–	6	10
Italy	396.0	450	540	2,330	6,440	2,130	5,510
Greece	190.0	450	130	2,000	1,720	320	3,950
Portugal	70.0	150	–	470	280	40	1,870
Spain	283.0	295	160	1,850	1,720	190	5,010
Turkey	598.2	640	310	4,320	5,270	2,350	14,900
USA	593.0	1,960	2,180	6,980	7,590	4,940	3,520
Canada	14.4	50	10	150	500	70	170
Iceland	–	–	–	–	–	–	–
TOTAL	3,660.23	7,130	5,270	30,690	46,900	18,070	57,060

Table 3.2 WTO estimates of the conventional balance of forces

	Personnel ('000s)	Combat aircraft	Combat helicopters	MBTs	IFVs and APCs	ATGMs	Artillery
B. WTO							
Bulgaria	117.5	234	51	2,220	2,365	360	3,990
Hungary	106.8	113	96	1,435	2,310	270	1,750
East Germany	173.1	307	74	3,140	5,900	620	2,435
Poland	347	480	43	3,330	4,855	435	3,065
Rumania	171	380	220	3,200	5,000	400	6,600
USSR	2,458	5,995	2,220	41,580	45,000	8,840	50,275
Czecho.	199.7	407	101	4,585	4,900	540	3,445
TOTAL	3,573.1	7,876	2,785	59,470	70,330	11,465	71,560

Note: MBT   Main battle tank
ATGM   Anti-tank guided missile launcher
IFV   Infantry fighting vehicle
APC   Armoured personnel carrier

Figures are as of 1 July 1988 and are for forces stationed in Europe and adjacent sea areas. For Soviet unilateral cuts of 1989 and 1990 see Ch. 2, n. 6.

Source: WTO 1989.

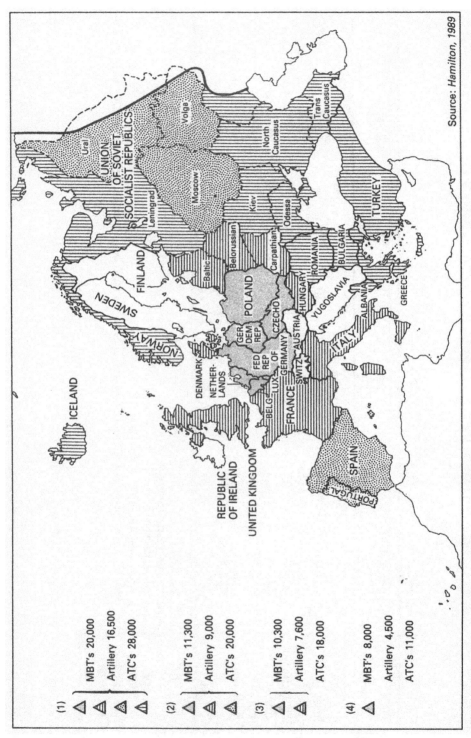

Figure 3.1 Atlantic to the Urals: proposed NATO sub-limits

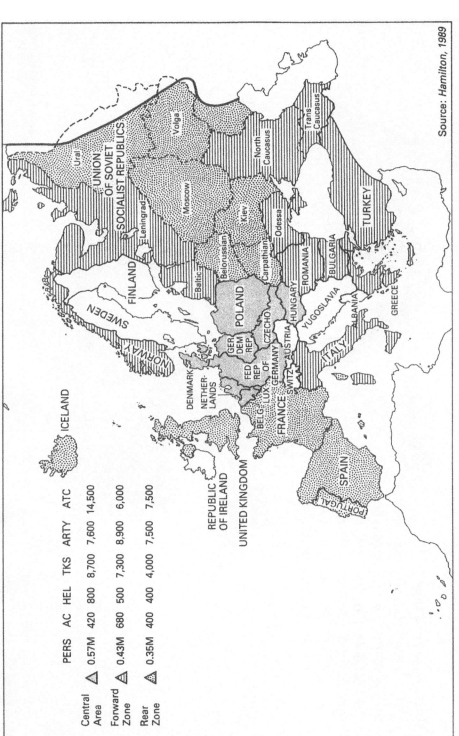

Figure 3.2a CFE: Warsaw Pact zoning proposal

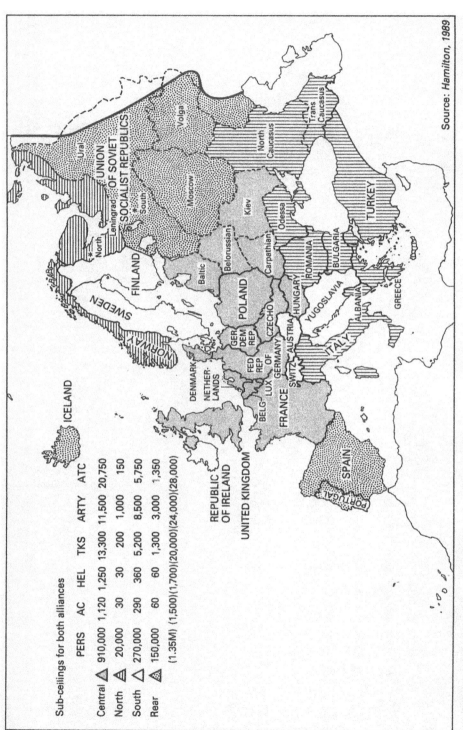

Figure 3.2b Warsaw Pact alternative regional proposals

and language difficulties are but two of the problems faced by Soviet commanders (Cockburn 1983; Suvorov 1981). These sorts of problems however are far from being exclusive to the WTO (US forces in Europe for example have often been accused of suffering from a drugs problem). Many Soviet units have also displayed high degrees of professionalism, while lack of *tactical* initiative is in part a deliberate product of a doctrine which prescribes clear methods and procedures (Donnelly 1985, pp. 15–17; *Statement on the Defence Estimates* 1988, p. 58). Claims of poor training may equally be applied to a variety of NATO forces, especially in periods of financial austerity. The performance of lead Soviet units in the Second World War was impressive and highly professional. Similar performances may not be beyond the current Soviet Army, particularly its forces in Eastern Europe (although category 2 and category 3 divisions based in the Soviet Union and some NSWP forces may fall well below this standard). As with the question of quality of equipment, although the balance appears to fall in NATO's favour, it cannot be considered to be decisively so.

Tooth vs. tail

NATO has outspent the WTO in defence every year since 1965, yet still appears to be in a numerically weaker position (Epstein 1987, p. 37). More, despite rough equality in manpower, the WTO has a considerably higher percentage of its troops in combat units and more main weapons systems deployed than NATO. Indeed, Stephen Canby has estimated that NATO requires twice the manpower to field a fighting force of a given size than does the Pact (Posen 1984, p. 68). NATO, and in particular the United States, appears to spend more for less. Why is this? One explanation is that the WTO is more efficient in its use of resources than is NATO. Although there have been examples of apparently gross inefficiency in resource allocation and procurement by NATO (Connell 1986; Falloows 1981), there is no convincing case that the Alliance is grossly and systematically more inefficient than the WTO (Luttwak 1982; Maddock 1988). An alternative explanation is that the WTO's offensive doctrine has been by its very nature cheaper than NATO's defensive role – that offence is cheaper than defence. Yet, as Epstein has pointed out, this is a curious reversal of Clausewitz's observation that defence is inherently easier than offence. Evidence that offence is cheaper than defence is also lacking. Finally, and most convincingly, there is the argument that NATO chooses to spend less on combat units ('teeth') in a deliberate decision to provide better support services ('tail'). Thus NATO troops enjoy superior C3I, logistics, maintenance, support and conditions of service than their WTO equivalents.

If this last point is correct, the question which emerges is whether this is the most efficient allocation of resources in terms of combat effectiveness. Barry Posen claims that these assets, invisible in a bean count, act as force multipliers up to a value of 50 per cent. According to Posen, the conscious decision to allocate more resources to support than to combat assets can only be logically explained by a conviction amongst NATO planners that it is more efficient to spend money in this way (Posen 1988, pp. 196–7).

Posen is correct that support assets can affect fighting effectiveness: combined arms forces which have run out of supplies cannot fight, commanders who cannot communicate and have no clear intelligence picture cannot command. But to explain NATO's allocation of resources as a logical step to improve force effectiveness overlooks a Western military style clearest in the US Army of the Second World War, when support assets received attention not as force multipliers but because of expectations of conditions of service derived from higher standards of living. NATO's emphhasis on rich support assets reflects Western society and the expectations of high standards rather than a logical analysis of military efficiency. Indeed it may be that in some areas NATO's military eeffectiveness *suffers* from its extensive support capabilities in addition to the opportunity costs of combat units foregone. In C3I for example a proliferation of intelligence sources, headquarters and communication facilities can lead to information overload, an unwieldy command structure, and a dependency on certain means of communication which may prove highly vulnerable in war. When this is added to NATO's relatively complex political command structure (to ensure maximum consultation between allies) the organization of command appears potentially confused, unwieldy and insensitive to battlefield needs.

The 'natural advantages' of the defence and offence

> the defensive form of warfare is intrinsically stronger than the offensive. (Clausewitz, quoted in Epstein 1987, p. 38)

Both offensive and defensive forms of warfare are credited with certain 'natural advantages' which cannot by their very nature be accounted for in a bean count. The two principal defensive advantages are that defenders can fight on familiar terrain which may have been prepared with defensive obstacles or a variety of strong points, and that to advance an attacker must expose himself and cross the 'empty battlefield', thus rendering himself vulnerable to attack. In contrast defenders can fight from concealed and/or protected positions. For NATO this latter advantage is lessened by a political limitation on pre-positioned hardened field defences. Many West Germans would object to their countryside being further dug up to provide steel and concrete shelters for the military. In addition there is a military objection, namely that constructing such defences would reveal the positions defenders would occupy. Instead NAATO troops would have the limited time available in a crisis to dig in. Against powerful modern field artillery it is doubtful whether such rough-and-ready trenches would provide much protection. NATO has therefore moved to emphasize greater manoeuvre in defence, reducing some of the natural advantages of the defensive in favour of the primary advantage of the offensive, namely surprise (see Ch. 5). For NATO, mobile forces would attack the advancing enemy at times and places of NATO's choosing, achieving surprise and disorienting the enemy.

The WTO would probably attempt to use the offensive advantage of surprise for primarily tactical and operational advantages rather than strategic, using deception (*maskirovka*) to gain a significant edge (see Ch. 4). Historically surprise has acted as an important and sometimes decisive factor in battle, from the small unit firefight to a campaign involving millions of men (such as Operation Barbarossa). Surprise however is not all or nothing, something which is either achieved or not, but rather something of degree. Thus the Soviets appear to accept that although they might not be able to surprise NATO completely, they hope that by deception they can reduce NATO's combat effectiveness. NATO may receive warning of a Soviet attack, but may be only partially mobilized and uncertain of where the attack is coming from (Cohen 1988, p. 61; Holmes 1988, p. 170). More, preventing surprise is not just a matter of gaining raw intelligence of an attack, but one of processing, interpreting and acting on that data. Judgements have to be made and the warning system is therefore vulnerable to the limitations of human psychology, military complexity and organizational viscosity (Betts 1977, p. 309). A force caught by surprise, off balance and without all of its assets fully deployed is much less effective than one fully alerted and prepared for enemy attack.

Other factors which might be added to this list of deficiencies in the bean-counting approach include: the quality of planning and preparedness; terrain; and the ability to trade space for time. The bean count fails to address many of the factors which can determine the outcome of combat. Some of these factors are intangible, and their impact inherently difficult to quantify. But others are more susceptible to attempts at quantification, and models have therefore been developed which attempt to measure force effectiveness and the dynamics of combat, rather than merely counting the men and matériel possessed by both sides.

Measuring force effectiveness

One of the more important failings of a bean-count approach is that it counts numbers rather than measuring effectiveness. The bean count also fails to give meaning to the figures produced: at what stage does an adverse force ratio become significant? When is a force 'decisively outnumbered'?

A much quoted rule of thumb is that a 3:1 advantage is required to ensure offensive success. The appeal of this is obvious: with the data from a bean count and this rule of thumb a simple 'meaningful' measure may be derived. But the 3:1 rule has been much abused, being essentially a tactical guideline inappropriate for operational or strategic judgements (Cohen 1988, p. 77). For example, two sides may be roughly equal overall, but if one commander successfully concentrates his forces for attack a local tactical superiority may be achieved and exploited. Thus offensive success may be achieved without an overall 3:1 superiority. Applying this tactical guideline as a ready reckoner for the forces on the central front is therefore not particularly meaningful. More, the guideline is based upon an assessment of force degradation through attrition in battle. In a war of manoeuvre, set-piece attritional battles might be less important than mobility and the ability to dislocate enemy forces. Thus the 3:1 rule might be inappropriate for this style of warfare. Nor is the rule a particularly reliable tool of analysis. In a major survey of some 600 battles the US Army concluded that a 3:1 advantage was not necessary for victory, nor could it guarantee victory (see Table 3.3). Finally this ready reckoner does not overcome the problem of how to judge between superiority in one weapon type and inferiority in another. For example, does it matter if NATO is outnumbered in terms of main battle tanks if it has more anti-tank helicopters and aircraft than the WTO? Bean counts do not produce a single figure to which the 3:1 rule can be applied, but rather a series of figures. The rule does not offer a means of determining the relative weight of imbalances in these various categories.

From these deficiencies with the 3:1 rule two requirements are apparent if force effectiveness is to be adequately measured. Firstly

Table 3.3 Battle outcome vs. force ratio

Force ratio (attacker: defender)	Outcome (percentage) Defender won	Draw	Attacker won
Less than 1:3*	40	0	60
1:3 – 2:3	51	2	47
2:3 – 3:2	36	6	58
3:2 – 3:1	31	6	63
3:1 or more	22	5	74

* Sample too small to be statistically significant.

Source: Combat History Analysis Study Effort (CHASE): Progress Report, August 1986, quoted in Epstein 1988, p. 156.

a standard unit of account is necessary to provide comparisons between forces of different composition. And secondly a more sophisticated understanding of combat dynamics is necessary to gauge the implications of an imbalance. This section deals with the first of these problems, the following section with the second.

A number of methods have been devised for assigning numerical values to variables such as quality and asymmetrical composition of forces. Such comparisons are made by devising a common unit of account based upon combat power. The most commonly used system is the armoured division equivalent (ADE) devised in the early 1970s by the US Army. The ADE uses a measure known as WEI/WUV (weapons effectiveness indices/weighted unit value) originally devised in 1973, but subsequently modified. The WEI component assesses the firepower, mobility and protection of weapons; the WUV assesses the importance of a weapon relative to other systems. The quantity and quality of weapons may thus be measured, though more intangible factors such as morale, or even some readily quantifiable elements such as ammunition stockpiles are excluded. The ADE is derived from the WEI/WUV score of one US armoured (heavy) division, one US division being one ADE (Cohen 1988, p. 79; Hamilton 1985, p. 134; Mearsheimer 1988, p. 175; Posen 1988, pp. 190–2).

A slightly different method used by William Kaufmann is to measure firepower in terms of FPUs (firepower units) which can then be weighted to account for armour and mobility. Other variables such as target acquisition, training and morale (measured by Kaufmann in terms of probability of firing a weapon), accuracy and reliability can also be factored in, in an attempt to measure force effectiveness (Kaufmann 1983, pp. 208–9). A third measure, developed by Andrew Hamilton, concentrates on 'fire teams' as the basic small-unit building blocks, assigning different values to different teams (e.g. an infantry squad, a tank and a howitzer would each be a given a numerical value according to its worth). By totalling these building blocks within a US armoured division Hamilton derives his basic unit of measure, the HDE (heavy division equivalent). By comparing this figure for an HDE with the building-block totals for other divisions, a figure for the military balance can be arrived at in terms of HDEs (Hamilton 1985, p. 135).

Each of these methods is subject to criticism on points of detail (Hamilton 1985, p. 135). But two fundamental problems exist for all such calculations. Firstly, there is the judgement to be made concerning the relative quality of weapons of the same type. It is difficult to determine whether one tank is better than another since a tank will often be better at some things and less good at others depending upon the design criteria. It is even more difficultt to decide how much better, and what figure to give. This is complicated by some weapons characteristics (particularly those of the WTO) being classified, making informed judgement difficult. Such calculations also tend to reflect the opinion of the analyst as to what is important (firepower, mobility or protection, for example) rather than objective criteria. Thus a factor unaccounted for in these measurements, such as C3I, may prove to be of critical importance in battle.

Secondly, judging the relative iimportance of different types of weapons is equally subjective. In his analysis Kaufmann assigns an infantryman with a rifle the value of one FPU and a main battle tank 100 FPUs. In contrast the US Army in 1974 assigned a weight of one for a rifle, but just 55 for a tank in defence, and 64 for a tank in the attack (Hamilton 1985, p. 135; Kaufmann 1983, p. 209). No matter how careful such estimates are, they remain estimates reflecting the opinion of an analyst. The use of figures gives an aura of objectivity, a 'scientific' feel to the measure. In reality they are maybe little more than guesses, albeit some more careful and better informed than others.

Thirdly, the reduction of weapons and forces to a common value tends to obscure the fact that different weapons and forces perform different functions. To use Eliot Cohen's analogy, a division is like an orchestra, requiring the balance of a variety of instruments. Reducing instruments to a common value will not reveal how the orchestra sounds or how good it is. Using such a calculation, an orchestra consisting solely of 200 violins might produce a higher score than the Berlin Philharmonic, but would not sound as good (Cohen 1988, p. 79). A division is a combined arms unit where balance is important. Calculations which reduce forces to a common unit of value are unable to reflect this necessary balance.[3]

Results from these calculations vary between analysts and between assumptions. Most of the results however show a balance between 1:1 and 2:1 favouring the WTO (Biddle 1988, p. 102; Hamilton 1985, pp. 115–16; Posen 1988, p. 190). This does not seem a decisive advantage, and is certainly well below the 3:1 rule. With WTO unilateral reductions, and the major reductions likely through a CFE treaty, this advantage will be further narrowed. But as Cohen has pointed out, when the Pentagon studied the military balance of May 1940 using the ADE methodology, the results showed that the Germans were 5–10 per cent *inferior* to the Allied forces. Within six weeks the Germans had routed the Allied armies and captured Paris (Cohen 1988, p. 78).

Two further factors need to be considered in this more complex static analysis, firstly mobilization schedules and the number of reserves, and secondly the impact of tactical air power. Asymmetrical mobilization can quickly lead to a rough balance on paper becoming a highly unequal contest. There are two parts to this mobilization question. The first is the number of reinforcements available, and the speed with which they can arrive at the front. The second is the amount of warning available to allow forces to mobilize and prepare themselves (and in particular the potential of a surprise attack).

Official wisdom claims that the WTO possesses an ability to build up its forces rapidly such that, even if NATO can absorb the first wave of a WTO attack (from forces based in Eastern Europe), the second strategic echelon will overwhelm the defenders. The 1976 Department of Defense analysis which underpins most subsequent analyses projects a 150 per cent build-up in Pact forces in the second and third weeks after mobilization (Posen 1988, p. 63; *Statement on the Defence Estimates* 1988, p. 65; Thomson 1989, pp. 85–7). Unofficial analyses similarly suggest impressive numbers of reinforcement divisions being available. One summary of a variety of such analyses claims that on mobilization the WTO would have 32 Soviet-style divisions available, that by M+9–10 this would have increased to 56–7 divisions, and by M+60–90 to 110–20 divisions. Thus two to three months into a war NATO would be outnumbered by 1.75:1 to 2.5:1 (Hamilton 1985, pp. 119–20).

This impressive WTO mobilizatiion is largely due to the use of reserve manpower to flesh out category 2 and category 3 divisions which in peacetime would have little more than skeletal staffs. Almost 80 per cent of the WTO divisions reinforcing the central front would rely on reservists compared to 40 per cent in NATO divisions (Hamilton 1985, p. 120). The fighting ability of these divisions is therefore open to some doubt. Soviet reservists have little of the training their NATO counterparts receive; category 2 and 3 divisions are rarely used in major exercises, denying them essential training; there is no guarantee that Soviet reservists would use the same equipment that they used when full-time soldiers; and there is similarly no guarantee that they will be fighting in the units they trained with (Posen 1984, p. 64). Thus if the WTO throws in large numbers of reserve divisons at an early stage, the quality of these divisions might be highly suspect.

NATO reserves are estimated to be capable of boosting in-place forces by 50 per cent within 14 days, and by up to 100 per cent within three months. Many of the front line European corps and divisions would have their strength increased by the addition of reservists, while yet more would undertake rear-area security duties, releasing regulars for the front line. Two key issues in the short to medium term after mobilization (M+7 − M+21) are the speed with which the six US REFORGER divisions and 60 tactical fighter squadrons can cross the Atlantic and be combat-ready (NATO plans estimate ten days for this; see Ch. 2) and the number of French divisions which would be committed to Germany. In the longer term (M+21–90) much is dependent upon the speed with which US National Guard divisions (reserve divisions comparable to Soviet category 2 and 3 divisions) can be mobilized. US estimates allow a minimum of three months for retraining to achieve combat readiness, a surprisingly long time since, unlike Soviet reserve divisions, US reserves undergo a minimum two-week annual refresher course with the units they will fight with. Limiting this retraining may reduce the time lag between mobilization and combat availability, as will the injection of increased finance in the early 1980s. Thus the critical gap between the arrival of Soviet and American reserves may be reduced (Posen 1988, p. 194).

As Hamilton has argued, however, this gap may be overstated, and may even bbe bridged by better use of European reserve manpower. Hamilton identifies the existence of a large under-utilized pool of trained manpower in Western Europe (see Table 3.4) and a large number of units which are either independent of divisions, or assigned rear-area security duties, or both (the equivalent of 20–23 divisions). More efficient use of these assets could improve NATO's medium-term manpower problems. In particular they may be organized into armoured divisions rather than infantry brigades, where although their training may be limited it will be roughly equivalent to that of the category 2 and certainly the category 3 divisions (Hamilton 1985, pp. 127–9).

Table 3.4 Hamilton estimates of NATO reserve manpower

	Active and reserve manpower committed to mechanized combat and support	Additional trained manpower available
Belgium	70,000	70,000
UK	120,000	200,000
Denmark	65,000	75,000
France	200,000	310,000/ 500,000
Netherlands	155,000	45,000
TOTAL	1,110,000	1,000,000/ 1,100,000

Source: Hamilton 1985, p. 128. Figures are for 1983–4. Estimates of the changing balance after mobilization can be found in: Hamilton 1985, p. 116; Kaufmann 1983, p. 60; Posen 1988, pp. 188 and 191; *Statement on the Defence Estimates* 1988, pp. 64–5; Thomson 1989, pp. 85–7.

The potential of these European reservists has recently engaged SHAPE's attention. In particular Deputy SACEUR General Sir John Akehurst has identified reservists as becoming increasingly important as the pool of available manpower shrinks in the 1990s through demographic changes. General Akehurst estimated that reserves would constitute between half and two-thirds of NATO's required wartime strength (van Loon 1989, p. 70).

The second half of the mobilization question concerns the amount of warning available and the associated problem of surprise attack. The combination of modern surveillance technologies and the probable large scale of any WTO mobilization suggests that NATO would receive technical warning of a likely WTO attack. Indeed, Soviet mobilization against Czechoslovakia in 1968, Afghanistan in 1979 and Poland in 1981, involving much smaller forces than would be required in a major assault on the central front, were all detected by NATO intelligence. The problem then is the correct interpretation of the raw intelligence and the political decision over what to do. History is replete with examples of raw intelligence being misinterpreted (the 1973 war in the Middle East and the 1982 war in the South Atlantic being two more recent examples). For NATO the major problem appears to be an unwillingness to act in a manner which might prove provocative. In particular there might be an unwillingness to risk the 'mad momentum' of competitive mobilization which preceded the First World War. Thus in the 1968 Czech crisis NATO reconnaissance flights were suspended and troops were ordered not to dig in. Similar 'non-provocative' moves were adopted during the Polish crisis of 1981. If this occurs when the Soviets are preparing to attack Western Europe a highly asymmetric mobilization pattern might emerge. Alternatively, since neither the Polish nor the Czech crises directly affected NATO security, a willingness to stand back was understandable; if NATO security was threatened, however, the practice might be different. As mobilization would be a political as well as military decision, the complex Alliance decision-making framework could limit or delay any decision. Thus despite strong indications from intelligence sources of imminent attack, NATO might be slow or reluctant to react (Holmes 1988, p. 169; Kaufmann 1983, pp. 59–61; Posen 1984, pp. 65–7).

Surpprise attack, though an ancient military tactic and strategy, is still of relevance in modern warfare. Surprise is more than a force multiplier; it can decide the course of battle. But surprise is usually relative not absolute. Thus claims that NATO is vulnerable to surprise attack are largely meaningless since what is important is the degree of surprise. Given the likelihood of any large-scale mobilization being detected by NATO the chances of achieving strategic surprise appear slight (though the early 1980s saw a scare over apparent Soviet attempts to develop such a capability with a 'standing start attack'; see Ch. 4). Soviet capabilities for a surprise unreinforced attack have been considerably limited by the unilateral reductions announced in the late 1980s, and are likely to be severely undermined by a CFE treaty. The possibility of achieving a degree of surprise sufficient to allow a decisive mobilization advantage, or of using in-place unreinforced forces alone, no longer seems a credible threat.

A final complication in attempting to assess combat power is the impact of air power on ground operations. From the Second World War on it has been apparant that the side with air superiority has a decided and sometimes decisive advantage over its enemy. Air power can be used not merely for reconnaissance and interdiction, but as a highly mobile source of firepower for units fighting on the front line (what is termed close air support, or CAS). This tactic was developed by the Luftwaffe in the Second World War to support panzer columns, given the lack of mobile artillery, and was subsequently used by Allied and Soviet commanders in that war. Since the Second World War CAS has come to be seen as a major component in land-air operations. The power of modern air-delivered munitions is such that a handful of CAS aircraft might wreak havoc and destruction upon an armoured division. Although NATO has a large number of aircraft capable of undertaking CAS missions, many of these are tasked with other missions as well. Accurately quantifying the effect of CAS on the conventional balance is not therefore possible as the number of aircraft available for CAS missions may vary substantially.

It is commonplace to grant NATO a considerable technological lead in air warfare (usually one of 5–10 years). Given the historical experience of technological advantage leading to highly favourable exchange ratios in this most technologically dynamic arena, NATO would seem to have a major advantage here. Further, the WTO have traditionally emphasized interdiction rather than CAS, and consequently have allocated fewer aircraft to the CAS mission. This generally favourable picture however must be mitigated by a number of factors. The WTO have made a significant investment in integral air defences. Modern WTO air superiority fighters will at least challenge NATO for control of the skies. NATO air bases may prove vulnerable to Soviet attack, either with improved conventional munitions, or with chemical agents. And what the Soviets lose in CAS they may gain in their interdiction capability threatening NATO's rear area, and in their considerable investment in attack helicopters rather than aircraft for the battlefield support role. On balance therefore NATO would seem to gain some advantage from its superior CAS. This capability is however challenged by the WTO, while the fact that the US Army is investing heavily in attack helicopters at the very least suggests that they consider NATO air forces pay insufficient attention to CAS.

Analysing combat dynamics

Static indices of combat power, whether simple bean counts or more complicated assessments such as the ADE methodology, reveal little about the likely result of a war. Does it matter if NATO is outnumbered? Or rather, at what stage does an imbalance in forces affect, or even determine, the outcome of battle? To arrive at some sort of conclusion about the effect of a force imbalance on battle it is necessary to analyse the dynamics of combat. A number of mathematical models have been constructed which attempt to analyse combat dynamics and act as tools to interpret static indices of combat power (inputs) into likely military gains and losses (outputs).

Frederick William Lanchester's laws of combat, devised during the First World War, have historically been the basis for most such analyses, including the US Department of Defense's computer models (Lanchester 1916; Lepingwell 1987, p. 89). Although Lanchester produced a number of mathematical models for combat dynamics, it is his square law which is most widely used and has received most critical attention. The square law may be illustrated by the following equation for stable conflict:

$$B^2 b = R^2 r$$

when B = the numerical strength of Blue forces
 b = the efficiency or fighting value of Blue forces
 R = the numerical strength of Red forces
 r = the efficiency or fighting value of Red forces.

If forces are unequal (i.e. if $B^2 b$ does not equal $R^2 r$), then Lanchester assumes that the superior side will concentrate its fire on the inferior, and casualties as a proportion of both forces will be asymmetrical. This will favour the superior side such that further concentration of fire will be possible until the weaker side surrenders, withdraws from combat, or is annihilated. A numerically inferior force may hold a superior force only if its superiority in fighting effectiveness (especially weapons) is much greater than its enemy's superiority in force size. This can be illustrated by the following example. Two lines of infantry face each other, each with the same fighting effectiveness (rates of fire, accuracy, etc.), but Blue has 32 men and Red has only 16. Assuming a 25 per cent hit probability, after the first round of fire Blue will have inflicted eight casualties on Red for the loss of just four men. The balance would then read Blue 28, Red eight. In the next round Red can inflict just two casualties on Blue, but will lose seven of its eight men. In the third round Blue will complete its annihilation of Red. To offset this a gross disparity in fighting effectiveness is required. To use Thomas F. Homer-Dixon's example, if Red has four units each capable of four rounds of fire per minute, and Blue has a single unit, Blue must fire 16 rounds a minute with the same accuracy as Red to ensure stable combat dynamics (Homer-Dixon 1987, p. 137).

Lanchester's square law therefore offers a means of assessing the attrition of forces as battle continues, and the likely results of combat. The square law predicts that an inferior force will rapidly become weaker and is doomed to lose. Thus as most static analyses, and in particular most bean counts, show NATO to be outnumbered, Lanchester-based analyses tend to predict the rapid defeat of NATO (Kaufmann 1983, pp. 210–4). As Joshua M. Epstein has pointed out, however, this is a somewhat unreal picture of combat since it excludes many of the tactics traditionally used by weaker forces to avoid the crushing defeats predicted by

Lanchester. In particular Epstein has pointed out that Lanchester concentrates on attritional warfare to the exclusion of movement. In reality weaker forces may withdraw and regroup, may trade space for time, or may attempt to undertake disproportionately successful flanking actions. Epstein also questions the reasoning behind squaring numbers relative to efficiency and the failure to account for diminishing marginal returns. Finally Epstein identifies the failure of studies of past battles to provide factual support for Lanchester as casting doubt on the validity of the square law (Epstein 1986, pp. 4–10; 1988, pp. 159–62).

As an alternative to Lanchester-based models, Epstein offers his more complex Adaptive Dynamic model. This model attempts to balance strategic and behavioural factors while reducing the importance of numbers. Most important though is Epstein's attempt to incorporate movement into his model by a mechanism which allows for the fact that forces adapt to changed battlefield circumstances. As battle continues both sides will adapt and the interplay of these two adaptive systems produces the combat dynamics of movement and attrition. Using this model Epstein produces much more optimistic results for a NATO–WTO conflict than the Pentagon's and Kaufmann's Lanchester-based calculations (Epstein 1986; 1987).

Finally the Attrition–FEBA Expansion model developed by Richard Kugler and used by Barry Posen attempts to grapple with the problem of what happens when breakthroughs occur. Starting with the rather artificial assumption that NATO will spread its forces evenly along its front line, holding in reserve what forces it can, the model examines the consequences of the WTO concentrating on three main axes and deploying minimum forces elsewhere to tie NATO down. As the WTO breakthrough develops, forces are moved by both NATO and the WTO to the sides of the salient. By factoring in assumptions on mobilization, force effectiveness, tactical airpower and force-to-space ratios (the space required for a given force to operate in, which can limit the amount of concentration possible), two curves are produced. The first shows force requirements over time, the second force availability (a combination of attrition and mobilization). By comparing the two curves judgements can be made about the likely results of battle. Posen points out that the model's results are highly dependent upon assumptions and judgements concerning variables, and that accordingly results favourable to both NATO and the WTO may be generated. Posen however clearly believes that NATO is not as decisively outnumbered as the Lanchester equations would suggest (Posen 1984).

Posen's caveat about the importance of assumptions made in determining the results from such models is applicable more generally than just to the Attrition–FEBA Expansion model. This point is illustrated by Stephen Biddle, who identifies the fact that most analyses assume *unstable* combat dynamics (i.e. that the weaker force will get progressively weaker, the stronger relatively stronger, thus exaggerating minor initial differences). But combat is not necessarily unstable. At some point an imbalance will be insufficient to generate the power necessary to impose asymmetrical attrition rates. Combat stability might also be highly scenario-sensitive, so that in certain circumstances (e.g. with tactical surprise) smaller forces may defeat larger. Thus the stability or instability of the combat process is dependent upon assumptions made over scenarios and over the point at which force ratios lead to asymmetrical attrition rates (Biddle 1988). John Mearsheimer has also argued that the space available on the central front may be insufficient for the WTO to concentrate its forces sufficiently to overpower NATO, and that by implication these models for combat dynamics are flawed (Mearsheimer 1983, pp. 181–3; 1988). Although Mearsheimer is correct in his underlying assumption that force may be constrained by space available, his analysis tends to suffer from inaccurate data over the degree to which Soviet forces are prepared to concentrate, over the possibility of long-range artillery and missiles spread over a considerable area being able to concentrate firepower onto very narrow sections of front, and over the attrition caused by successive WTO echelons eventually contributing to a WTO numerical advantage (Cohen 1988).

Conclusion

Attempts to measure the conventional balance are constrained by three major factors. Firstly, results from models are highly sensitive to changes in underlying assumptions. Different assumptions over the availability of tactical air power, weapons effectiveness, and the importance of C3I, for example, can produce major variations even in static bean counts. Secondly, assessments are highly sensitive to different politico-military scenarios. NATO and WTO cohesion, mobilization, surprise, and the direction, size and purpose of attack, for example, can all vary, producing different balances (Cohen 1988, p. 85). Barry Posen for example has identified three possible types of WTO attack: a smash and grab raid with limited objectives; an attempt to overthrow the central front by seizing West Germany, Belgium and the Netherlands; and an attack against the whole of Western Europe from the Pyrenees to the North Sea. In each scenario the size of the WTO force varies, as does the mobilization time required. NATO cohesion may similarly vary according to the type of attack (particularly French commitment against a limited attack). Questions must also be raised about the reliability of the NSWP forces. Finally the sheer complexity of any assessment is a major problem. This is not merely because the more sophisticated analyses attempt to cover a variety of scenarios and a range of assumptions, but because the number of factors involved in any sophisticated assessment are so great.

What emerges from this is a necessary caution over statements concerning the defensibility of the central front. Although analyses have been produced which argue that NATO is not decisively outnumbered, thus challenging official orthodoxy (Epstein 1988, p. 163; Holmes 1988, p. 172) this is less important than the revelations concerning the methodologies for measuring the balance. Quite simply the methodology does not exist for any definitive statement over the balance of forces, or the implications of that balance. By adopting certain methodologies and making certain assumptions, a particular result might be obtained. By changing the methodology and assumptions a different result is possible. The important point is that analyses are unable to demonstrate definitively that NATO's conventional forces *cannot* defend the central front. The conventional balance and its implications for the defensibility of the central region are uncertain partly due to methodological deficiencies, but also because so much depends on the way in which forces are handled, and what actually happens on the day of battle. In other words the balance is such that the way in which forces are used will be as or more important in determining the outcome of battle than the number and quality of forces available.

Notes

1 Notable examples of this include US estimates over Soviet strategic bomber and missile strength in the late 1950s–early 1960s, and German assessments of Red Army strength pre-Operation Barbarossa.
2 Most NATO weapons systems undergo some evolutionary development (for example the US F 4 Phantom jet fighter underwent considerable development over two decades of production), and almost all receive some sort of mid-life modernization. Similarly, complex systems may work very reliably if the technology is mature and well understood. Forty years ago televisions were considered

complex electronic systems and were prone to break down. As the technology matured so reliability has dramatically improved.

3   For example the Israelis found in the 1973 Middle East war that their divisions were too armour-heavy and lacked sufficient infantry. This was corrected by the time of the 1982 invasion of Lebanon, but would not have been revealed as an improvement by this form of measurement.

4

Soviet military doctrine

Whereas NATO has a rather vague idea of what constitutes military doctrine, the Soviet Union has a clear idea of doctrine as a structured, 'scientific' discipline.

> A military doctrine is a structured set of views, accepted in a country at a given time, which covers the aims and character of possible war, the preparation of the country and its armed forces for such a war, and the methods of waging it. (*Soviet Military Encycoplaedia*, quoted in Donnelly 1985, p. 20)

Soviet military doctrine is rooted in the Clausewitzian dictum that war is an extension of politics, a view of war adopted by Lenin, and in the nuclear age by writers such as Sokolovskiy (Donnelly 1985, p. 21; Dziak 1981, pp. 17–22). Its doctrine exists on two levels, the political and the military technical, so that it concerns not merely the employment of forces for battle, but wider questions concerning the purposes for which military power may be used. This latter point became increasingly important as nuclear stockpiles grew. If large nuclear stockpiles meant that war would lead to the destruction of the Soviet Union, Soviet strategists were forced to confront fundamental issues of the utility of war in the nuclear age. The development of Soviet military doctrine outlined below concentrates on the military-technical side, since this is the primary problem facing NATO. But as will become apparent, this cannot be divorced from developments on the political side. The analysis also concentrates upon the offensive component in Soviet military doctrine, not just because it is this which concerns NATO, but because of the emphasis in Soviet writings on the offensive as the basic form of military actions. But although there is some consensus in the West that (at least until recently) if the Soviet Union were to fight a war in Europe it would prefer to be on the offensive, there is no such agreement over whether at the political level Soviet military doctrine was offensively oriented. In other words, there was no agreement that the Soviet Union was intent upon attacking NATO. Gerard Holden has identified five reasons offered by Western analysts for the Soviet offensive posture.

1. To invade and occupy Western Europe, or by threatening to invade to gain influence there (to 'Finlandize' Western Europe).
2. To deter the USA from attacking the USSR by threatening a retaliatory invasion of Western Europe (war avoidance).
3. To deter attempts by West Germany or any other Western power at intervention in Eastern Europe.
4. To maintain control of Eastern Europe and enforce the Brezhnev doctrine.
5. Sheer inertia. The combination of a traditional emphasis on the offensive and the strength of the military in the Soviet political system. (Holden 1989, p. 12)

From this it is clear that there is no consensus on the nature of the Soviet threat to NATO. What this chapter therefore attempts to do is to trace the development of Soviet ideas on how to fight a war with NATO, if such a war were ever to become necessary. The starting point for this is to examine Soviet military doctrine in the Second World War (the Great Patriotic War). This provides an important data base and reference point for Soviet military thinkers, and casts several long shadows on Soviet attitudes to war.

The Great Patriotic War

The scale and ferocity of fighting on the Eastern Front from 1941 to 1945 was awesome. Estimates of losses on both sides are uncertain in all but their scale. According to John Erickson, the Soviets suffered over 12 million battle casualties (with perhaps 10 million of those fatalities) and a further 10 million civilian casualties. Between June 1941 and May 1945 the Red Army was fully engaged in fighting 88 per cent of the time, with a scant 145 days of relative quiet (Erickson et al. 1986, pp. 9–10). In so doing, Soviet estimates claim that the Red Army destroyed 607 German divisions (compared to an Anglo-American total of 176) and three-quarters of all German military equipment. No less dramatic was the impact upon the Soviet civilian population. For long periods of the war substantial areas of the Soviet Union were occupied and brutally oppressed by the Nazis. Over 70 per cent of housing and industry in the European regions of the USSR was totally destroyed. One in four Soviet citizens was killed or injured in the war – compared to 1 in 150 US citizens, and 1 in 40 British. Victory for the Soviets was dearly bought, and the experience has not been forgotten (nor has it been allowed to be). The result was an awareness of the cost of war which was without parallel in the West, an awareness which both served to sustain a high budgetary priority for the military, and a desire to avoid another long and bloody struggle (Donnelly 1988, p. 79).

The Soviet war effort was run by Stalin. Command was marked by strict centralization, with higher staffs merely acting as a means to channel information up to the supreme headquarters, the *Stavka*. The *Stavka* itself was dominated by Stalin, who kept a tight grip on not just strategic, but operational and even tactical issues. The *Stavka* maintained control by means of strict discipline, a strong emphasis on following orders, and by sending its representatives to the front to chivvy army commanders along (sometimes in a most ruthless fashion) and to report directly back to Stalin. The three key *Stavka* representatives in this were amongst the highest and most respected Soviet officers – Marshals Zhukhov, Vasilevskiy and Voronov. The result was a system which functioned very poorly in the early years, being prone to inflexibility, information overload, alienation of the upper command levels, and a lack of initiative (Erickson *et al.* 1986, p. 19). As the war progressed so some of these problems were overcome, and the system began to work more efficiently. Although tactical initiative was generally lacking, at the higher command levels Soviet generals displayed considerable talent. The use of the 'flying circus' of Zhukhov, Vasilevskiy and Voronov also served to overcome the alienation effects endemic to a centralized system (van Creveld 1985). But these developments were clearly an attempt to make Stalin's strictly centralized command system work rather than developing a new style of command.

A key feature of Stalin's centralized command system was his identification of 'permanently operating factors' which determined the outcome of war. Outlined early in 1942, these rapidly assumed the status of dogma, guiding the planning and conduct of military operations. The five factors Stalin identified were

- stability of the rear
- morale of the troops
- quantity and quality of divisions
- armaments of the army
- organizational ability of command personnel of the army

(Scott and Scott 1988, p. 18)

A number of features arise from this which are worth commenting upon. First, surprise is excluded. Stalin considered surprise a transitory not permanent factor, of operational but not strategic importance. In this way he was able to play down the significance of the Germans achieving surprise in Operation Barbarossa, the 1941 invasion of the Soviet Union. Surprise, and deception in particular, nevertheless remained an important part of Soviet operational planning. In Operation Bagration (the destruction of the German Army Group Centre in June 1944) the Soviets were able to deceive the Germans into believing that their main blow would fall further to the south against Army Group North Ukraine. The Soviets were therefore able to attack with a considerable superiority in men, tanks, guns and aircraft. This superiority was fundamental to the Soviets inflicting on the Germans a defeat greater in both scale and significance than that at Stalingrad (Niepold 1987, pp. 10–16 and 49–50).

A related feature to that of surprise is that of readiness. The German invasion demonstrated that the Red Army was in no fit state for a major war. The disastrous first few weeks displayed weaknesses in training, leadership, equipment, supplies and organization. This resulted in huge numbers of Soviet troops being out-fought, out-manoeuvred, surrounded and defeated. For the Red Army it was an unprecedented catastrophe of near fatal proportions (Erickson 1975).

The success of Barbarossa also demonstrated the vulnerability of an army geared for offensive operations which is suddenly forced onto the strategic defensive. This is a lesson the Soviets have continued to pay considerable attention to. As Christopher Donnelly has argued:

> Operationally, [the Soviets] recognise the vulnerability of an offensive system to disruption by surprise attack. It is not for nothing that almost all major Soviet and Warsaw Pact exercises start with a simulated attack by NATO (Donnelly 1988, p. 80)

Stalin's permanently operating factors also reveal an emphasis upon mass: in terms of numbers of men and equipment, and in the emphasis on stable rear areas being able to produce and supply weapons in sufficient numbers. The staggering quantities of weapons and ammunition produced by Soviet industry or procured through lend-lease with the United States were matched only by the manner in which forces at the front guzzled them up: over 100,000 tanks and self-propelled guns, 110,000 lorries, 17 billion rounds of small arms ammunition, 427 million artillery and mortar rounds, 13 million tons of fuel, 40 million tons of food, 73 million army tunics. Stalin was insistent that the war would be won and lost in the machine shops and, with US lend-lease providing not inconsiderable assistance, it was the Soviets who eventually outproduced the Germans (Erickson *et al.* 1986, p. 10). Complementing this emphasis upon volume production was an emphasis on achieving decisive numerical superiority at the critical points in battle. Forces would be echeloned into successive waves to achieve a pile-on effect, placing the outnumbered German troops under continuous pressure. Sheer weight of artillery fire and infantry would overwhelm defences at the selected points of breakthrough, rupturing lines and allowing mobile armoured groups to be released deep into the enemy rear. Artillery, not the tank, was the main striking force, the 'God of War'. Large artillery formations (artillery divisions) were created, able to concentrate massive firepower upon the selected breakthrough areas. In the final assault upon Berlin, Zhukhov concentrated a minimum of 189 artillery tubes on each kilometre of the front, increasing to 295 for the breakthrough sectors (Erickson 1985, p. 743). Artillery barrages developed in weight and sophistication as the war progressed, suppressing enemy defences to over a kilometre behind the front line, and offering support to the mobile groups once they were released. Tactical air support also developed, coordinating with artillery and infantry attacks. Eventually the combined arms battle emerged, where infantry, artillery, aircraft, engineers and armour coordinated their actions into a process of fire, shock power/attack and manoeuvre (Erickson *et al.* 1986, pp. 15–16).

Although the Red Army entered the war committed to manoeuvre operations, it was woefully ill-equipped for that form of warfare. The basic unit of organization in 1941 was the rifle division, a large (14 483 officers and men) predominantly infantry unit lacking the mobility and communications for effective manoeuvre. The huge Soviet tank park (consisting of more tanks than in the rest of the world put together) was almost entirely obsolete, though the excellent new T 34s and KV 1s were just entering production. By 1942 matters were improving with the greater availability of the new tanks, and the formation of tank corps and tank armies. These new tank formations were designed primarily for deep operations as a weapon of exploitation. Used for the first time in summer 1942, they initially proved too cumbersome. By the time of the Stalingrad counter-offensive in November 1942, however, the tank army had matured into a powerful weapon consisting of two tank corps and a mechanized corps (35 000–50 000 men and 550–700 tanks). The tank army was used as the mobile group for fronts, while independent tank corps acted as mobile groups for armies. From the battle of Kusk (1943) on, these mobile groups were used extensively by the Red Army: out of a total of 67 operations by tank armies, 11 were in the period 1942–3 and 56 from 1944–5 (Erickson 1975, pp. 53–75; Erickson *et al.* 1986, p. 12; Glantz 1983, pp. 6–7).

The Soviet mobile group finds its roots as an operational concept in the 1930s, and in the writings of Marshal Tukhachevskiy in particular. Both deep battle and Tukhachevskiy fell victim to Stalin's purges, so that in 1942 few commanders had any significant appreciation of the concept, and much had to be learned by trial and error. Simpkin identifies a three-phase pattern of attack which quickly emerged:

> independent tank brigades and battalions were assigned to all-arms and infantry formations for the break-in. These included the heavy tank regiments . . . equipped initially with the interim KV85, then with the Josef Stalin I. Tank and mechanized corps were given the tasks of completing the penetration, screening the flanks of the shock/mobile group, and/or seizing short-range operational objectives. And the tank armies . . . formed the front's mobile group (Simpkin 1987, p. 61)

Once launched, the mobile group would range deep into the enemy's rear, seizing key objectives or encircling the operationally static German defences (Niepold 1987, p. 63).

In contrast to this emphasis on manoeuvre, the Soviets developed considerable respect for the defensive potential of fixed fortifications and urban areas. Fighting in built-up areas was found to consume huge numbers of troops and slow advances considerably. The defence of Stalingrad and Leningrad, and the enormous effort required to take Berlin (where two divisions were required merely to take the Reichstag) stand as testament to the defensive potential of cities. Defended fortifications similarly posed enormous problems, and were bypassed wherever possible (Donnelly 1977; 1989, p. 81; Erickson 1975; 1985).

A final feature of Stalin's permanently operating factors is the considerable emphasis paid to morale, and the associated problem of discipline. Tight discipline was enforced throughout the forward units to maintain control. Tactical initiative was subordinated to the unquestioning obedience to orders. Tactical units as low as companies could order the execution of a soldier for failure to obey orders. Others guilty of disobedience might be assigned to the brutal penal battalions and given (literally) suicidal missions.

But this system worked in forcing soldiers to fight and to fight well. It was felt particularly necessary when dealing with Soviet ethnic minorities, who were understandably less highly motivated by the patriotic call to defend Mother Russia; the unreliability of the ethnic minorities was a major source of concern, particularly in the early years of the war when the Soviets stood on the brink of defeat, and substantial non-Russian areas passed out of Soviet control (Donnelly 1985, p. 85).

Finally a feature not brought out by the permanently operating factors, but crucial to the Soviet conduct and success of the war, was their ability to think at the operational level of war. This level sits between the strategic and tactical, and concerns the use of major formations within a theatre of operations (armies and fronts). Although the Germans regularly outfought the Soviets at the tactical level, they were defeated by the Soviets' ability to mass sufficient force to overwhelm defences almost regardless of how well they fought. It was this operational level of superiority which, for the Soviets, epitomized the military art: the fact that, despite having no overall superiority for much of the war, they were able to create local superiorities of decisive significance by their mastery of the operational art. The lack of initiative and flexibility at the tactical level was therefore overcome by the ability of the higher commands to outperform their German counterparts in operational thinking (Donnelly 1988, pp. 81 and 86).

Stalin and the nuclear age

Despite the advent of nuclear weapons, postwar Soviet doctrine atrophied along the lines of the permanently operating factors. The Red Army (renamed the Soviet Army) was reorganized into tank, mechanized and rifle divisions, emphasizing mobility and firepower. Numbers were reduced from a wartime peak of $c.$ 11 million to an armed forces total of $c.$ 4 million in 1948 (of which 2.75 million were in active army units). What doctrinal thinking there was concerned improving the sort of operations undertaken during the war. Ground forces remained the arbiter of victory, the quantity and quality of ground forces being the most important constituents of victory, and the conventional strategic offensive the means for achieving victory. By holding Western Europe at risk with its overwhelming advantage in numbers of divisions, Soviet conventional offensive capabilities were seen as the most effective – and only available – counter to the American nuclear monopoly

(Donnelly 1988, pp. 86–7; Erickson *et al.* 1986, pp. 20–4; Scott and Scott 1988, p. 19).

The conventional offensive therefore became the single most important operation for the Soviet military. Not surprisingly, given the first-hand experiences of 1941–5 and the conceptual straitjacket imposed by Stalin, the postwar offensive drew heavily on wartime operations. Major offensives would be undertaken by groups of fronts, each consisting of 3–4 armies with an air army in support. Combined arms armies would break through at a number of points, releasing the tanks in mechanized armies once they had reached operational depth. These would execute pincer movements of up to 200 miles depth, enveloping the enemy. A classic double encirclement would ensue, with follow-on rifle divisions establishing the inner perimeter of the trapped pocket, and the mechanized forces moving to establish the outer perimeter, preventing outside relief. The major developments from wartime norms concerned the replacement of the mobile group with augmented second echelons, the increased role of tactical airpower, a general increase in firepower and mobility, and consequently an increase in the size and tempo of battle (Erickson *et al.* 1986, pp. 24–5). More fundamental changes were not apparent.

The 'revolution in military affairs'

The death of Stalin in 1953 released Soviet military thinking from the straitjacket of the permanently operating factors, and allowed a major reassessment of the impact of nuclear weapons on military doctrine. This reassessment was termed the 'revolution in military affairs', and revolved around a number of key issues. Some of the changes were quickly accepted, others developed throughout the late 1950s and the early 1960s until Kruschev's removal from power, while yet others proved a major source of debate throughout this period.

At the political level three key issues emerged – the inevitability of war, whether victory was possible in a nuclear war, and whether nuclear escalation was inevitable. At three key Party Congresses (the 20th, 21st and 22nd), Kruschev developed the idea that nuclear weapons had made war no longer inevitable between the capitalist and communist blocs, and that peaceful coexistence was possible. The Third Party Program, which was adopted at the 22nd Party Congress in 1961, declared that the main objective of Soviet foreign and defence policy was to prevent nuclear war. Peace was to take precedence over socialism in foreign and defence policy. If war

SOVIET MILITARY DOCTRINE

did occur, then it would be a product of Western aggression. But once this aggression occurred, the Soviets would move onto the offensive to win the war as quickly as possible. A distinction was therefore drawn between the aggressive nature of imperialism which might lead to war, and the offensive nature of Soviet operations should war occur.

The possibility of war led to two further questions: would such a war inevitably escalate to a strategic nuclear exchange? And if it did, would there be a victor? On the first question there was some debate, the balance (including Kruschev) tending to see escalation as inevitable. This seems to have been reassessed in the wake of the Cuban missile crisis, and the possibility of limited local wars was acknowledged. There was a general consensus however that, despite the catastrophic nature of a nuclear war, socialism would survive, but capitalism would be finished by such a war. Socialist victory was therefore inevitable (Holden 1989, p. 5; Scott and Scott 1988, pp. 21-58).

The growing emphasis on nuclear war prompted a reassessment of the relationship between nuclear and ground forces. For Soviet military commentators, the nuclear armed missile was a revolutionary development comparable in effect to the introduction of gunpowder. As a result ground forces were no longer the decisive element in war. Instead the strategic rocket forces, created as a separate armed service in December 1957, became the paramount service. As nuclear forces were built up, so the army was reduced in size and importance. In January 1960 Kruschev announced his 'new look', the essence of which was that a third world war would be short and determined by nuclear strikes, not land operations. This view was reflected in the key military text of that period, Sokolovskiy's *Military Strategy*:

> a third world war will be primarily a nuclear rocket war . . . Consequently, the leading service of the Armed Forces will be the Strategic Rocket Forces . . . The basic method of waging war will be massed nuclear rocket attacks inflicted for the purpose of destroying the aggressor's means of nuclear attack and for the simultaneous mass destruction and devastation of the vitally important objectives comprising the enemy's military, political and economic might, and also for crushing his will to resist and for achieving victory within the shortest time possible . . . the initial period of the war will be of decisive importance for the outcome of the entire war . . . Consequently, the main task of Soviet military strategy is the development of methods of reliable repulse of a surprise nuclear attack of

the aggressor. (Sokolovskiy, quoted in Scott and Scott 1988, pp. 37–8)

In stark contrast to Stalin's permanently operating factors, surprise attack was considered a central, strategic concern – although Kruschev was careful to emphasize that an American first strike would still leave some Soviet missiles untouched, and would not therefore be a decisive, war-winning move (Goure 1987, p. 148; Scott and Scott 1988, pp. 22–62).

Things were not quite so simple as this however. Kruschev's public relegation of ground forces to a subsidiary role in 1960 may have owed much to deteriorating Sino-Soviet relations and Mao's declared willingness to sacrifice 100 million Chinese in a world revolution. By downgrading the role of ground forces, Kruschev was maintaining the Soviet Union's position in the socialist hierarchy in the face of a growing Chinese threat (Scott and Scott 1988, p. 60). Petersen and Hines also argue that, rather than being persuaded of the utility of nuclear weapons, it was in the Soviets' interests for the war to stay conventional, and it was NATO's explicit commitment to early and massive nuclear use which prompted the Soviets down the same path. The combination of NATO's superiority in tactical and strategic nuclear weapons, Soviet conventional superiority, and the likelihood that nuclear war would destroy the spoils of victory (i.e. Western Europe) created a preference for a conventional war tempered by the nuclear orientation of NATO strategy (Petersen and Hines 1983 p. 696). What therefore seems to have emerged is a doctrine rather less clear-cut in its emphasis on nuclear weapons. Although Kruschev recognized that a war might be short, fought with strategic (nuclear) weapons before operational (ground) forces could be deployed, he also acknowledged that war might be protracted. Similarly, although the strategic rocket forces assumed the primary role in Soviet doctrine under Kruschev, he also recognized that other forces would be required to consummate any victory – in particular by invading and occupying enemy territory. Thus Kruschev seems to have adopted a compromise position between the competing interests of the nuclear advocates and the ground forces (Erickson *et al.* 1986, p. 16; Scott and Scott 1988, pp. 41 and 56).

At the military–technical level, doctrine was influenced both by the developments at the political level outlined above, and by the increased mobility of ground forces and the availability of tactical nuclear weapons. From the early 1960s on, Soviet tactical nuclear weapons started to become available in sufficient numbers to have a major impact upon battle. At the same time infantry divisions were motorized, and the Soviet Army restructured into just two standard divisional formats, motorized rifle divisions (MRDs) and tank divisions. A combined arms army would consist of 3–4 MRDs and a tank division (1000 tanks in all), and a tank army of 3–4 tank divisions (1500 tanks). As important as this increased mobility for the infantry (which enabled higher speeds of advance), were the increased numbers and importance of tanks in both types of division (Donnelly 1983, p. 52; 1987, p. 87; Erickson *et al*, 1986, p. 27; Scott and Scott 1988, pp. 39 and 56).

Although army generals from Zhukhov down argued for the continued importance of ground forces, it was clear that these forces would have to operate on a nuclear battlefield. The NATO strategy of early use and the widespread US deployment of tactical nuclear weapons meant Soviet ground forces would be targeted by nuclear weapons. But equally the Soviet armed forces would have their own tactical nuclear weapons. Thus a nuclear dimension was incorporated into Soviet operational planning. Whereas in the past enemy lines would have been ruptured by a first echelon attack, and the second echelon or mobile group would exploit this, tactical nuclear weapons now became the means of rupture, to be exploited by a succession of echelons. As the first echelon was exhausted, so it would be replaced by a subsequent echelon, maintaining momentum in a steamroller fashion. To avoid creating targets for NATO nuclear strikes, enemy lines would be ruptured in a number of places, and Soviet forces would advance along multiple axes splitting NATO into small packets of surrounded troops. Thus the requirement to concentrate forces (and so create tempting targets for NATO nuclear strikes) would be reduced. Vulnerability to nuclear attack would also be reduced by high rates of advance and the avoidance of clear lines of battle. In this confused battlefield NATO would be unable to identify targets for attack, or would find Soviet forces too close to NATO forces for nuclear weapons to be used (Donnelly 1983, p. 52; 1988, p. 87; Erickson *et al*. 1986, pp. 26–8; Karber 1979, p. 29; Petersen and Hines 1983, p. 706).

Developing a conventional variant

With the removal of Kruschev from power in 1964, little change was apparent in the military leadership, nor at first in military doctrine. In the mid-1960s, however, changes began to appear, particularly on the questions of escalation and victory, and by 1966–7 it was clear that the Soviets were beginning to consider that a war in Europe might not necessarily go nuclear; a conventional variant to the Soviet offensive was under consideration. Although MccGwire identifies 1966/7 as the time of a decisive shift to a conventional option, discussions were certainly spread over a greater period of time than this, and even in the late 1960s Defence Minister Grechko bemoaned the fact that troops in exercises were still relying on nuclear strikes to destroy the enemy and allow subsequent exploitation (Bluth 1989; Erickson *et al.* 1986, p. 30; MccGwire 1987; Scott and Scott 1988, pp. 44, 48 and 61).

This shift can be seen as a product of a number of factors. The adoption of flexible response by the United States in the early 1960s and subsequently by NATO in the mid-1960s raised the possibility that NATO might not use its nuclear weapons until some time into a conflict. When coupled to the apparent reluctance of certain NATO members to sanction nuclear use, and the likely delays in release authorization, the conventional period might amount to a number of days. If the Soviets could conduct a fast, *Blitzkrieg*-style operation, they might be able to win the war in Europe before NATO could arrive at a decision to use nuclear weapons. The Soviets would therefore be able to present NATO with a *fait accompli* (Donnelly 1988, p. 87; Goure 1987, p. 150; Petersen and Hines 1983, pp. 695–6; Scott and Scott 1988 pp. 46 and 49).

The problem, as Snyder comments, is that as the Soviets approached conventional victory so they would create the situation whereby NATO *would* use nuclear weapons: this was exactly the scenario flexible response foresaw, and Soviet writings acknowledged this. Rather Snyder claims that the crucial change in 1966–7 was a result of bureaucratic politics within the Soviet Union, not the changing strategic environment. Snyder identifies a key meeting in December 1966 in which a deal was struck between Defence Minister Grechko and Brezhnev, the result of which was the public proclamation of a conventional option. For Grechko, a conventional option justified a large standing army and high military expenditure. For Brezhnev it created the illusion of some control over escalation, but more importantly secured both his position as commander in chief of the armed services and the political support of the military (Snyder 1987, pp. 123–4).

Although Snyder's argument is important, and goes some way to explaining the shift in 1966–7 identified by MccGwire, it does not fully evade the case that flexible response had some effect on Soviet military doctrine. As has been stated earlier, even under Kruschev a preference for conventional operations can be identified, but the NATO strategy of early nuclear use seemed to preclude this. The reform of NATO strategy went some way to removing this problem. Additionally NATO's political weakness and unwillingness to use nuclear weapons might enable a rapid conventional operation to be completed before escalation was authorized. If nothing else, the possibility was tempting.

But the 1970s provided another reason for optimism that NATO might be reluctant to escalate and that a conventional option might succeed. The Soviet achievement of parity at the strategic and theatre levels removed NATO's position of escalation dominance. NATO could no longer escalate to a position of relative superiority. Rather escalation would increase the level of destruction for no real advantage. Therefore the incentive to cross the nuclear threshold was substantially reduced (Donnelly 1988, p. 87; Karber 1979, p. 31; Petersen and Hines 1983, p. 696).

Soviet confidence in a conventional variant was further boosted by a belief in the mid-1970s that the Soviet army was more than a match for NATO, and that the NATO policy of forward defence rendered it vulnerable to attack (Erickson *et al.* 1986, p. 30; Petersen and Hines 1983, p. 698). Thus when Brezhnev adopted a policy of no first use of nuclear weapons in the early 1980s, he was reflecting a well-established preference for a conventional rather than nuclear war. This preference was based both on a belief in the capacity of the Soviet armed forces to win such a war and win it quickly, and in the belief that if the war escalated there would be no victors, only mutual catastrophe – another departure from the Kruschev line (Donnelly 1985, p. 20; Scott and Scott 1988, pp. 116 and 124; Warner 1989, pp. 15–16).

At the military–technical level, changes were required in terms of doctrine, equipment and organization to match the shift away from Kruschev's 'one variant war'. Soviet divisions in the mid–late 1960s were seen as lacking the weapons for a credible conventional option. A major build-up followed, improving both the quality and numbers of weapons with divisions based in Eastern Europe. Divisional strength increased by around 20 per cent, with the most dramatic changes occurring in the motor rifle divisions (whose tank strength increased by over 40 per cent to 266 tanks per division). In line with the combined arms concept, artillery strength was increased and self-propelled guns introduced to keep pace with a fast-moving assault. Engineering assets were improved, and logistic stockpiles increased. Tactical conventional missiles and precision-guided weapons (ATGMs and SAMs) were introduced, frontal aviation was greatly strengthened (particularly for close air support), and combat helicopters were developed. All this seemed to indicate a serious attempt to improve the mobility, firepower, sustainability and general strength of Soviet conventional forces. One estimate suggested that as a result of these improvements, the Group of Soviet Forces in Germany's 20 divisions in the mid-1970s were the equivalent of some 25–30 divisions of the mid-1960s (Erickson 1977, pp. 51–2; Erickson *et al.* 1986, pp. 30–1 and 41; Karber 1979, p. 30; Petersen and Hines 1983, pp. 672–3).

Throughout this period Soviet military thinking continued to concentrate upon the offensive (Scott and Scott 1988, p. 154). New doctrinal methods therefore had to be developed to replace the previous reliance on nuclear weapons for the breakthrough. Of particular importance were the lessons from the Arab–Israeli wars of 1967 and 1973. In the 1967 war, the Israeli use of air power demonstrated how a combination of pre-emption and close air support could help achieve decisive victories very quickly. A conventional *Blitzkrieg* still seemed viable. Less satisfactory were the lessons of 1973. Aside from the rather disappointing performance of the Soviet-backed Arab armies, attention focused on the use of anti-tank and anti-air precision-guided weapons (ATGMs and SAMs respectively). The implication of these weapons seemed clear: these new weapons had placed the tank and the aircraft, the key weapons of the *Blitzkrieg*, in a new position of vulnerability. Faced with a prepared NATO defence using these weapons (in which the West had, or would have, a lead), could the Soviets launch a successful *Blitzkrieg*? This question prompted a major debate in the two years following the 1973 war. The result was a series of operational and tactical changes which formed the basis for Soviet operational doctrine in the late 1970s (Donnelly 1978, p. 1406; Erickson 1977, p. 53; Karber 1976a, p. 13; 1979, pp. 30–1).

Soviet doctrine as it emerged in the mid to late 1970s displayed a number of key features. The first of these was the requirement to avoid a war of attrition. Such a war would allow NATO the time to unite politically, to mobilize its powerful reserves, and above all to make decisions on nuclear release. If a Soviet attack was to succeed, it had to be over in a matter of days. Speed was essential, with very high rates of advance maintained along key sectors (Karber 1979, p. 31; OTA 1987, p. 61).

Secondly, fire support had to be improved to compensate for the loss of nuclear weapons. Artillery and air support would provide a volume of fire throughout the depth of the enemy defences. A sophisticated fire support plan was devised to suppress enemy defences, enable a breakthrough in key sectors, and support the forces exploiting the breakthrough. The weight of fire in breakthrough sectors would be sufficient to destroy 50–60 per cent of NATO's major weapons systems (including ATGMs) before the manoeuvre elements reached the point of contact. The emphasis also shifted to even shorter barrages, cutting the time down to a handful of minutes to allow maximum surprise and avoid NATO firing against Soviet artillery (Petersen and Hines 1983, pp. 711–15).

Even with these improvements in speed and firepower, Soviet commentators doubted whether they could penetrate a thick, prepared defensive belt. Interestingly it appeared that the Soviets were more concerned with the density of defences (particularly ATGMs) than with the abilities of specific weapons. A third feature to emerge then was that of pre-emption. The Soviets identified NATO's 'layer cake' structure of national corps as a potential source of weakness (see Ch. 2). Whereas some corps might achieve high states of readiness very quickly, others might be slower. Thus pre-emptive manoeuvre would be used to find those sectors of NATO less well prepared, and to attack the defences there before they mobilized (Donnelly 1983, p.38; 1985, p. 23; Karber 1979, pp. 31–2).

The method of attack envisaged by Soviet planners was an assault across the entire length of NATO's defences (possibly including Austria as well), breaching these defences at a number of key points and penetrating deep into NATO's rear to paralyse its command and control. Some flexibility was shown in the location of breakthrough sectors, with an emphasis being placed on finding those areas where NATO was weakest or less well prepared. Forces would be echeloned at all levels from a front to divisional. This would create the weight and momentum necessary for attack while avoiding over-concentration (and thus offering targets for nuclear attack). Initially the method of echeloned attack was a simple 'steamroller' approach of one echelon piling onto another. As will be seen below, however, this developed into a rather more sophisticated idea with the introduction of the Operational Manoeuvre Group (Donnelly 1983, pp. 38 and 49; Erickson 1977, pp. 55–6; Goure 1987, p. 158; OTA 1987, p. 61; Petersen and Hines 1983, p. 729).

A fourth feature was a priority on destroying NATO's nuclear weapons. Soviet planners were well aware that a conventional attack against a nuclear power might provoke a nuclear response. Even if this could be limited to the battlefield (something the Soviets remained sceptical about), it would have catastrophic results. To reduce the risk of nuclear attack, NATO's nuclear weapons would have to be destroyed by pre-emptive attacks, and by Soviet forces in NATO's rear (Petersen and Hines 1983, p. 705).

The new Soviet doctrine was also marked by an emphasis on air power. Fire support from ground-attack aircraft and helicopters went some way to offsetting the loss of nuclear strikes. Airborne and air assault operations were devised as a means of overcoming NATO defences, or of bypassing them and creating havoc in the rear. And the more offensive use of air power would help achieve air superiority, protecting ground forces from NATO air attacks (Karber 1979, pp. 33–4; Petersen and Hines 1983, pp. 707–8; Warner 1989, pp. 17–18).

Finally surprise was considered essential for the success of a major conventional operation. The Soviets paid some attention to minimizing NATO's preparations, both in peace and in crisis situations, but acknowledged that strategic surprise was unlikely. A war with NATO was likely to begin with an international crisis which would alert NATO to the possibility of attack. But the degree of NATO's readiness for an attack, the location of key points of effort, and the timing of an attack were all open to some degree of influence. Soviet deceptive methods would therefore attempt to prevent or minimize NATO mobilization by playing down the crisis, and would attempt to conceal the key areas of advance until as late as possible. There was even talk of an unreinforced attack to obtain maximum surprise. In this scenario WTO forces would mobilize at the last possible moment and attack out of garrisons with what they had rather than waiting for reinforcements (what was termed the 'standing start attack'). Surprise was considered a force multiplier, and achieving surprise was a prerequisite for the rapid defeat of NATO (Donnelly 1983, pp. 44–7; 1985, pp. 26–7; Karber 1979, p. 32; Petersen and Hines 1983, p. 734).

In the late 1970s and early 1980s the Soviets began to introduce a major new development to this conventional variant, the Operational Manoeuvre group. The origins of the concept can be traced back to Tukhachevskiy's 1930s ideas of deep battle, and to the wartime experience of mobile groups. First publicly revealed in the Polish military press in 1981, the OMG was a powerful fighting body which would break away from the main echeloned attack to raid deep in the enemy's rear. It would operate there independently for a limited period of time, neutralizing key installations and generally wreaking havoc. (Donnelly 1983, pp. 44 and 51–4; Glantz 1983, pp. 4–5; OTA 1987, p.62; Petersen and Hines 1983, pp. 720–1; Simpkin 1987; Swan 1986, pp. 43–6).

The composition of the OMG was to some extent unclear in the West. This was partly due to the flexibility of the concept, so that the size of the OMG could be varied depending on whether it was operating as part of an army or front. It was also partly a product of some confusion in the West over whether the OMG was a specialized force incorporated into Soviet/WTO military organization, or whether it was a concept which would have forces assigned to it if and when it was implemented. However, a number of features were identifiable. The OMG was an all-arms unit, with strong air support acting as mobile artillery (particularly from helicopters). At army level it would be of divisional strength, at front level it would be roughly the size of a corps. It would consist of either tank or motorized rifle divisions, with integral logistics support. Finally the OMG would be drawn from existing units rather than involving the creation of additional forces (Donnelly 1983, pp. 44 and 55–7; OTA 1987, pp. 66 and 71; Swan 1986, p. 46). Although the OMG was to act independently of the main thrust, it would be assigned a number of specific targets by the army or front commander. Priority would go to destroying nuclear forces, command posts, electronic warfare assets and anti-aircraft defences, as well as to the general aim of creating havoc and confusion in the enemy rear. The OMG would force NATO to change its focus away from forward defence to rear-area security and thereby help speed up a WTO advance (Donnelly 1983, pp. 51–3).

By the mid-1980s two distinct methods of inserting the OMG into NATO's rear could be identified, reflecting perhaps some disagreement in the WTO, or alternatively the development of the concept. The first method identified was similar to that used by mobile groups in the Second World War, namely to exploit a breakthrough by first-echelon forces. At the army level this would mean inserting a divisional-sized OMG in the wake of the first echelon divisions. In this instance the OMG might even replace the second echelon divisions. Against stiffer defences, the OMG might be held back until second echelon divisions had secured the breakthrough. The second method, which began to appear in the mid-1980s, was for the OMG to exploit a gap in NATO's defences. The OMG would act as a pre-emptive raiding force rather than exploiting a first echelon success. In both cases, however, OMG operations were characterized by speed, surprise and an early introduction into battle (up to 1–2 days after first contact). These characteristics were essential if the relatively vulnerable OMGs were to survive once committed. When in NATO's rear they might remain as a single force, or sub-groups (perhaps of regimental size) might split off to attack individual targets. Finally the OMG concept tended to reinforce the value of secret behind-the-lines operations by such forces as *Spetsnatz*, and *desanty* operations by air assault forces. These again would help sow confusion in NATO's rear, reducing military efficiency, and transferring attention away from the front line (Donnelly 1983, p. 56; OTA 1987. p. 66; Swan 1986, pp. 46–7).

By the late 1970s the Soviets had developed a formidable capability for conventional warfare. The introduction of the OMG in the early 1980s added a doctrinal refinement which alarmed some NATO commanders. But a number of significant weaknesses could also be identified. The raw skills of conscripts, particularly from the central Asian republics, left much to be desired. There was a lack of advanced technical skills for the repair and maintenance of modern systems. Recruitment was increasingly a problem, as was bullying, corruption and alcohol abuse. Training often did not approximate to battle conditions. There were doubts over the reliability and capabilities of non-Soviet Warsaw Pact units. The inflexible command and control system and the general lack of initiative were perennial deficiencies exacerbated rather than eased by modern battle conditions. The key element of surprise was becoming more difficult to achieve as technology rendered the battlefield increasingly transparent. Increased rates of fire and the requirement for rapid advance placed great strains on logistics. The increased urbanization of West Germany threatened to slow any Soviet advance (some Soviet estimates reckoned on having to take a major city every 40–60 km of an advance, that is every other day). Concerns were apparent over the ability to provide the necessary volume of artillery fire on breakthrough sections as technology improved the responsiveness and accuracy of NATO's counter-battery fire (i.e. NATO's ability to identify and target Soviet artillery formations). And finally there was concern over the lack of infantry in the tank heavy units assigned to penetrate and exploit NATO's defences, particularly given NATO's extensive use of ATGMs (Bracken 1976; Erickson 1977, p. 53; Mearsheimer 1982, pp. 30–5; Petersen and Hines 1983, pp. 716 and 733; RUSI 1989a, p. 17).

The OMG was also vulnerable on a number of counts. Its speed of advance made it difficult for sub-groups which had peeled off to re-join the main force, while its size limited the number of sub-groups available. Keeping the OMG supplied deep in the enemy rear would be difficult at best. Local air superiority was essential, but could not be guaranteed. Adverse weather could slow an advance, as could scatterable mines. Incorrect timing when commiting the OMG (the trickiest part of wartime mobile group operations) could lead to disaster. The failure to maintain speed and surprise would allow NATO the opportunity to attack the OMGs vulnerable rear and flanks. Lack of integral firepower meant prepared defences would have to be avoided. And finally lack of initiative amongst the Soviet officer corps raised serious question marks about the viability of such a 'daring thrust' (Swan 1986, p. 48). In short the OMG was a risky concept which, if incorrectly executed, could leave key Soviet forces trapped and without supplies deep in NATO territory.

The Ogarkov revolution

During the early to mid-1980s the Soviet military hierarchy became increasingly aware that modern warfare was changing. Two successive Chiefs of the General Staff, Marshals Ogarkov and Akhromeyev (Chiefs of the General Staff 1977–84 and 1984–8 respectively) began referring to a 'revolutionary transformation in military affairs'. The result was what became known as the 'Ogarkov revolution'.

As Chief of the General Staff, Ogarkov was officially second in the military hierarchy behind the Minister of Defence. But his forthright writings, interviews and television appearances made him the dominant military figure of the early 1980s and drew considerable attention from the West (Scott and Scott 1988, p. 99). Ogarkov's concerns were not exclusively doctrinal. He was critical of arms control, argued for further increases in the military budget, and pressed for greater military influence in defence decision-making. His successor, Akhromeyev, was rather more circumspect in his political pronouncements, but appeared to share many of Ogarkov's concerns, particularly on doctrine (Herspring 1986, pp. 524–31).

Both Ogarkov and Akhromeyev appeared to place less emphasis on nuclear weapons. Escalation remained possible, and conventional forces had to remain 'nuclear scared', but strategic parity and new conventional force multipliers made nuclear war less likely and less necessary respectively. The General Staff publicly rejected Sokolovskiy's 1962 belief that war would inevitably escalate. Rather they appeared concerned with limiting nuclear use, and replacing nuclear weapons with new conventional technologies for some missions. The greatly improved range, accuracy and firepower of conventional weapons allowed them to be used with confidence against targets throughout the entire depth of NATO's force deployments (Goure 1987, pp. 154–5; Herspring 1986, p. 528).

These improvements in conventional weapons, coupled to improvements in nuclear and electronic systems, constituted a revolution in military technology. But as important as the systems themselves was the fact that the pace of technological change was accelerating, and that the modern battlefield was dominated by high-technology weapons systems. In addition there was the prospect of entirely new weapons systems based on 'new physical principles'. The implication seemed clear. Numbers were no longer sufficient. The Soviet Union had to match the West's accelerating rate of technological change and had to become more technologically aware in order to compete on the modern battlefield (Goure 1987, pp. 154–5; Herspring 1986, p. 526; Scott and Scott 1988, p. 114).

This recognition of a revolution in military affairs affected Soviet thinking about war and consequently organization for war. Ogarkov was clear that technological changes would increase the tempo and destructiveness of war. Accordingly the size of military operations and the requirement for close coordination between all services were to be increased. The result was not just a belief in dynamism, manoeuvre and the need to seize and retain the initiative, but the creation of a new command structure to better coordinate operations on the modern battlefield. As technology increased the range of weapons, so operations would be conducted at a level higher than that of front or even groups of fronts. Similarly, to coordinate the actions of a number of services a high-command post had to be established. Thus the theatre of military operations (TVD) was created to coordinate the actions of a variety of fronts and services (Goure 1987, p. 157; Scott and Scott 1988; pp. 119–20).

Soviet doctrine in the mid-1980s therefore emphasized a fast-moving combined arms offensive to be conducted across the breadth and depth of NATO's defences. Although the Soviet Union claimed to be defensively oriented, if a war occurred the offensive remained the key to military success. This would be conducted with conventional weapons as far as possible, and with greater attention to high technology systems.

Gorbachev and 'new thinking'

Whereas the Ogarkov revolution was largely confined to developments at the military-technical level, the mid to late 1980s saw a fundamental review of Soviet security policy at all levels. Under the leadership of Mikhail Gorbachev a new flexibility, self-restraint and willingness to make concessions has been used to defuse US/Western hostility. Ideological conflict has been replaced by the promotion of 'all-human' or universal values, principally war prevention. Lying behind these changes has been the emergence of a new package of ideas termed 'new political thinking'. Although some of these ideas were emerging in Soviet security policy before Gorbachev, and others have subsequently been identified with various Soviet writers and thinkers in the early 1980s, it is apparent that the Gorbachev leadership has provided the political climate whereby these new, sometimes radically different ideas have been combined and incorporated into official thinking.

The key strands to this new thinking are relatively easy to identify. The first is the rejection of the use or threatened use of force as a tool of foreign policy. In particular the disutility of nuclear weapons is acknowledged. Nuclear deterrence is portrayed as inherently unstable and politically dangerous, and nuclear disarmament has therefore received particular attention. Complementing this has been the belief that security can only be achieved at the political level, not the military-technical, and that security involves economic, humanitarian and ecological concerns as well as the more traditional military concerns. This has led to the acknowledgement of the interdependence of survival and hence security in the modern world. In a radical departure from traditional Soviet zero-sum thinking about security (that security is a national problem which can be best solved by achieving unilateral advantages over a perceived hostile power), 'new thinking' portrays security as a shared problem requiring cooperative action. Gorbachev has displayed a clear recognition of the security dilemma, and has promoted common security as the principal means of overcoming this problem (see Ch. 1). The acceptance of the security dilemma and espousal of common security has led Gorbachev to argue for reasonable sufficiency in Soviet forces, and a defensive defence doctrine. Continued military build-ups are recognized as not only expensive (and probably too expensive for the Soviet economy to bear) but ultimately self-defeating through the workings of the security dilemma. The traditional preference for offensive military operations has similarly been recognized as self-defeating in creating a threatening image of the Soviet Union and insecurity in the European system (Allison 1989, pp. 4–5; Holden 1989, pp. 2–6; Meyer 1988, p. 133; Snyder 1987, pp. 118–20; Warner 1989, p. 14).

Considered as a package, new thinking implies major changes for the Soviet military. Doctrine at both the political and military-technical levels, force organization, the size and shape of military budgets, and the military's role in defence decision-making will all be significantly affected – and in some cases already have been. The changes also have major implications for the West's appreciation of the Soviet threat, and its own approach to security. But this raises fundamental questions over the extent and durability of new thinking. Is it a temporary phenomenon which may be replaced at a later stage by a more aggressive policy, or does it represent a fundamental and irrevocable shift forced on the Soviet leadership by economic or other constraints? And is new thinking limited to the political leadership and some in the upper echelons of the Soviet military hierarchy, therefore lacking a solid long-term foundation, or is it percolating through and being gradually accepted throughout the Soviet security establishment?

An important indicator for this is the motivation behind 'new thinking'. Explaining why the Soviet leadership has changed its views on security policy goes some way to revealing the extent and durability of this change. Unfortunately there is no consensus over the motivation lying behind the Soviet Union's new approach to security. Rather five different types of explanation have been offered by Western analysts.

The first explanation of the motives behind new thinking links two of the dominant features of the Soviet economy in the 1980s: economic stagnation and high defence expenditure. By the time of Gorbachev's ascendancy in 1985 the Soviet economy had stagnated to the point of crisis. The exact figures to support this vary in degree. (One Soviet analyst, Abel Aganbegyan, has claimed that by the late 1970s the Soviet economy had reached a standstill.) But the common conclusion is that the Soviet Union had reached a point of economic stagnation of crisis proportions, and consequently that something had to be done to prevent further deterioration. At the same time defence spending was occupying a more than significant share of Soviet GDP – the exact figures again being uncertain, but US and UK defence intelligence agencies placed it as around 16–17 per cent of GDP. More importantly it was claiming one-third of all machinery production, and even greater proportions in the high technology sectors. To solve the Soviet economic plight, Gorbachev instituted a series of changes termed *perestroika* (restructuring). Part of this included the transfer of resources (including management skills and industrial capacity) away from defence and into the civilian sector. To justify this, a new security framework was required which reduced the threat of conflict. Thus new thinking was driven by the economic necessity of cutting back on the defence sector (Holden 1989, pp. 6 and 20; Hooper 1989, pp. 15–17).

The implication of this is that new thinking is more than a temporary phenomenon associated with the current leadership. But a second explanation can be offered drawing on the same arguments. This is that the Soviet Union has recognized that, because of economic stagnation, it is no longer in a position to compete with the West in the same manner as it has previously. This is particularly so in the new high-technology areas. New thinking is effectively an admission that the West has won this stage of the arms race. But with economic recovery, and the spread of *perestroika* to the Soviet armed forces, a leaner, fitter military may be produced. Even in the short term, resource constraints may lead to greater efficiency and hence more effective armed forces. Under this interpretation, new thinking may represent less a fundamental shift in Soviet thinking than a hiatus or breathing space (*peredyshka*) in the East–West competition (Holden 1989, p.7; Hooper 1989, p. 19).

An alternative though related explanation concentrates upon Soviet domestic politics. Jack Snyder and Stephen Meyer have both argued, though in slightly different terms, that Gorbachev's new thinking is an attempt to gain control of defence policy and smash the entrenched, conservative institutions which have previously controlled the defence agenda. Snyder bases his analysis upon the creation of a number of key institutions by Stalin to promote economic change, and which have since clung on to power despite a changing domestic and international world. Thus 'historical Soviet expansionism and zero-sum thinking about international politics have largely been caused by the nature of Soviet Stalinist domestic institutions' (Snyder 1987, p. 94). The failures of the late Brezhnev years discredited these institutions, while a new political constituency emerged (what Snyder identifies as the 'intelligentsia') whose needs were not represented by these conservative and repressive institutions. Gorbachev has therefore launched an attack upon these institutions, which include the various security and defence groupings, both to satisfy the growing demands of the intelligentsia, and to allow greater initiative and autonomy from below to further his economic reforms (Snyder 1987, pp. 94–5 and 110-12).

Meyer is less convinced of the role of the intelligentsia, and places greater emphasis on Gorbachev using new thinking as a tool to gain control of the defence agenda and set his own priorities. This gives him the control over defence spending necessary to rebuild the Soviet economic and industrial base (Meyer 1988, p.125). A key development here has been the use of civilian defence specialists to create alternative centres of expertise and to devise defence agendas to compete with those of the entrenched military establishment. The military's position as a monopolistic supplier of advice on security has therefore been undermined, and its influence accordingly reduced (Allison 1989, p. 2; Warner 1989, p. 19). Similarly Gorbachev's new appointments to key posts in the military hierarchy have strengthened his hand. This combination of new personnel and alternative centres of expertise has helped to 'tame' the military, and has allowed Gorbachev to impose his views on security issues on the defence establishment.

These explanations of the motivations behind new thinking offer no easy answers to the question of its permanence. If Snyder is correct that the intelligentsia have emerged in the 1980s as a key political grouping, with aspirations to a better material way of life and greater intellectual freedom, then the mould created by Stalin may have been shattered and the military's grip on Soviet politics may have been irrevocably broken. But this assumes the continuing strength of the intelligentsia in Soviet politics. A military backlash and reimposition of Stalinist-style bureaucracies still remains a possibility. Meyer's analysis similarly indicates that the military's grip is slipping but has yet to be broken. Meyer explicitly identifies Gorbachev as the key agent of change, and implicit in this is the possibility that if Gorbachev fails a reaction may set in taking the Soviet Union back to 'old thinking' (Meyer 1988, p. 127).

A final explanation of the shift in Soviet thinking about security is that it is a product of a fundamental reassessment of strategic logic. Drawing upon the lessons of Brezhnev's failures in foreign and security policy, it is a genuine recognition of both the security dilemma and the implications of the nuclear age. It may also be in part a reaction to what are perceived as the more offensive NATO weapons and doctrines developed in the 1980s (weapons such as Assault Breaker/MLRS, ATACMs and the F-15E, and doctrines such as Follow-on Forces Attack and AirLand Battle). These forced the Soviets to consider the possible requirement for a defensive phase before launching a crushing counter-offensive. They also brought home the implications of the West's technological lead and the requirement to react in some way to this (Holden 1989, pp. 18–19; Snyder 1987, p. 129). The problem with this is that lessons can be unlearned, and the new assessments reassessed. If strategic logic drives new thinking, then its essentially subjective and value-sensitive nature does not guarantee its permanence.

The origins and permanence of new thinking are therefore somewhat uncertain. But two major and connected initiatives have already emerged as products of new thinking, the concept of reasonable sufficiency in armed forces, and a defensively-oriented defence policy. Both are concepts initiated and endorsed at the highest political levels. But the precise meaning and implications of these terms are somewhat vague, and are the subject of some dispute within the Soviet Union (in rather stereotyped and simplified terms, the views of the military establishment confronting those of civilian analysts).

Reasonable sufficiency was publicly introduced to the Soviet defence debate by Gorbachev at the 27th Party Congress in February 1986. It was not immediately apparent what the term involved, nor how it would be applied. In part it seems to have been an attempt by Gorbachev to set the military agenda and widen the security debate. It also seems to have some basis in the Soviet Union's economic plight: 'reasonable sufficiency in defence has been forced upon the Soviets in part by a weakened economy and by Gorbachev's conviction that the huge defence spending for the arms race has been futile' (Hooper 1989, p. 18).

Reasonable sufficiency is clearly a product of new thinking in its belief that a unilateral pursuit of military power will not yield security, but rather might prove self-defeating. Security is not a product of military strength alone, but of economic and political factors as well. The concept of reasonable sufficiency therefore lies behind a number of the Soviet defence cuts, including those announced in Gorbachev's December 1988 UN speech, the Soviet CFE proposals for deep conventional cuts, and the announcement that the military budget is to be cut by 14.2 per cent and arms production by 19.5 per cent over the next few years (Herspring 1989, p. 327; Holden 1989, pp. 14, 23–4 and 30–1). These constitute part of a process towards reasonable sufficiency, but the end point of what level of forces constitutes reasonable sufficiency remains undecided (Warner 1989, p. 22). Rather a number of issues can be identified around which the debate is revolving.

The first of these issues concerns the extent of limitations on an offensive capability. It is here that the link between reasonable sufficiency and defensive defence is most apparent. Reasonable sufficiency is defined as the level of forces necessary for defence but insufficient for offensive operations or surprise attack. Thus primarily offensive forces (such as assault bridging units) are to be withdrawn, and other forces reduced to a level consonant with defensive defence (Herpsring 1989, p. 322; Holden 1989, p. 3; Hooper 1989, pp. 18–19; Scott and Scott 1988, p. 102). The problem here is twofold: the nature of the defence, and defining force levels. On the first problem there are various operations which may be called 'defensive'. These range from the initially defensive preceding a devastating counter-offensive (as at Kursk) through to non-offensive defence which is structurally incapable of offensive operations. Each of these involves a different concept of force structure. The level of forces considered necessary may also vary considerably. As the Soviet debate on defensive defence is far from resolved, the level of armaments which constitutes reasonable sufficiency may similarly vary. But even if a particular defensive scheme is approved, the process of then determining the forces required to implement this scheme is as much a political process subject to value judgements as an objective calculation.

These problems underpin the second issue, namely defining reasonable sufficiency in terms of numbers of men and equipment. It is not even clear whether reasonable sufficiency is a purely quantitative measure, or whether it includes qualitative elements as well. This has led some analysts to question whether the Soviet Union might not be creating 'leaner but meaner' armed forces: Herspring for example has interpreted the personnel cuts as a means of getting rid of incompetent officers (Herpsring 1989, pp. 322–3). Although efficiency might be improved as a result of some of the changes instituted under Gorbachev, it is difficult to see how the result will be more powerful armed forces given the scale of the cuts already announced. Nevertheless it is clear that for the moment reasonable sufficiency is more a process of reduction than an agreed force size. Thus the end result remains unclear and a source of issue.

A third related area of contention concerns whether the reductions involved in moving to reasonable sufficiency should be determined unilaterally or with reference to NATO force levels. Marshal Kulikov, the commander in chief of WTO forces, has defined reasonable sufficiency as conventional parity between NATO and the WTO but at a lower level of armaments. Thus WTO force limits would be set to match NATO's. In contrast some civilian analysts have argued that the Soviet Union should develop its forces in relation to its own requirements. Rather than attempting to match NATO forces it should accept the possibility of force asymmetries and be willing to make unilateral cuts so that force levels reflect what iis *necessary* for security rather than what the military may find desirable (Allison 1989, pp. 6–9; Holden 1989, p. 14). This also highlights the gulf which exists on many of these issues between civilian analysts and the military establishment. Reasonable sufficiency has featured more strongly in the civilian literature, and has generally been interpreted in a more radical fashion than has been the case with the rather more conservative military (Phillips and Sands 1988, pp. 164–78).

Finally, although reasonable sufficiency primarily concerns conventional forces, it has a nuclear dimension. In his first years as General Secretary, Gorbachev placed considerable emphasis upon nuclear disarmament in his foreign policy. The nuclear test moratorium, the proposal for the elimination of nuclear weapons by the year 2000, and the successful completion of the INF treaty are the key landmarks of this. Although interest now seems to have shifted towards conventional forces, the reduction of nuclear weapons still appears to be part of the Soviet, or at least Gorbachev's, conception of reasonable sufficiency (Holden 1989, p. 8; Hooper 1989, p. 18; Scott and Scott 1988, p. 102).

Complementing reasonable sufficiency is the shift in policy towards a more defensively oriented doctrine, with the emphasis on war prevention rather than war winning. To some extent the interest in defensive operations pre-dates Gorbachev, being a part of the Ogarkov revolution. In the early 1980s a number of factors seem to have combined to force something of a rethink on the status of the defensive. New long-range high-precision conventional weapons blurred the distinction between offensive and defensive operations – forces were now able to engage simultaneously in offensive and defensive battles. This point was reinforced by new NATO doctrines (particularly the deep-strike elements of AirLand Battle and Follow-on Forces Attack) which placed greater emphasis upon offensive operations. The lessons of 1941 might have played some part here, where the Red Army's failure to orient itself for defensive operations proved a major source of weakness. Thus some interest was apparent in developing a new relationship between offensive and defensive operations, including the possibility of conducting a temporary defensive operation before launching a decisive strategic offensive (Allison 1989, pp. 9–16; Holden 1989, p. 16).

As with reasonable sufficiency, one of the problems which emerged with the policy shift towards a more defensive doctrine was in defining what constituted a defensive posture. A variety of different ideas concerning the relationship between defence and offence were outlined by civilian and military analysts. One method of understanding this variety is to adopt the framework devised by two Soviet analysts, the civilian Andrei Kokoshin and Major-General V. Larionov (a comparatively innovative and radical figure within the Soviet military establishment). Kokoshin and Larionov identify four basic variants in the offence–defence relationship:

1. Both sides are committed to decisive strategic offensives (the traditional posture of the Soviet Army).
2. An initially defensive phase (emphasizing positional aspects) to be followed by a decisive counter-offensive (modelled on the 1943 battle of Kursk).
3. A limited counter-offensive capability within a defensive framework, sufficient to remove invaders from friendly territory but not to undertake strategic counter-offensives into enemy

territory (the model for which is the 1939 campaign against the Japanese at Nomonham/Khalkhin Gol).
4 Both sides adopt a structurally defensive posture, with mobility at the tactical level alone (similar to some of the Western ideas of non-offensive defence).

Kokoshin and Larionov favoured the fourth variant as the most stable, but it is clear that the Soviet debate on defensive doctrine has encompassed all three defensive variants (Allison 1989, pp. 22–3). Initially (1985–7) the Soviet military had little interest in non-offensive defence, preferring to think in terms of the second Kokoshin/Larionov variant. Although priority was given to defensive operations and emphasis was placed on the development of defensive tactics, statements by Soviet military leaders (including Akhromeyev, Gareyev and Yazov) made it clear that the defensive was merely the initial phase in a conflict; the decisive phase remained a strategic counter-offensive launched deep into enemy territory. This interpretation can also be placed on the document produced by the WTO at their 1987 Berlin meeting, which claimed WTO doctrine was strictly defensive[1] (Allison 1989, pp. 16–18; Herspring 1989, p. 333; Holden 1989, p. 15; Scott and Scott 1988, pp. 102–3; Warner 1989, pp. 25–6).

In contrast, civilian analysts were beginning to develop concepts of non-offensive defence based upon the structural inability to undertake offensive operations. Although this was partly a product of a belief in the capabilities of defensive technologies to halt an offensive, its primary motivation was political, stemming from new thinking. As Roy Allison has commented: 'While Soviet military officials may accept a revision in the offence-defence ratio out of military necessity, civilian specialists appear opposed to offensive capabilities as a matter of political principle' (Allison 1989, p. 2). By 1988, then, two competing approaches to defensive doctrine were apparent in the Soviet Union. The first, largely associated with the military hierarchy, corresponded to Kokoshin and Larionov's second variant and appeared to be modelled on the 1943 battle of Kursk. In this an initial positional defensive would be followed by a decisive strategic counter-offensive which would win the war. The second approach was largely civilian-inspired and appeared to draw heavily upon the ideas of Western alternative defence thinking about non-offensive and non-provocative defence. The themes here were structural limitations on offensive actions and the exploitation of defensive technologies (particularly anti-tank guided munitions). In Roy Allison's analysis, a synthesis of these two approaches began to appear in 1988. Statements from Akhromeyev and Gareyev in particular began to indicate the emergence of a less offensive orientation. In explaining a March 1988 WTO exercise, Akhromeyev stated that the aims were to expel the enemy invaders from friendly territory and attempt to negotiate a settlement to the dispute. Only if this attempt at a political solution failed would WTO forces go onto the offensive. A similar exercise in April 1989 required WTO forces to re-establish the original battle lines, while one report suggested that there might be a defensive period of 3–4 weeks before a counter-attack was undertaken (Allison 1989, pp. 25–8). Thus by the late 1980s Soviet defensive doctrine appeared to correspond to Kokoshin and Larionov's third variant of an initial defensive with limited counter-attacks to regain lost ground. The model for this appeared to be Zhukhov's 1939 defence against the Japanese in Khalkhin Gol/Nomonhan (Coox 1985; Drea 1981).

What is clear from this is that Soviet doctrine has undergone a radical shift of emphasis. The belief in the necessity for an all-out offensive has been replaced by much more limited aims. Indeed if Allison's analysis is correct there is considerable doubt as to whether the Soviet Union intends to cross into enemy territory. The capability for surprise attack – a major feature of doctrine under Brezhnev – has been eroded, not least by the cuts announced by Gorbachev to the United Nations in December 1988. Implicit in all of this is that whereas the East European members of the WTO previously provided a launch pad for a pre-emptive offensive, they now constitute more of a buffer zone.

Conclusion

The heady combination of new thinking, reasonable sufficiency and defensive defence promises fundamental changes to Soviet military doctrine and to the West's perception of the Soviet military threat. The old emphasis upon overwhelming mass, offensive operations and surprise has been overthrown. Major changes have already been implemented and more are promised. For some commentators these changes are indications that the cold war is over and the West has won (Booth 1989, p. 3). The economic failure of the Soviet Union has forced it into a fundamental reassessment of its foreign and security policy such that the old cold war confrontationalism has been replaced by a new spirit of cooperation and commonality. Others are less optimistic over these developments. Alarmists fear that this is merely a temporary phenomenon to allow the Soviet military to regain the ground lost to the West's technological advances. The end result might therefore be 'leaner and meaner' Soviet armed forces

> The Soviet military is undergoing a process of change greater than anything it has faced at least since the introduction of nuclear weapons, and perhaps since the purges of the late 1930s. These changes, if fully implemented and supported by a more viable economic infrastructure, will over the long run produce a more efficient and effective military force. (Herspring 1989, p. 321)

Alternatively there are the pessimists who fear that new thinking will remain thinking and that the in-built conservatism of the military or the failure of *perestroika* to produce an improvement in the economy will undermine Gorbachev's reforms (Allison 1989, p. 1; Meyer 1988, p. 124).

For NATO this creates a problem as well as an opportunity. Each of the three possibilities outlined above are plausible, though they may vary in their likelihood. Each places different requirements upon NATO in terms of its response to change. The temptation is to be cautious, to wait and see what happens before acting decisively. But this is too simple. Failure to act may confound the process of change and may, directly or indirectly, help to undermine the very changes NATO wishes to see. This obviously applies to the third possibility, but also to the first and second. Both are vulnerable to reactionary pressures created by the West's failure to reciprocate on Soviet initiatives. This applies to the first in that the lessons of the failure of economic and foreign policy pre-Gorbachev may be replaced by lessons from the failure of *perestroika* and new thinking. For the second, more alarmist posture, that new thinking is a conspiracy to lower the West's guard, given the scale of unilateral change in the Soviet Union this seems highly unlikely. But that these changes may produce a more efficient military is an undeniable possibility. When matched to the CFE process of reducing forces in Europe, the much-reduced Soviet Army will face a reduced NATO. But this fear of a leaner and meaner Soviet military is only justified if NATO allows the political situation to slide back into a position of confrontation.

Thus the problem NATO faces in the 1990s is not one of managing a massive Soviet military threat, but of ensuring that the process of change continues in the current direction while maintaining forces and doctrines capable of managing the threat if it does reappear.

Notes

1 This mid-way posture was also probably influenced by other factors than simply new thinking. Concern over the implication of NATO's introduction of new doctrines and weapons, a lack of confidence in Gorbachev's willingness to authorize a surprise attack, and the possibility of a multi-theatre war in which the Soviet Army could only undertake a limited number of offensives may all have contributed to this revision.

5

NATO operational doctrine

To defend its central front, NATO will attempt to fight and win a number of key interrelated battles (what may be termed 'mission concepts'). These include: the air superiority battle, fought primarily between the two opposing air forces for control of the skies over the battlefield; the close battle, fought by the two opposing land forces and supported by aircraft and helicopters, for control of the ground of the central front; the deep battle, involving interdiction strikes against enemy forces before they reach the forward edge of the battle area (FEBA); and the rear-area security battle, involving the protection of key NATO installations (such as command posts) against enemy special forces. This chapter considers the three key NATO doctrines formulated in the 1980s which guide operational thinking for two of these battles (the close battle and the deep battle). These doctrines are the US AirLand Battle, the British Corps Concept/NORTHAG concept of operations, and NATO's Follow-On Forces Attack (FOFA). Although the air superiority battle does involve some degree of doctrinal thinking, particularly in the development of offensive counter-air (airfield attack), that battle is governed more by tactics than by operational concepts. This is even more the case with the rear-area battle. Thus although these latter two battles are critical NATO missions, the key operational thinking involves the close and the deep battles.

AirLand Battle and US Army doctrine

After the Bundeswehr the US Army provides the single most important contribution to NATO ground forces on the central front. In CENTAG it maintains two full strength corps (V and VII Corps), while III Corps would be quickly mobilized under the REFORGER programme into a reserve for NORTHAG (see Ch. 2). The US is also extensively represented at the higher levels of NATO's political and military decision-making apparatus. Thus US army doctrine can have an important impact upon NATO military thinking. But this can be a source of tension. US Army doctrine is determined nationally, not by NATO, and although the central front is an important area for the US Army it is not its sole area. Nor do US Army commanders in NATO write US Army doctrine. That task is performed principally by TRADOC (Training and Doctrine Command) stationed at Fort Monroe in Virginia. Although consultations do take place with US commanders in Europe, and with other NATO commanders (particularly the West German commanders with whom the US shares responsibility for CENTAG), and although personnel may move between the US Army in Europe, NATO military headquarters (SHAPE) and TRADOC, US Army doctrine is not NATO doctrine. It is not written by nor exclusively for NATO, and hence the opportunity for tension exists. Nevertheless US Army doctrine does have a major impact on NATO. It acts as a source of ideas for NATO military commanders. It determines much of US Army training. And it acts as a guide for the actions of US forces in war. Although the current AirLand Battle doctrine is not NATO doctrine, nor is it formally approved by NATO commanders, its influence on US and NATO thinking about conventional war on the central front is profound.

Active Defense

AirLand Battle was preceded as US Army doctrine by Active Defense. This was formulated by TRADOC under its first commander, General William E. De Puy, in the early 1970s. In the aftermath of the Vietnam War the US Army faced reduced budgets and a change of focus away from South-East Asia and towards Europe. It also had to reorient itself away from the requirements of an airmobile war against ill-equipped troops to an armoured war against opponents deploying large quantities of modern, sophisticated weaponry. In addition the 1973 war in the Middle East had indicated that the battlefield was changing. Precision-guided munitions (PGMs) had been used extensively in that war, and the success of Soviet-supplied anti-tank and surface-to-air missiles with the Egyptian Army had received considerable coverage. This was closely studied by TRADOC in 1974, and the lessons played out in war games and computer simulations. The results led De Puy to advocate a major revision of the Army's 'how to fight' manual, FM 100–5 *Operations*, the then current version of which had been written in 1968 at the height of the Vietnam War. Through a series of meetings and conferences in 1974–5 with a wide range of US Army and Bundeswehr officers a number of ideas began to emerge (what became known as the 'pot of soup'). These ideas were then taken by TRADOC and formulated into the doctrine of Active Defense, published in 1976 in a new version of FM 100–5 (Romjue 1984, pp. 2–5; Starry 1978, pp. 3–4).

The key problem faced by TRADOC was to devise a doctrine to enable the US Army to 'fight outnumbered and win' on the central front. TRADOC assumed that the enemy would not only be numerically superior, but would be likely to use weapons as lethal as those deployed by US forces. High weapon lethality would lead to high losses on both sides, and forces would be destroyed if they were not properly deployed. New technology had also increased the tempo of war so that in TRADOC's assessment the first battle could also be the last. Thus the US Army had to be prepared to *win* the first battle, and not to rely on a period of mobilization during war.

The key themes which emerged from the 'pot of soup' and TRADOC's studies were those of: fighting outnumbered; the use of terrain as a force multiplier; rapid suppression of enemy forces; an emphasis on firepower rather than manpower; constrained manoeuvre to support firepower; and the use of battlefield intelligence. TRADOC depicted a complex 'scientific' battle, determined by weapons characteristics – numbers of weapons, rates of fire, engagement ranges and kill probabilities. The talk was of 'servicing' targets – of destroying a certain number of enemy targets within a set timeframe – and of using a combination of firepower, manoeuvre and the natural advantages of the defensive (particularly terrain) to offset Soviet numerical strength (Romjue 1984, pp. 5–9).

Soviet doctrine was portrayed as one dominated by mass, momentum and continuous land combat by successive waves (echelons). The problem for NATO was seen not as one of an attack across a broad front, but one which concentrated on a few key points. A Soviet tank division of *c*. 300 tanks might therefore mass on a 5 km front. In contrast a US armoured division would be tasked with defending a front of perhaps 40 km. To counter this Active Defense emphasized battlefield intelligence to determine the point of main attack, manoeuvre to meet that attack, and firepower to destroy it. A strong covering force would be deployed to meet the main threat axis and allow defensive forces to concentrate behind it. Through a series of lateral movements, seven or eight armoured battalions would concentrate from across the divisional frontage to meet this attack. By manoeuvring in this manner, force ratios could be decisively altered. Defensive forces would form a succession of battle areas. By picking the ground on which to fight with some care, and by the extensive use of cover and concealment, the defender could gain an extra advantage over the attacker – a force multiplier of perhaps ×3 or even ×6. By concealing forces the defender would also have the advantage of firing first, a factor which was particularly significant given the increased lethality of modern weapons. In the words of a subsequent TRADOC commander: '[The Active Defense would] see deep to find the following echelon, move fast to concentrate forces, strike quickly before the enemy can break the defense and finish the fight quickly before the second echelon closes' (Starry 1978, p. 7). By massing seven or eight of a division's 11 or 12 battalions in such a small area flanks would obviously be exposed. These gaps would be covered by airmobile forces (air cavalry and attack helicopters), trading lack of firepower and numbers for speed of response (Romjue 1984, pp. 8–9; Starry 1978, pp. 7-8).

Active Defense was a clearly defensive doctrine. Counter-attacks were limited to small-scale ventures to inflict disproportionate casualties or recover vital ground. Large-scale counter-attacks were all but ruled out through the unavailability of sufficient reserves – when fighting a battle heavily outnumbered, maintaining large reserves for possible counter-attacks was considered an unjustifiable luxury. Even the traditional 'two up, one back' fighting formation was sacrificed for greater concentration of force at the decisive point of battle.

This defensive orientation was reinforced by a perception that, with the advent of large numbers of relatively capable PGMs, technology had shifted to favour the defence. This in turn militated against counter-attacks: 'For the same reason that we believed it possible to annihilate large numbers of armoured forces coming at us in mass formation, it was possible for them [the Soviets] to do likewise unto us' (Starry 1978, p. 9). But despite this defensive emphasis, offensive operations were considered necessary if the initial defence proved successful, particularly to regain lost ground. Here the Soviet concept of echeloning in depth would be a crucial consideration, and hence the requirement to 'see deep' and identify these echelons before undertaking operations. Rear-area attack, though, was considered particularly promising given the perceived vulnerability of Soviet command and control and logistical resupply units (Romjue 1984, p. 8; Starry 1978, p. 9). But attention was clearly concentrated on fighting the defensive battle, and not on the (remote) possibility of subsequent offensive operations.

The debate on Active Defense

The new FM 100–5 of 1976 quickly produced a spirited debate in American military journals. This debate revolved around a number of key criticisms levelled at the new doctrine.

1 *Firepower and manoeuvre.* Active Defense was criticized both for an overemphasis on firepower, and for its assumption that new weapon technologies (PGMs) favoured the defence. Active Defense was not a manoeuvre doctrine but one which emphasized firepower as the decisive element in the defensive battle. What manoeuvre elements there were in Active Defense concerned the concentration of forces to improve the weight of firepower. But given NATO's numerical disadvantages, was the available firepower sufficient to defeat WTO echelons? For TRADOC the key to this question lay in the perceived defensive potential of new weapon technologies. Using PGMs from concealed positions, TRADOC estimated that defenders could repel attacks from forces three or more times their number. But it was also recognized that the Soviets were concerned over the implications of these new technologies (particularly ATGMs), and that consequently they might devise counter-measures (tactical or technological) to overcome this threat. Further, the Egyptians had used PGMs whilst on the strategic *offensive* not defensive, indicating perhaps that PGMs did not decisively favour the defensive but had implications for both offensive and defensive forces. In addition there were strong indications that the effect of PGMs on Israeli tanks and aircraft had not been as significant as was at first believed. So not all were convinced by the argument that PGMs gave the defence the advantage it needed to offset WTO numbers, while the weight of Soviet artillery and the lack of fixed NATO defences caused some concern over the vulnerability of ATGM-armed American troops to indirect fire (Lind 1977, p. 58; Syrett 1977; TRADOC 1976, p.27).

2 *Lateral movement.* The key defensive idea of the new doctrine was the lateral movement of forces to concentrate at the decisive point of a Soviet breakthrough. This complicated movement was considered by some commentators to be too difficult in battlefield conditions. It required a series of precisely choreographed moves which would be vulnerable to delays and disruption. Effective command and control was vital for the coordination of these defensive movements, but would be vulnerable to jamming and other forms of disruption. If commanders failed to identify the main Soviet axis of advance correctly, the whole defence might be scuppered. The concentration of force left flanks vulnerable and created the tempting prospect of a Soviet encirclement. Lateral movement might be obstructed by terrain. Active Defense appeared to deploy forces in a linear fashion which was vulnerable to manoeuvre by a mobile opponent such as the Soviets. And finally it was criticized as a doctrine for a face-saving defeat, and not one for winning the war (Lind 1977, pp. 62–3; Romjue 1984, pp. 19–20).

3 *Reserves.* The emphasis on lateral movement replaced the traditional 'two up, one back' divisional formation, and therefore robbed divisions of a strong reserve in favour of a more fluid system which strengthened the front line. This radical and innovative move was criticized as risky and unproven. If something went wrong, there were no reserves to shore up the defence. TRADOC replied that the degree of Soviet superiority necessitated a forward emphasis. Holding substantial forces in reserve would critically weaken the front line and endanger the whole defence (Jones 1978, pp. 33–5; Romjue 1984, p. 17).

4 *Soviet doctrine.* Active Defense was designed to counter a Soviet threat based on mass, momentum and the concentration of force at a few key breakthrough points. By the mid-1970s it was clear that Soviet doctrine was changing. Like the Americans the Soviets had studied the 1973 Middle East war closely and had revised their doctrine accordingly. Instead of concentrating on a few key points, Soviet doctrine began to emphasize a multi-pronged assault across a broad front, seeking gaps and weak points in NATO's defensive line. Active Defense's acceptance of weak flanks appeared to play into the hands of this doctrine (Karber 1979; Romjue 1984, pp. 16–17).

5 *Winning the first battle.* FM 100–5 identified the critical necessity of winning the first battle since the first battle might also be the last. Critics however argued that the Soviet practice of echeloning their forces created a situation whereby the second and third battles were equally important. The overcommitment of forces to win the first battle might hinder the chances of winning subsequent battles. But this argument tended to misunderstand at least some of the concerns of Active Defense. The new doctrine was not concentrating on the first echelon to the detriment of later battles. Rather it attempted to shift American thinking away from mobilization to a 'come as you are' war (Lind 1977, p. 57; Romjue 1984, pp. 15–16).

6 *Defensive emphasis.* Finally, Active Defense was criticized for being too defensive in its outlook. Despite assurances that the US Army would eventually move over to the offensive in a war, the doctrine was clearly more interested in defensive concerns. It therefore acquired a somewhat negative and pessimistic reputation in certain quarters (Jones 1978, p. 30; Romjue 1984, p. 14).

Developing AirLand Battle

The debate over Active Defense led to misgivings over the doctrine at the highest levels of the Army, including the Army Chief of Staff

General Edward C. Meyer (Romjue 1984, p. 30). This provided an important force for change, but other factors also contributed significantly to the decision to develop a new doctrine. Amongst these was the appointment in 1977 of General Donn A. Starry as the new TRADOC commander. As commander of V Corps in Europe, Starry had inaugurated a series of studies which were to provide the basis for a number of the key ideas developed at TRADOC in the subsequent years. Amongst these were an interest in attacking and disrupting second-echelon forces, the decisive importance of close air support, and the use of historical analyses.

Once at TRADOC Starry picked up on criticisms of Active Defense's first-battle emphasis, and began to encourage planners to 'look deep' at the follow-on echelons. The relatively predictable echeloning of forces enabled planners to look beyond the first battle, and created potential targets for corps artillery. Once they had been encouraged to look deep, TRADOC planners began to think of attacking deep. Studies indicated that no matter how successfully the close battle was fought, forces would eventually be ground down by successive WTO echelons. But by attacking these echelons, pressure could be relieved at the FEBA and WTO momentum disrupted. Although interdiction as such was not new, TRADOC's ideas were in that they linked deep attack to concepts of echeloning in an attempt to shape the central battle. Deep attack became more than the random interruption of an offence by interdiction. Rather it became a closely defined concept involving corps artillery as well as air support.

TRADOC's planning period was also increased under Starry. Whereas De Puy had been concerned with the immediate future, Starry looked at developments up to eight years ahead. This enabled TRADOC to assess the impact of new and emerging technologies on the battlefield. From this perspective technology was considered as having a major impact on the US Army, and of being the main area of change for the Army at the turn of the decade (Romjue 1984, p. 23–5 and 33–6).

A second source of influence were the nuclear and chemical systems programme reviews undertaken at TRADOC in 1979–80. In the nuclear systems programme review, the Field Artillery School had for the first time combined tactical nuclear options, second-echelon attack, and fire and manoeuvre schemes into a single general scheme of action. In this, nuclear weapons were not to be viewed separately from conventional operations but were to be incorporated into an integrated battlefield. Moreover nuclear weapons were to be used to win the battle, not to avoid defeat. From this emerged the concept of the integrated battlefield, which in July 1980 Starry ordered all TRADOC commanders to incorporate into their work on doctrine (Romjue 1984, pp. 32–9).

The third factor contributing to this process was the series of US Army reorganization studies conducted at the turn of the decade. In October 1979 General Meyer was presented with the Division 86 study. This prompted the army chief of staff into undertaking a wider series of studies entitled Army 86. The most important of these to the doctrinal review process was Corps 86. This reintroduced the corps as a major element on the battlefield, and enabled it to play a number of key roles in the emerging doctrine. The corps became the major point of coordination with the air force, would conduct nuclear operations, and could look deep and attack the second tactical echelon up to 150 km (72 miles) from the FEBA. Above all the corps allowed commanders to think above the tactical level, and therefore assisted in the development of an operational level of war (Hanne 1983, p. 4; Romjue 1984, pp. 27 and 33–5).

The two final factors contributing to the review process were a developing interest in manoeuvre warfare, and a movement away from a single-theatre war. Active Defense had emphasized firepower and used manoeuvre (or more accurately mobility) as a means of concentrating firepower. By the early 1980s TRADOC was becoming interested in opening up the battlefield, and in moving towards a more manoeuvre-oriented doctrine to counter Soviet firepower and tactical rigidity (Starry 1981). With the crises in Afghanistan and Iran, the army was also becoming concerned that its narrow focus on a European war might be misplaced. Doctrine had to cover worldwide contingencies, but Active Defense had been devised almost exclusively for the problem of a European war. A new degree of flexibility was therefore required to cover operations in the Third World (Romjue 1984, pp. 33 and 39).

These developments culminated in March 1980 when General Starry commenced the process of rewriting FM 100–5. Although the work was supervised by Starry and his deputy, General William R. Richardson, and TRADOC staff had a key input, the new manual was written in the Department of Tactics at the Army's Command and General Staff College, Fort Leavenworth.

The initial focus of the rewriting was on correcting the deficiencies of the existing field manual in the wake of the debate over Active Defense, and in adapting the doctrine to Third World contingencies. It was initially seen as a revision of the 1976 FM 100–5 rather than the development of a new doctrine, but this soon changed as writing progressed. A coordinating draft appeared in January 1981, and pamphlets were produced from March 1981 on introducing and explaining the new doctrine. Publication of the new FM 100–5 was delayed by two factors. Firstly, Starry's initial term for the new doctrine – 'the extended battlefield' – was replaced by the more descriptively accurate term AirLand Battle. And secondly Starry's successor at TRADOC, General Glenn K. Otis, had decided to incorporate the concept of the operational level of war into the new doctrine as the level at which AirLand Battle would be fought.

When the new FM 100–5 was finally published in August 1982 it was clear that it represented more than a revision of the 1976 field manual. Rather it constituted a new and highly controversial doctrine. As a result of this controversy (which stemmed in part from a lack of clarity over certain aspects of the doctrine), and as the new ideas were worked through, so it became apparent that a revision of the manual would be required. This was published in May 1986. While reaffirming the main thrust of the 1982 manual, a number of changes and modifications were apparant in the revised manual (FM 100–5, 1986, pp. i-ii; Richardson 1986; Romjue 1984, pp. 43–4, 57 and 60).

AirLand Battle

> The AirLand Battle will be dominated by the force that retains the initiative and, with deep attack and decisive maneuver, destroys its opponents' abilities to fight and to organize in depth. (FM 100–5 1982)

The new doctrine depicted a battle consisting of four components, each of which would be undertaken simultaneously:

1. defeating enemy forces in the first battle with a combination of firepower and manoeuvre;
2. deep attack missions to disrupt second echelon forces and influence future battles;
3. wresting the initiative from the enemy and exercising it in a series of daring and unpredictable counter-attacks;
4. actions directed at the collapse of the enemy's fighting ability, both physical and moral (Romjue 1984, p. 58).

To this end FM 100–5 identified four key concepts as lying at the heart of AirLand Battle doctrine: initiative, agility, depth and synchronization (FM 100–5, 1986, pp. 14–18).

1 *Initiative.* Whereas Active Defense had been an essentially reactive doctrine, AirLand Battle identified seizing the initiative as one of the major determinants of battlefield success:

[AirLand Battle is] based on securing or retaining the initiative and exercising it aggressively to accomplish the mission. The object of all operations is to impose our will on the enemy – to achieve our purposes. To do this we must throw the enemy off balance with a powerful blow from an unexpected direction, follow up rapidly to prevent his recovery and continue operations aggressively to achieve the higher commander's goal. (FM 100–5 1986, p. 14)

Seizing the initiative required a vigorous offensive spirit. In contrast to Active Defense which was seen as excessively defensive in its orientation, AirLand Battle developed an explicit offensive emphasis. Early offensive actions would end the war on US terms. War termination would not be a return to the *status quo ante bellum*, but a resolution of the conflict on new terms advantageous to the US. This would give the political leadership something to bargain with.

This dramatic new emphasis on the initiative jarred with many of the accepted tenets of NATO strategy. In particular the emphasis on offensive actions appeared inappropriate for an ostensibly defensive alliance. As a result the 1986 field manual was somewhat more circumspect in its treatment of the offensive. It drew attention to the fact that AirLand Battle concerned winning at the tactical and operational not strategic level. Strategic war aims were beyond the realm of army *doctrine*, but tactical and operational offensives were considered essential for a successful defence (FM 100–5 1986, pp. 15–16; Richardson 1986, pp. 6–7; Romjue 1984, pp. 57–8 and 68; TRADOC 1981).

2 *Agility*. In place of Active Defense's rather mechanical emphasis on firepower (the 'servicing' of targets and the 'calculus' of battle), AirLand Battle reintroduced manoeuvre into battle. Manoeuvre was no longer to be merely the precursor to battle allowing the concentration of firepower. Rather it was to be incorporated *into* battle. This idea was termed 'agility':

Agility – the ability of friendly forces to act faster than the enemy – is the first prerequisite for seizing and holding the initiative ... [It] permits the *rapid concentration of friendly strength against enemy vulnerabilities*. This must be done repeatedly so that by the time the enemy reacts to one action, another has already taken place, disrupting his plans and leading to late, uncoordinated and piecemeal enemy responses. It is this process of *successive concentration against locally weaker or unprepared enemy forces* which enables smaller forces to disorient, fragment and eventually defeat much larger enemy formations. (FM 100-5 1986, p. 16, emphasis added)

Battle would not be one of defending set areas against enemy breakthrough, but of rapid movement and intense volumes of fire. The doctrine advocated powerful blows from unexpected directions – 'violent effort' and (borrowing from Liddell Hart) 'the indirect approach'. These would throw the enemy off balance, disrupting his plans, slowing his momentum and spreading confusion. This succession of surprise attacks would be so rapid that the enemy would be unable to react quickly enough to use his strength efficiently. This idea of getting within the enemy's decision-making cycle was important in allowing a numerically weaker but more agile force to overcome the large but cumbersome enemy forces. The German idea of the *schwerpunkt* (the concentration of main effort) was also important. But whereas Active Defense had seen this in terms of concentrating against the enemy's *strongest* point (the point of attempted breakthrough), AirLand Battle used the idea for the concentration of friendly forces against enemy *vulnerabilities*. From this it is clear that AirLand Battle is an opportunistic doctrine. Centres of effort would be shifted as new opportunities emerged. Thus agility was not merely the physical capacity to move quickly, but the mental ability to spot and exploit opportunities. Its keynotes were simplicity, flexibility, concentration and audacity (FM 100-5 1986, p. 16; Romjue 1984, pp. 67- 70).

3 *Depth*. Extending the battlefield had been a major preoccupation of TRADOC's throughout this period. In its key 1981 pamphlet *AirLand Battle and the Corps Concept – 1986*, deep battle – attacking enemy echelons beyond the FLET (forward line of enemy troops) – had been identified as a necessity to disrupt momentum and reduce Soviet firepower advantages. Commanders at every level were to be responsible for seeing and attacking deep up to a certain distance or time ahead, the degree to be determined by the level of command (the higher the commander, the further ahead he must look). By disrupting momentum deep attack could also create windows of opportunity in which the initiative could be seized and offensive actions undertaken (TRADOC 1981).

By the time of FM 100-5's publication in 1982, the rather mechanical time–distance approach to deep attack had been dropped in favour of greater flexibility. Depth also emerged as meaning something more than simply deep attack:

Depth is the extension of operations in space, time and resources. Through the use of depth, a commander obtains the necessary

NATO OPERATIONAL DOCTRINE

space to manoeuvre effectively; the necessary time to plan, arrange and execute operations; and the necessary resources to win . . . Commanders must see beyond the requirements of the moment, actively seek information on the area and the enemy in depth, and employ every asset available to extend their operations in time and space. (FM 100–5 1986, pp. 16–17)

Battle was to be extended in depth by hitting forces in enemy territory, in time by monitoring developing threats, projecting trends and attacking enemy forces before they were committed to battle, and in command by placing greater emphasis upon the higher levels and operational art. But depth also meant deploying in depth for defence, and sustained operations when in attack. When on the defensive, deploying reserves in depth gave them room to manoeuvre and strike at exposed enemy flanks and other weak spots. In attack, a sustained and concentrated operation would create the momentum necessary to rupture a defence. Reconnaissance and attack ahead of an offensive (i.e. looking and striking deep when attacking) would also serve to disrupt enemy defences (FM 100–5 1986, pp. 16–17).

4 *Synchronization.* Synchronization involves coordinating the various elements of battle to produce the maximum combat power at the decisive moment. These elements of battle might be concepts such as fire and manoeuvre, or combat units such as reserves, armour, or artillery. Synchronization is necessary at both the operational and tactical levels. At the tactical level, for example, fire can support a force on the move; at the operational level, one force can fix the enemy while another manoeuvres to attack an exposed flank. This emphasis upon synchronization implicitly places greater burdens on higher level commanders to organize their forces and time their actions. But such commanders may be removed from battle by enemy disruption of communications or the fog of war. Thus AirLand Battle identified the requirement for subordinate commanders to understand the plan and intentions of the commander, and for training to promote the necessary degree of understanding to allow coordination without direct higher level command (FM 100–5 1986, pp. 17–18).

In addition to these four key concepts, AirLand Battle was distinguished by a number of other features. Firstly it introduced the idea of an operational level of war into American doctrine for the first time. This involved the use of major commands (corps and above) in a single plan of operation. Divisions and units below corps level were considered as fighting at the tactical level – that is, within this overall plan. The corps acted as the link able to fight at the tactical or operational level (Richardson 1986, p. 5).

The introduction of an operational level of war was an important innovation. It provided a framework for coordinating and prioritizing air and land operations. Since the Second World War the air and land battles had become increasingly interrelated. Air superiority, close air support and battlefield air interdiction were all seen as major – even essential – elements in support of the land battle. In emphasizing this, AirLand Battle created a requirement for the better coordination of air and land operations at a level above that of the tactical. The operational level provided this. It also allowed commanders to concentrate their forces sufficiently to inflict decisive blows against the enemy, as opposed to the pennypacket forces available at the tactical level. By creating a plan at the corps or Army Group level, major formations could be used to concentrate mass and firepower to a degree unattainable at the divisional–tactical level. Finally commanders at the operational level could raise their eyes from the immediate battle to project future developments and plan accordingly. This would enable battle to be extended in time and space, with commanders looking deep into enemy territory to monitor and attack forces beyond the FEBA.

A second feature was the integration of chemical and nuclear weapons into conventional planning to allow an easy transition from one to the other should it be required. It was considered important that, should the decision to use nuclear or chemical weapons be made, forces should not be required to fight with a different doctrine, but could continue to fight and operate as before. This led to some criticism that the US Army was insensitive to concerns over nuclear warfighting and failed to distinguish clearly between nuclear and conventional war. In the 1986 revision of FM 100–5, therefore, the language used was rather more circumspect, emphasizing that nuclear use would be controlled by political authorities and geared to strategic rather than tactical concerns (FM 100–5 1986, pp. 45–6; Richardson 1986, p. 7).

AirLand Battle also paid much greater attention to the 'human' side of battle. Intangible elements such as training, motivation, leadership and individual initiative received considerable attention, contrasting with Active Defense's 'calculus of battle' approach. For example:

> The most essential element of combat power is *competent* and *confident* leadership. (FM 100–5 1986, p. 13, emphasis in original)

and:

agility is as much a mental as a physical quality. (FM 100-5 1986, p. 16)

The destruction of enemy morale became a target, and some US commanders (such as General Richard E. Cavazos, Commander US III Corps) began talking of battle in terms of a clash of wills (Romjue 1984, pp. 53 and 69).

Finally AirLand Battle reintroduced the use of 'principles of war', not so much as a recipe for success but as a guide or checklist for battle. An initially lengthy list was cut to seven 'combat imperatives' in 1982, which increased in 1986 to nine principles of war. These nine principles were:

1 *Objective.* A clearly defined and attainable objective.
2 *Offensive.* Seize, retain and exploit the initiative.
3 *Mass.* Concentrate combat power at the decisive place and time.
4 *Economy of force.* Allocate the minimum force to secondary objectives.
5 *Manoeuvre.* To place the enemy at a disadvantage.
6 *Unity of command.* A single commander for each operation.
7 *Security.* Deny the enemy information and intelligence which might be of advantage.
8 *Surprise.* Strike the enemy when he is unprepared.
9 *Simplicity.* Make sure plans are clear and thoroughly understood. (FM 100-5 1986, pp. 173-7)

The debate on AirLand Battle

As had been the case with Active Defense, so AirLand Battle sparked a lively debate. But unlike the 1976 field manual, this debate was not largely confined to military journals but spilled over into the wider defence debate. To some extent this was a product of the times. Defence had become a major political issue, regularly making the headlines. Concern was particularly apparent over US attitudes to a war in Europe. With its talk of 'offensive operations', 'seizing the initiative', 'aggressive spirit', 'deep strike' and integrated nuclear operations, the tone of the new field manual matched the confrontational rhetoric of the new cold war. But it also fitted all too easily the preconceptions of some of the peace movement that the US was an aggressive and warlike power.

Concern over AirLand Battle was in part a product of a misinterpretion of FM 100-5 as defining US strategy rather than doctrine. AirLand Battle's emphasis on offensive actions and seizing the initiative, and what some saw as its implicit condoning of cross-border operations, was criticized as provocative and inappropriate for a defensive alliance. As Ben Dankbaar commented, 'winning' was the wrong sort of objective in the nuclear age (Dankbaar 1984, p. 145). But FM 100–5 was not concerned with winning at the strategic level, or undertaking strategic offensives. Its concerns were with the tactical and operational levels and the use of offensive actions to win these battles: 'defining strategic goals and strategic victory is beyond the purview of FM 100–5' (Richardson 1986, p. 8). Similarly Richardson claimed that fears over cross-border operations were misplaced, and reflected a lack of clarity and sensitivity in the 1982 field manual rather than a clear commitment to such operations: 'AirLand Batte does not espouse a need for cross-border operations . . . The decision to cross an international border must reside with the strategic command authority' (Richardson 1987, p. 9).

But concerns over AirLand Battle's offensive emphasis cannot simply be negated by pleading that it is a doctrine and not a strategy. The emphasis on manoeuvre, seizing the initiative and deep battle all have connotations which go beyond merely the defence of West Germany. The intention may not be there (though Richardson carefully avoids ruling out strategic offensives, placing the decision in the hands of political authorities) but the capability is – if not necessarily in the sense of numbers then at least in the doctrinal sense. The distinction between an operational offensive when on the strategic defensive or offensive may be little more than semantic. An offensive drift in doctrinal thinking may lead to an offensive drift in strategic thinking; more likely, though, is that it may be misperceived as such. As with the British Corps Concept and NORTHAG concept of operations, this creates a number of dangers in terms of its effect on crisis stability, on confidence building, and on any movement towards a common security framework (see Chs 1 and 6).

On a more technical level, doubts can be raised over the emphasis on manoeuvre. As with the NORTHAG concept of operations detailed below, it is by no means a foregone conclusion that manoeuvre is the best form for the defence to take. But AirLand Battle poses a number of specific problems. The close battle portrayed in FM 100–5 is characterized by a series of unexpected, fast, hard-hitting synchronized attacks. These will get inside the enemy's decision-making cycle, throw him off balance and therefore seize the initiative. But achieving tactical surprise may become significantly more difficult as new real-time sensors and other intelligence aids create an increasingly transparent battlefield. This, and the depth of striking power available to Soviet divisions and armies, is likely to force reserves deep to hide them and to protect them from attack. Moving reserve forces from deep holding areas to battle will therefore take time, time in which they may be spotted, or in which the battefield may change, making the planned attack less effective. In other words, the concept of rapid blows against vulnerable targets requires reserve forces to be stationed close to the battle area, but new sensors and improved firepower create the opposite requirement. Synchronizing these attacks may also be difficult in the fog of war. C3I (command, control, communications and intelligence) will be a target for enemy attack, and its survival cannot be guaranteed in its entirety. Relying on training and understanding seems optimistic for peacetime exercises; in war, with the problems of friction, and with new and unfamiliar commanders replacing battle casualties, it could spell disaster. Synchronizing attacks could therefore fall foul of one of FM 100–5's nine principles of war, namely simplicity.

The requirement for attacks to be hard-hitting may be constrained by lack of ammunition and spare missiles. Recent academic studies on sustainability have indicated that after just a handful of days NATO will start to run out of key stores (Pay 1988). 'Hard-hitting' means a significant weight of firepower. In implementing this forces may quickly exhaust the limited stocks available, and might therefore be unable to undertake further counter-attacks through lack of ammunition.

But a number of mitigating factors must be set against these problems. Transparency upon the battlefield is dependent upon sensors working effectively. They may be prevented from so doing by attacks against them or by a wide variety of deceptive measures. Tactical surprise may therefore still be possible. The West also appears to have a significant lead in many of the key technologies in surveillance, tracking and target acquisition (particularly in computer hardware and software). Attacks may also be designed to bring a variety of smaller forces together at the decisive point rather than moving a single large force from the rear, so easing the problem of deep basing, while other assets may be sufficiently mobile (particularly helicopters and long-range artillery and missiles) that deep basing is not a major problem. But this places an even greater strain on coordination and synchronization, and hence on C3I. Again the West may take some comfort from its apparent lead in C3 technologies and the increased redundancy of modern systems. But C3 cannot be guaranteed to work in all circumstances, and the likelihood is that some C3 will be inoperable most of the time and most will be inoperable for some of the time.

Finally, as regards sustainability, although stores may be used up very quickly this applies to both sides. Similarly, given the high lethality of modern weapons systems, if they work as well as expected attrition will be extremely high. Therefore although the numbers of weapons available might be limited after the first few days of combat, so might the number of targets left on the battlefield (Pay 1988).

Executing the manoeuvre operations envisaged by AirLand Battle would not be easy. They would place high demands on troops and particularly on commanders. If they succeeded then the payoff would be substantial. But if they failed the result could be a disorganized mess with forces used inefficiently. AirLand Battle is a risky doctrine – though no doctrine is without some risk, and all involve the balancing of various competing factors.

Problems can also be identified with a second key component of AirLand Battle, namely depth. Placing defensive forces in depth raises a number of political problems within the Alliance. Defending deep in West Germany would involve military operations over large areas of friendly soil, and would consequently place greater numbers of people and property at risk. It might also be seen as displaying a willingness to sacrifice those areas near the inner German border. But if this resulted in a more effective defence of West Germany as a whole, and particularly if it reduced the likelihood of early nuclear use, then these objections are difficult to sustain.

More problematic are operations deep in the enemy's rear. Some of these problems are dealt with elsewhere (see the section on FOFA below), but two are of particular relevance to AirLand Battle and the close battle. The first concerns the opportunity costs of striking deep. If divisional and corps firepower is used against second-echelon targets, then the weight of firepower available for use against the first echelon will, logically, be reduced. Manoeuvre forces may not receive the fire support they require and the outcome of the first battle may be placed in doubt. If this first battle is lost, then the follow-on forces are less significant. The opportunity costs of deep attack are therefore felt in the close battle. This does not necessarily mean that deep attack should be abandoned, but rather places an emphasis on the close and deep battles being coordinated to avoid this situation arising. The correct allocation and successful coordination of resources between these two battles would be a major task for commanders fighting the AirLand Battle (Richardson 1986, pp. 6–7). Success in this would be highly dependent upon real-time intelligence and on the judgement of individual commanders. That both are suspect to failure again highlights the risky nature of AirLand Battle. But if the task were managed successfully, then the result would be a highly efficient and effective use of firepower.

The second problem involving attacks in the enemy's rear concerns battlefield air interdiction. AirLand Battle identified corps commanders as the key personnel for identifying and prioritizing targets for battlefield air interdiction (particuarly divisions in the second tactical echelon). Given the many demands on air forces, their possibly very high attrition rates, and delays if NATO airfields were attacked, there can be no guarantee that an air strike requested by a corps commander could be executed. Thus attacks to disrupt and delay the second tactical echelon, which might be necessary to allow friendly forces to go on the offensive and seize the initiative, might not go in. As Richardson frankly admitted, this is a problem, but one which could be mitigated if corps commanders planned operations well in advance so that the availability of airpower could be assessed (Richardson 1986, p. 7). Whether such time would be available on the hectic battlefield may be questioned, but it should also be remembered that a major reason for the creation of the operational level of war was to allow commanders in this position to be able to lift their eyes from the immediate battle and project trends perhaps up to 72 hours ahead.

A further problem area concerns the integrated battlefield. Although at a tactical level there was a requirement for a doctrine which addressed the issue of how to fight in a nuclear or chemical war, the integration of this into standard operational doctrine raised concerns of a more political and strategic nature. The problem concerns the perceived failure to distinguish sufficiently between conventional and chemical-nuclear warfare. Rather than creating a sharp dividing line in the minds of commanders, AirLand Battle might serve to blur distinctions. Nuclear and chemical use was made psychologically easier for commanders, who might therefore be less unwilling to use these weapons, lowering the nuclear threshold and increasing the perception of nuclear reliance (Dankbaar 1984, p. 145).

AirLand Battle also raised problems over the complexity of battle, possible changes in Soviet doctrine, and relations with non-US corps on the central front. Although FM 100-5 emphasized the necessity of simplicity, it was apparant that the doctrine was far from simple. The deep attacks and series of fast-moving opportunistic blows envisaged in the doctrine required a high level of coordination (synchronization) and a sophisticated understanding of the developing battle. In particular there was a very real danger that corps commanders might be overwhelmed with tasks, and might be unable to cope with the demands of fighting a fast-moving, large-scale, opportunist battle involving a wide variety of air and land assets to over 150 km in depth and continually projected 72 hours into the future. The possible effects of a change in Soviet doctrine were unclear, particularly if the Soviets launched a broad-fronted attack with most assets placed in the first wave rather than relying on subsequent echelons to develop momentum and exploit mass – the so-called front-loading of forces (OTA 1987, pp. 68–9). This would obviously affect the deep-attack requirement, but might also affect the viability of operational offensives when on the strategic defensive. Similarly the implications of a more defensive Soviet doctrine, possibly designed with a more aggressive US doctrine in mind, are unclear. Finally there was a residual concern over the US unilaterally changing its doctrine without closer coordination with other corps on the central front. Concern was expressed that not only might certain elements of AirLand Battle conflict with NATO strategy (particularly the offensive elements and the integrated battlefield), but over harmonizing operations between corps fighting under different doctrines (Flanagan 1988a, p. 90).

Defending northern Germany: the British-NORTHAG concept of operations

Current NATO plans to defend the northern of its two Army Groups on the central front originated in ideas for the reform of 1 British (BR) Corps by its commander in the early 1980s, General Sir Nigel Bagnall. When Bagnall was appointed commander of NORTHAG he took these reforms with him and used them as the basis for a wider Army Group concept of operations. As similar reforms were being undertaken within the Bundeswehr, and had been underway for some time in the US Army, the thrust of Bagnall's thinking was very much in line with developments elsewhere in NATO.

The British Corps Concept

British Army doctrine had already been revised during the 1970s. Early ideas had envisaged a mobile linear defence. The corps would be deployed in two echelons, the forward echelon of two divisions being deployed close to the inner German border in accordance with the principle of forward defence. There it would hold a line until forced by attrition to withdraw through the second echelon, which would then assume the role of the forward echelon. The weakened divisions would then reform to provide a further echelon, and so the process would continue.

Although adhering firmly to the overriding political requirement of forward defence, this rather unimaginative concept did not offer much hope of defeating the numerically superior WTO forces. It was therefore replaced in the mid-1970s by a concept of 'killing zones' – mobile sacs into which enemy forces would be sucked. The defending forces would inflict high rates of attrition in a relatively positional battle, and would then withdraw before WTO second-echelon forces arrived. The position of these sacs was not rigidly determined, rather being responsive to WTO axes of advance. But terrain would be reconnoitred during peacetime, and likely avenues of advance identified. Thus defenders would have the benefit of intimate knowledge of the ground over which they would probably fight.

By the late 1970s this concept was under threat from developments in WTO forward air assets (against which killing zones, once formed, would be vulnerable), and *desanty* operations which could bypass such zones and create havoc in the rear. In particular the development of the Operational Manoeuvre Group as a powerful raiding force independent of the main echeloned advance posed a major threat which could only be dealt with by the creation of powerful reserve forces capable of operating in the corps rear if necessary. Thus by the early 1980s British Army doctrine required revision in response to an evolving threat.

As the architect of change, Bagnall's central concern was to avoid a static linear defence. In particular he emphasized that the NATO strategies of flexible response and forward defence did not imply the sort of Maginot Line defence critics so often portrayed it as being: 'Forward defence and flexible response are broad strategic objectives . . . What has happened is the interpretation of forward defence has been taken in some geographic areas . . . as being over-literal' (Bagnall 1986, Q. 633). A linear defence of the central front would be unable to respond to WTO axes of advance as they developed, spreading NATO assets along the central front rather than concentrating them against WTO thrusts. Such a defence could also become a matter of attrition, and static attritional warfare when in a position of inferiority would be a formula for early defeat.

> Static defence can only lead to a war of attrition, while the new concept would allow the defenders to seize the initiative from the aggressor, giving the Alliance a much better chance of defeating

the enemy rather than delaying him. (*Statement on the Defence Estimates* 1986, p. 33)

These concerns were far from new. And Bagnall's responses were not particularly novel: instead of a static or positional defence, manoeuvre was to be encouraged; linear defence was to be replaced by defence in depth; and rather than responding to a WTO operational plan NATO forces were to seize the initiative themselves. Similarities between this and the US Army's AirLand Battle doctrine are evident. Though the two are distinct in detail, they reflect similar lines of thinking: that the largely positional warfare of the 1970s would be unable to hold, let alone defeat a WTO advance, and that manoeuvre warfare designed to seize the initiative would offer a greater prospect of defeating the enemy. Thus rather than defending a front line with the bulk of available forces deployed forward, only vital areas would be held positionally and a strong reserve created. The defence would be so designed as to permit a small number of major penetrations rather than a larger number of 'penny-packet' breakthroughs. This would allow the concentration of reserves in a decisive counter:

> We must accept that the enemy will penetrate through and between our forward formations and so we must be prepared to destroy him in depth by the resolute use of mobile forces capable of concentrating sufficient firepower at the right point in time and space. (Burton 1986, p. 44)

These counters would be offensive in character, designed to destroy the enemy's first operational echelon and gain the initiative:

> there is no alternative to us attempting to seize the initiative ourselves at an early stage. Unless we achieve this we will only be reacting to Soviet moves and, as a greatly numerically inferior force, would inevitably be ground down in a battle of attrition. (Bagnell 1984, p. 60)

Having developed these principles of mobility, defence in depth, and securing the initiative, Bagnall proceeded to devise a four-phase framework for battle.

Phase 1   The covering force battle.[1] 1 A major concern of the early 1980s was how to deal with a surprise attack by the WTO. Surprise is not something which is either achieved or not, but is rather a matter of degree. Thus even if NATO received detailed information of WTO mobilization, it might still be surprised by the direction and timing of an attack and caught out of position. This is important since, as Field Marshal Viscount Montgomery noted, forces which begin a battle off balance rarely gain that balance necessary to fight efficiently. Rather than being in a position to gain the initiative and dictate the course of battle, they would be forced into reacting to enemy moves – the very position Bagnall was concerned to avoid. Thus a covering force would be deployed ahead of the main force to delay the enemy advance and allow the corps to deploy.

The strength and role of the covering force was the subject of some debate. Discussion has centred around how long such a force should (and could) delay a WTO advance. Initially a strong force was advocated. This would force advancing troops to stop, deploy off the line of march, and engage in time-consuming attacks. WTO momentum would thus be disrupted allowing sufficient time for the main defensive force to deploy correctly. The problem with this was that a force would have to be so strong that those forces committed to the main defensive battle would be diluted by up to one-third. Doubts were also raised as to whether even a strong covering force could delay an advance sufficiently as to be worthwhile. Thus an alternative, lighter force was advocated with a role less that of delay but of identifying major axes of advance and destroying enemy reconnaissance. By the late 1980s plans envisaged the early deployment of a strong covering force capable of delaying the enemy if NATO forces were not fully mobilized. The covering force battle would then meld into the main defensive battle as the attack developed. If NATO forces were successfully deployed before a WTO attack began, however, the covering force would be thinned out to little more than a reconnaissance screen, and forces redeployed to the main defensive battle.

Phase 2   The main defensive battle. Prior to Bagnall, British military planners envisaged a main defensive battle which used obstacles to canalize enemy forces into prepared 'killing zones' where favourable rates of attrition could be exacted. Bagnall emphasized a much more fluid approach to battle exploiting mobility and depth. Positional aspects would remain in the form of 'vital ground' which would be held and if lost recaptured. But rather than a linear defence or the tactically positional killing zones, the new concept would lure enemy forces deep into corps territory where they would be caught by surprise counter-moves. This was likened to a modern-day battle of Alam Halfa, where Montgomery lured Rommel's Afrika Korps onto well-prepared, mutually reinforcing anti-tank positions, with his own armoured reserve ready to burst forward in aggressive counter-attacks. In this defensive battle Montgomery forced Rommell to react to his (Montgomery's) plan, secured the initiative, and paved the way for the offensive battle of El Alamein (Hamilton 1981, pp. 601–70; Montgomery 1958, pp. 107–115). This is a slightly false comparison, however, as Montgomery's Eighth Army assumed a tactically positional defence, whereas Bagnall emphasized tactical mobility wherever possible.

Phase 3 The counter. Montgomery's conduct of the battles of Alam Halfa and El Alamein was essentially attritional (particularly the 'crumbling' operations used to weaken Rommel's forces in the second battle of El Alamein). In contrast Bagnall eschewed attritional elements and concentrated upon the use of mobile reserves, moving towards a more manoeuvre-oriented doctrine. One-third of the corps' forces (i.e. one armoured division) would be used for these reserve operations, making viable the traditional 'two up, one back' formation. Although most interest has focused on the counter-stroke, both counter-penetration and counter-attack options are available. Counter-attacks are operations to *regain lost ground*, and would probably be mounted by forces involved in the main defensive battle rather than the corps reserve. Counter-penetration operations are moves designed to *block* enemy penetrations. The counter-stroke is an *offensive flanking action* against forces either on the move or who have yet to take up defensive positions. Catching the enemy by surprise on his flanks, off-balance and unprepared, a numerically inferior force may dislocate and destroy the enemy. Historically even hastily conducted counter-strokes (such as the Arras operation in 1940) have created considerable confusion and delay, while more carefully planned and better executed manoeuvres (such as von Manstein's counter-stroke in the Dneiper campaign, the template for the British plan) have achieved a disproportionate success.

Phase 4 Subsequent operations. As General Sir Martin Farndale, Bagnall's successor as commander of I BR Corps, stated: 'Once the initiative has been seized it must be held at all costs' (Farndale 1985, p. 7). The question though is how the initiative is to be used. One possibility would be a more general move to the offensive, attacking into enemy territory. Evidence of support for this idea is slight, however, and largely indirect, while NATO has formally stated that it will not sanction land operations east of the inner German border. What seems more likely to British planners is that there will be a natural pause in the conflict after the defeat of the WTO first echelon. NATO forces would attempt to re-establish prewar boundaries, but would lack the forces to mount a more general offensive. Troops would be dead or dead tired. Both NATO and the WTO would be attempting to bring strategic reserves up to the front, but would be hindered by problems with lines of communication (in particular the delaying effect of FOFA operations for the WTO and the distances involved for US reserves). In this pause diplomatic efforts at war termination might be undertaken.

Maintaining the initiative is therefore an attitude of mind rather than an indication of a precise plan of action. The priority would be the re-establishment of the territorial integrity of the Federal Republic rather than excursions into Eastern Europe. Cultivating an offensive, aggressive spirit and emphasizing maintenance of the initiative might, however, be interpreted as implying a possible move to the general offensive, not least by the WTO. Identifying possible actions this far into the battle is hazardous, though, since (to use von Moltke's famous dictum) no operational plan can predict what will happen after the first encounter with the enemy's main force.

Towards a NORTHAG concept of operations

By the mid-1980s Bagnall's Corps Concept was becoming well established in plans and exercises for 1 BR Corps. Although similar developments were apparent in American and West German thinking, these changes were less well integrated into a wider NATO concept of operations.

The appointment of Bagnall as commander of NORTHAG in 1983 acted as a catalyst for change. Bagnall publicly bemoaned the lack of standardization and doctrinal harmonization in forces under his command: 'National planners and analysts tend to focus on the requirements within their respective Corps areas, with scant regard being paid to what the overall battlefield requirements are' (Bagnall 1984, p. 62). Plans called for a coordinated line along which the main defensive battle would be fought (the FEBA), and behind which a corps could not withdraw without Army Group authorization (lest it expose the flanks of other corps). Bagnall was distinctly unhappy with the manner in which this arrangement was put into practice: 'Currently this instruction is interpreted in different ways in the four Corps, without an overall design for battle at the Army Group level' (Bagnall 1984, p. 62).

Bagnall therefore attempted to use the British Corps Concept as the basis for a wider Army Group concept of operations. This was by no means an easy task. His position in NORTHAG resembled more that of a chairman than military commander. Indeed it was only in the event of war that control of individual corps would pass into his hands. Moreover there were doubts from the West Germans over the possible implications of the concept for forward defence. With an estimated 30 per cent of the West German population living within 100 km of the inner German border there was an understandable reluctance to advocate defence in depth. Bagnall emphasized that if the end result was a more credible conventional defence then such a doctrine would be to West Germany's advantage. Nevertheless the Germans argued for a stronger covering force, and that the emphasis be as much on the main battle as on the use of mobile reserves as the means of defeating the WTO. For the Germans, the defence of NATO territory (in particular *their* territory) should start as far to the east as terrain would permit, and everything possible be done to hold terrain. But German operational guidelines did begin to emphasize more strongly the use of reserves, attacks against follow-on forces and the importance of gaining the initiative; the operational level of war began to be emphasized and reserve formations strengthened; and particular attention began to be paid to the potential of high-technology barriers (such as advanced anti-armour mines) to divert and delay enemy attack and allow mobile counter-operations. Thus although the Germans appreciated and endorsed the general shift in thinking, they retained their concern for defending territory and holding any attack as far to the east as possible.

Progress on developing a NORTHAG concept which would be anything more than a paper plan or too general to have any real meaning was slow. By the late 1980s a degree of agreement had been reached over the covering force and over the main defensive battle. Moreover Farndale, Bagnall's successor as commander of NORTHAG, had advocated the use of the counter-stroke as an Army Group rather than corps operation, involving at least a division acting under Army Group command, and aimed at destroying large WTO breakthroughs – an operation which individual corps, with their smaller reserves, might be unable to undertake effectively.

Issues raised by the NORTHAG concept

Bagnall's reforms at corps level have therefore been translated into a concept of operations for NATO's Northern Army Group as a whole. This concept, when coupled to improvements in equipment, has led to a belief amongst NORTHAG military commanders that NATO is now capable not merely of holding any invasion of what has traditionally been seen as its weakest sector, the North German plain, but of defeating the WTO's first operational echelon without having to use nuclear weapons. However, Bagnall's concept of operations also raises a series of issues which require some careful examination.

1 *Finance*. Bagnall's concept of operations emphasizes the importance of avoiding static defence, and of conducting a campaign oriented towards manoeuvre. Conducting this manoeuvre defence requires a high standard of training and quality of equipment. Neither comes particularly cheaply, and NATO defence budgets appear to be facing a period of relative austerity. American defence spending is already under considerable pressure, while the British defence budget faces decline and a possible review 'by stealth'.[2] The Belgian government has already agreed to a 4.3 per cent cut in military expenditure, and its equipment budget is facing a lean future. Some reports suggest that Belgium is unable to fulfil over 50 per cent of its NATO tasks. NATO's financial position could be further worsened by the opportunity costs involved in the major funding required for the deep-strike mission. Thus the training and equipment of forces involved in the close battle may suffer, eroding their effectiveness and therefore their defensive capabilities. The British in the late 1970s, for example, facing real cuts in expenditure, cut back training to a point where efficiency was seriously degraded and the Army suffered a crisis in morale. Risky operations like the counter-stroke require highly trained forces, confident in their equipment and their own ability. Cuts in equipment and training may erode these.

Alternatively it may be argued that the early 1980s have raised defence budgets to a plateau from where some relaxation is possible, particularly given the progress in arms control. The problem also tends to vary from nation to nation. In the NORTHAG area, the Belgians are a major source of concern, while the British and West German corps pose fewer immediate worries (though there is some cause for future concern). The three US corps based in Europe (the lead elements for one of which are based in the NORTHAG area) have seen major improvements over the past decade in terms of men, material and morale, but require continued substantial funding to maintain this high level – funding which might not be available if the US defence budget declines substantially in real terms. US concerns over burden-sharing and the prospect of troop withdrawals pose an additional uncertainty over the numbers and quality of forces available.

2 *The conventional balance*. Bagnall's emphasis upon manoeuvre warfare was based upon the belief that static attritional warfare when in a position of inferiority would lead to early conventional defeat. This reflects two assumptions: that NATO forces on the central front are outnumbered to a significant degree; and that a more favourable kill ratio can be achieved with manoeuvre rather than positional warfare. This debate on the conventional balance is

of obvious importance to the wider debate on conventional defence: if NATO is decisively outnumbered then conventional defence is, to all intents and purposes, a non-starter; if on the other hand the WTO's numerical superiority can be offset by less tangible factors, then not only might conventional defence be possible, but the character of conventional operations might be affected. Bagnall's assessment of a pronounced imbalance – a key factor underpinning his emphasis on manoeuvre – reflects a pessimistic judgement of the conventional balance which can be and has been challenged. Moreover with the WTO unilateral reductions, and the prospect of a CFE treaty, the degree of WTO superiority has declined considerably from that of the mid-1980s, and the prospect of a surprise attack with little or no mobilization appears now to be beyond WTO capabilities.

3 *Manoeuvre warfare.* The second assumption made by Bagnall was that manoeuvre, and in particular seizing the initiative, offered a greater likelihood of success in defensive operations than a more positional defence - a view paralleled by the US Army and its AirLand Battle doctrine (FM 100–5 1986, pp. 134–7 and 140; Romjue 1984, p. 71). The defence that Bagnall was advocating, however, was not a completely fluid battlefield, but rather one which included positional as well as mobile elements. Ground considered vital would thus be held by positional warfare. What Bagnall was striving for was the optimum balance between positional and mobile elements, while effecting a shift towards a more manoeuvre-oriented doctrine. The ground on the central front, even on the North German plain, is littered with sufficient obstacles as to make fluid battles with no positional elements impractical (see Ch. 2). The defensive potential of these positions might be such that, in attempting to take them, the enemy suffers heavy casualties. Thus positional warfare may act as a force multiplier. Positional defence of vital areas may also be important in forcing the enemy to stop, deploy and engage in a fixed battle, thus disrupting offensive momentum. Although mobile operations may also disrupt momentum, they are much more difficult to execute, and there is the danger that if they are not succesfully executed they become little more than skirmishes. Thus Bagnall retained positional elements in his defensive scheme, but emphasized mobility to effect the shift in thinking towards manoeuvre warfare. Bagnall was not forsaking positional for mobile warfare, but rather shifting the balance between the two elements.

Balancing these two elements is a perennial feature of military history. Unfortunately history offers no easy answer to the problem. Although the Maginot Line is often portrayed as an example of the folly of static defences against mobile, armoured formations, its vulnerability lay as much in the inadequacies of the French army (the series B divisions), the lack of mobile reserves, the flawed design of the fortifications (notably in the Ardennes), the lack of defences on the Belgian border and Allied disunity as in any intrinsic weakness of positional defence (Gunsburg 1979, pp. 266-77). In contrast the Soviet defence at Kursk and Montgomery's conduct of Alam Halfa offer examples of armoured offensives battering in vain against well-constructed positional defences (Erickson 1985, pp. 128-49; Hamilton 1981, pp. 601-70). Indeed one historian has concluded that, if there is any lesson to be learned from military history, it is that, without surprise or an overwhelming superiority of firepower, and against a well-organized positional defence, armoured offensives are rarely successful (Griffith 1981, pp. 96 and 98-9; Griffith and Dinter 1983, p. 104). There is an important distinction to be made however between strategic and tactical positional defence. In the latter (e.g. Kursk and Alam Halfa) positional defence acts as an element in a wider campaign involving both positional and mobile elements. Thus both Kursk and Alam Halfa were followed by offensive battles and mobile operations. In contrast the less successful Maginot and Bar-Lev Lines used the positional element as the essence of the defensive campaign, and based operational and strategic planning upon that.

There are grounds other than military history for examining closely the value of mobile defence and manoeuvre warfare on the central front. Mobile forces rely on speed and surprise for survival. Even the most heavily protected mobile platforms – main battle tanks – remain vulnerable to attack, while less well-protected but nevertheless essential platforms (such as infantry combat vehicles and self-propelled guns) have displayed an alarming propensity to become death traps against heavily armed opponents.[3] A manoeuvre-oriented defence of the central front would be no different in relying on speed and surprise. With ongoing improvements in C3I and battlefield surveillance aids some may begin to question the survivability of such forces. Hiding a large armoured force, perhaps of divisional size, in the battlefield of the future might be no mean feat (Mackenzie 1989, p. 7).

A second problem is the massive Soviet investment in attack helicopters. These helicopters when operating closely with ground forces would be able to spot NATO ground forces before a WTO column comes into range, thus denying surprise. Moreover, combining speed and mobility, helicopter-mounted anti-tanks weapons can engage tanks at long range with relative impunity (Gabriel

1984, pp. 212–13). Against this however must be set the vulnerability of helicopters, particularly to fixed-wing aircraft. If the WTO failed to achieve air superiority, then their large helicopter fleet could prove exceptionally vulnerable to NATO tactical aircraft. In short, without air superiority mobile forces may be extremely vulnerable and air superiority can probably be guaranteed for only comparatively short periods of time.

Thirdly, the operational mobility of modern armour is surprisingly limited. A reserve corps travelling on six major routes would take 24 hours to pass a given point, longer if there were any enemy interference. The 400 km-long columns would also prevent for up to 36 hours the logistic resupply of those corps at the FEBA whose rear areas are crossed. This would have a major effect on the combat power and sustainability of those corps. And as Mackenzie comments:

> despite the considerable efforts made in recent years to speed up the necessary battle procedure, it still takes some 96 hours to commit a reserve Corps to battle. Consequently decisions on the time and place of decisive counter actions have to be taken extremely early in the conflict and with the barest of intelligence information. This makes commanders susceptible to enemy deception measures and encourages them to delay their critical reserve committal decisions until dangerously late in an attempt to improve the intelligence picture. (Mackenzie 1989, p. 7)

Finally, with the revolution in mine-laying capabilities, a flank may be protected from attack by the rapid laying of intelligent anti-armour mines. Much attention has been paid to the potential of mines for the defence. Their use by offensive forces however has tended to be ignored. Against an imminent counter-stroke, the quick laying of a minefield (by artillery or rocket forces) could be an effective counter. The problem here however is that even with the development of rapid mine-laying techniques a degree of warning is required to create an effective barrier. Modern minefields can be sown at the rate of 2 km an hour. Since the counter-stroke emphasizes speed and surprise, sufficient time might not be available for this. Minefields may be of use against a potential or developing threat, or to hinder the mobility of defensive forces; it seems unlikely, however, that they could be used against a well-executed counter-stroke.

Mobile forces therefore face a number of potential threats: improved battlefield C3I may not only rob them of surprise but render them vulnerable to attack; WTO forward air, and in particular anti-tank helicopters, may prove formidable opponents if unchecked by NATO air defences; operational mobility for reserves is limited, and may be even more so if new mine-laying capabilities are used to hinder movement. But equally positional defence faces major problems. Political constraints impede the construction of pre-placed field defences. Defensive positions would have to be rapidly constructed and could prove vulnerable to the very powerful WTO artillery. If a degree of construction was possible in peacetime, such sites could be extensively surveyed by enemy intelligence and plans designed to overcome them. Positional defences, even when rapidly constructed in war, pose a set problem which can be planned against. NATO would risk revealing both the place where it had chosen to do battle, and the nature of its defences, thus surrendering two important battle assets: surprise and the initiative.

This however would be to overstate the case agaist positional defence. Positional defence does not necessarily involve relinquishing surprise or the initiative. The criticism that such defences pose a set problem assumes perfect intelligence. NATO may engage in deceptive measures which, if successful, would allow it to surprise the WTO over the nature and extent of its true defences. Though modern intelligence and battlefield surveillance have rendered this more difficult, improved engineering capabilities have equally provided new opportunities. New technology imaginatively used might have considerable success in deceiving attackers. Although great store is set in both British and American circles by the value of the initiative, this is easily misunderstood as meaning offensive operations. Rather what makes the initiative so attractive is that the enemy, unable to implement his plan, conforms to the plan of the defensive commander. This was the key to Montgomery's successful defence at Alam Halfa and the Russian defence at Kursk. The initiative does not equate with offensive actions or mobility. Rather it means developing a sound plan to which an attacker is forced to respond.

The benefits of manoeuvre warfare are therefore by no means as clear-cut as might at first be imagined, nor are the arguments totally one-sided. While positional defences have some serious problems, they also offer a number of advantages which may be exploited in modern warfare.

4 *Offensive action.* Critics of the Corps Concept have noted in its advocacy of mobile warfare a willingness to consider offensive actions (*NATO's Northag Concept* 1987, pp. 6–10). Does mobile warfare imply an ability (if not willingness) to conduct offensive operations? And, if so, is this a matter of concern?

Manoeuvre in itself does not enable deep offensive operations. Logistical planning and preparation alone would need to be addressed in much more detail. Combined force operations use enormous amounts of fuel and ammunition, and keeping these forces supplied deep into enemy territory requires a considerable logistical capability which NATO lacks. However, more limited offensive actions *are* possible – indeed in this respect there appears little difference between planning a counter-stroke and planning an opportunistic raid into Eastern Europe. It is the destabilizing consequences of this potential for limited offensive action which must therefore be addressed.

For some advocates of mobile warfare an offensive potential is welcomed as improving NATO's warfighting capability (Huntington 1984). Offensive operations into Eastern Europe from corps which are not under heavy attack might be used to relieve pressure on other sectors and create considerable problems for Soviet planners (Brinkley 1986). But aside from the not inconsiderable question of whether these underemployed forces might not be better used as reserves for corps under heavy pressure, it is difficult to see how such ideas equate with NATO's position as a purely defensive organization (though some such capability might be important for the defence of West Berlin).

But should NATO be a purely defensive alliance, and why should it avoid limited offensive actions? The major problems with an offensive capability are its implications for stability and confidence-building. As advocates of common security have pointed out, developing a counter-offensive potential might be dangerously destabilizing and provocative, and might ultimately undermine rather than strengthen NATO's security (See Chs 1 and 6).

5 *Force disposition.* The manner in which forces are organized is an important component in their fighting effectiveness. Indeed classical strategists paid considerably more attention to the organization of forces than to the more modern preoccupation with the impact of technology. The current organization of NORTHAG creates two possible problems when implementing the new concept of operations. First, uncertainty over the size of the covering force creates uncertainty over the forces available for the main defensive battle. In the event of a surprise attack one-third of the forces allocated to the main defensive battle might have to be used to strengthen the covering force. If this happens the fighting power of the force engaged in what is the *main* battle would be reduced, which could in turn affect the planning of that battle. In particular, if a strong covering force is deployed there is a danger that the forces remaining

for the main battle might be insufficient to inflict major losses on WTO formations. This problem may be lessened by the fact that the covering force in this situation would meld into the main battle and that plans could cover this eventuality. But this would not remove the possibility that defensive commanders would be unable to concentrate sufficient force to exact high casualties.

Second, and more importantly, the Army Group commander lacks substantial in-place reserve forces under his direct control. But if the WTO breaks through in strength on a limited number of axes (one per first-echelon WTO army) then corps reserves would be inadequate to deal with this. An Army Group reserve force could be wielded much more effectively against major penetrations. Given the reliance placed on reserve operations to gain the initiative, the lack of substantial in-place Army Group reserves is a major problem. Although III US Corps is allocated as a powerful reserve for NORTHAG, the majority of the force is located in the continental US. Mobilizing the corps would require a major logistical and political effort – at a time of great political sensitivity. The alternative of creating a reserve from those corps already on the central front is beset in peacetime by the problems of who would pay and where loyalties would ultimately lie. The practice has therefore been to assume that in a war situation NORTHAG's commander in chief would have sufficient military authority to create a substantial Army Group reserve if necessary. But as Major General J. J. G. Mackenzie has noted:

> While the need for counter action reserves at Army Group level is not disputed, the danger is that the FEBA corps will be so weakened by their removal that they will end up being committed early merely to bolster the self-induced weakness on the FEBA. (Mackenzie 1989, p. 6)

What is apparent is that with the emphasis on strong reserves, and on the possibility of a strong covering force as well, NORTHAG corps are being stretched across considerable depth. There is therefore a danger that corps may be overstretched and unable to concentrate sufficient force at the decisive moment in battle.

6 *Sustainability and interoperability*. Improved conventional defence capabilities may be used to reduce NATO's reliance on nuclear weapons and raise the nuclear threshold, and indeed one of the aims in developing the Corps Concept was to reduce dependency on early nuclear use. But this also requires a capability to fight for an extended period with conventional weapons alone. A feature to emerge from conflicts using modern high-technology weapon

systems is the speed with which stockpiles of such weapons can be eroded. Given the cost of the weapons and their launch platforms, limited numbers are bought, stockpiles are small, and structural disarmament occurs. In addition modern guided weapons offer kill probabilities well in excess of Second World War standards. One is therefore left with a potential scenario where, if the weapons work even half as well as expected, platforms will be quickly destroyed, and if they don't work then the limited stockpiles will quickly be used up and platforms become weaponless (Pay 1988). Advocates of raising the nuclear threshold must therefore confront the probability that modern, high-technology armies cannot fight long wars against each other. Simple mathematics suggests that attrition will be high, stockpiles of sophisticated weapons will be rapidly exhausted, and the war (or at least the high-technology war) short. Within a very few days either one side will have won or a stalemate will have been reached. The use of nuclear weapons to reverse a defeat in this scenario is possible. In the case of a stalemate, however, a number of possibilities arise. The most optimistic of these is that diplomacy will end the war. Alternatively a longer war using less sophisticated weapons might ensue. In the medium term this might favour the WTO's stockpiling of obsolete weapons (providing they have been well preserved). In the longer run it might favour the West with its higher industrial capacity. Finally, nuclear weapons might be used in an attempt to break the stalemate. The problem is particularly acute for NORTHAG, in that some of its corps exhibit alarmingly low stockpile levels. Cordesman estimated I Belgian Corps as possessing balanced stocks for less than 10 days of intensive armoured combat (Cordesman 1988, p. 183). This is exacerbated by the lack of interoperability. With four separate national corps in the Army Group, NORTHAG displays alarmingly poor standards of interoperability, not merely in logistics but in communications and tactical doctrine (including basic subjects such as terminology and fire-support measures). This affects not just sustainability, but the ability of divisions to cross corps boundaries in counter-attacks (Mackenzie 1989, p. 6).

Conclusion

Bagnall's Corps Concept has provided a framework for conventional operations which is seen by both British and NATO military commanders as improving the chances of not merely holding but defeating WTO first echelon forces. But the concept is not above criticism – indeed it raises many of the key issues in the debate over strategies for conventional defence, issues also raised by AirLand Battle. Is the emphasis on modern sophisticated, heavily armoured and highly trained forces the most cost-effective means for conventional defence, and what are the implications of emerging resource constraints for these forces? Is the balance of forces such that a more positional defence, keeping to the letter as well as the spirit of forward defence, is impractical? Does the modern battlefield favour a movement towards manoeuvre warfare? Does the emphasis on mobile reserves overly weaken forces at the front line? And is the offensive potential of manoeuvre forces desirable in the broader NATO political framework? The NORTHAG concept provided a militarily acceptable formula for the latter half of the 1980s. Whether it will continue to do so in the 1990s remains to be seen.

Follow-on forces attack (FOFA)

Whereas AirLand Battle and the NORTHAG concept of operations are primarily concerned with the close battle, the FOFA mission concept concerns attacking enemy forces *before* they reach the FEBA. Drawing upon some of the deep attack ideas emerging from TRADOC, planners at SHAPE technical centre produced a study in the early 1980s for the systematic attack of WTO second-echelon forces (what were termed follow-on forces by NATO). The plan received strong backing from the then SACEUR, General Bernard Rogers, who saw it as a means of improving NATO's conventional capabilities and thus raising the nuclear threshold. FOFA was approved as NATO policy by the Defence Planning Committee in November 1984, and was then passed on to NATO's international staff for refinement. During the process FOFA passed from a general concept of the destruction, disruption and delay of follow-on forces at a variety of distances from the forward line of enemy troops (FLET), to a set of specific tasks linked to new and emerging weapons (OTA 1987, pp. 50–2).

Attacking enemy forces beyond the line of battle was hardly a novel idea, and an interdiction mission already existed for NATO. What was new was the idea that new technologies (called 'emerging technologies' or ET) enabled conventional weapons to attack targets previously assigned to nuclear weapons (thus raising the nuclear threshold), and the direct coupling of interdiction strikes to Soviet echeloning. Deep strike could exploit echeloning in a number of ways. By metering the arrival of Soviet follow-on forces it could prevent NATO conventional defences from being overwhelmed. Moreover by attacking these forces before they reached the FEBA it could reduce their capabilities and fighting effectiveness. Thus deep strike could help compensate for Soviet numerical advantages, while the new technologies offered the potential of a new generation of force multipliers. Studies at TRADOC and elsewhere produced strong indications that an emphasis on fighting the close battle alone would lead NATO to being ground down by successive waves, but that deep strike could have a major impact on the outcome of battle by attacking these forces. FOFA allowed NATO to shape the battlefield and to compensate for its own lack of depth by extending the battlefield into the enemy's rear. This would enable NATO commanders to create 'windows' in time and space where they could seize and use the initiative. Finally the new weapons and sensors would enable corps to provide long-range fire support to bolster other corps under heavy pressure (OTA 1987, p. 4; Romjue 1984, pp. 36 and 46).

The mechanics of FOFA

As originally conceived by SACEUR General Bernard Rogers, FOFA would attack forces ranging from those within a few kilometres of the FEBA to those several hundred kilometres deep in the enemy rear. This led to some confusion, as it encompassed such a wide variety of targets and potential weapons with which to attack these targets. The US Air Force, for example, tended to view FOFA very much along the lines of traditional interdiction tasks, while for the US Army the concept fitted neatly into the deep-battle component of AirLand Battle. As FOFA evolved in the 1980s however there was a narrowing of interest in the near term towards the shorter range tasks, partly due to doubts over the technology for longer range tasks, and partly because shorter range systems were already being developed or procured.

FOFA is intrinsically connected to the Soviet concept of echeloning. This concept is schematically illustrated in Figure 5.1. From this a number of categories of FOFA operations can be devised, closely related to particular echelons. These categories and their roles are shown in Table 5.1. It is important to note that current FOFA plans envisage a progression from the destruction of enemy forces near the FEBA, to their disruption further from the FEBA, to their delay hundreds of kilometres behind the FEBA. This creates a variety of approaches and requirements: from that of finding, targeting and attacking mobile columns near the FEBA, to the creation of

NATO OPERATIONAL DOCTRINE

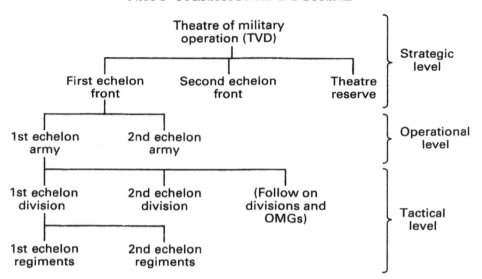

Figure 5.1 Schematic illustration of Soviet/Warsaw Pact concept of echeloning

choke points by the destruction of static targets deep in Eastern Europe.

This variety has led to some dispute within NATO. For some, Soviet forces should be attacked and *destroyed* well behind the FEBA. This view is supported by technical analyses indicating the value of such attacks in *delaying* and reducing WTO forces. For others this task is too technologically demanding for it to be a feasible proposition. In particular the surveillance, tracking, target acquisition and destruction arrangements, involving a number of separate and distinct platforms (which will all require sophisticated coordination) appear extremely difficult in a time–urgent, fast-moving battlefield with substantial enemy disruption likely. Debate has also focused on how effective the destruction of key choke points might be in delaying Soviet forces, and analyses have differed markedly over this. In contrast the advantages of attacking enemy C3I assets is well recognised, but it is not at all clear whether they could be found. Similarly there is an as yet unresolved debate over the effectiveness of attacking logistics, some arguing WTO combat vehicles carry large supplies into battle, others arguing that combat battalions have little integral excess supply and are heavily dependent upon resupply.

In general however it has been noted that the further attacks are made from the FEBA, the less is their direct effect on the battlefield and the greater is WTO ability to compensate; but equally the greater is NATO's opportunity for further attacks to produce the desired effect (OTA 1987, p. 7).

Table 5.1 Categories of FOFA operations

Category	Range (km)	Target echelon	Desired effect	Operations
1	5–30	2nd echelon regiments of engaged divisions	Destruction	Attacks vs. regiment columns by air, artillery and missile forces
2	30–80	2nd tactical echelon (2nd echelon divs of 1st echelon armies)	Destruction	Air and missile attacks vs. divisional columns; air and missile attacks vs. regiment assembly areas
3	80–150	2nd tactical echelon	Disrupt	Air and missile attack of divisional columns and assembly areas; air attack of chokepoints and halted units; air and missile attack of command posts
4	150–350	2nd operational echelon (2nd echelon armies of 1st echelon fronts)	Disrupt/delay	Air and cruise missile attack of units on roads
5	350–800	2nd strategic echelon (2nd echelon fronts)	Delay	Cruise missile attack vs. bridges and rail network and vs. units on rails

Source: OTA 1987, pp. 78–9 and 203–8.

Requirements for FOFA

In 1983 SACEUR General Bernard Rogers identified three key areas of technological change which would be exploited by FOFA (Rogers 1983, pp. 45–50). In the field of intelligence gathering and data fusion technological improvements were producing real-time surveillance and target acquisition capabilities. Since FOFA would be dealing with mobile rear-echelon forces, accurate and up-to-date intelligence on enemy movements hundreds of kilometres behind the FEBA would be essential. Moreover, at the FEBA real-time intelligence would also be required to locate and identify second tactical echelon forces attempting to penetrate and exploit gaps in NATO's front line. Once the intelligence had been collected it would have to be processed as quickly as possible and decisions made equally quickly over action to be taken. Improvements in C3 were therefore essential not just for the better management of forces in battle, but to reduce the time lag between the identification and attack of enemy units. Thus advances in computer hardware and software would be harnessed to provide real-time battle management (DeLauer 1986, p. 41). Finally enemy forces would have to be delayed or destroyed once located. Developments in microelectronics would allow sensors to be built into small warheads to provide terminal guidance and thus high accuracy regardless of range, while the warheads themselves would be smaller yet more destructive than the current generation. Weapons could be developed for use against armoured formations which dispensed a host of terminally guided sub-munitions with very high kill probabilities, while longer range weapons (such as conventionally armed cruise missiles) could be developed for use against static targets such as choke points which would have previously been targeted by nuclear weapons. In the short term the bulk of FOFA missions would be carried out by strike aircraft (such as Tornado, the F-15E and the F-111). Ultimately many of these missions would be undertaken by missile systems such as MLRS and ATACMs, though with the signing of the INF treaty in 1987 ground-based long-range missiles could no longer be based in Europe, forcing the long-range FOFA missions on aircraft or missiles from submarines or aircraft.

In addition General Rogers identified offensive counter-air (OCA) as a priority to limit WTO attacks on NATO C3 and the support of WTO troops at the FEBA. New runway denial weapons such as JP 233 would be used for this where previously only nuclear weapons might have been effective. It should be noted that many of these new technologies could also be used at the FEBA improving NATO's capabilities against first-echelon forces.

The current state of technology

When FOFA was officially endorsed in 1984 NATO possessed only a limited capability to execute FOFA tasks. In 1987 the US Office of Technology Assessment identified major shortcomings in three critical areas: in adequate reconnaissance, surveillance and targeting resources; in sufficient numbers of capable munitions and platforms to distribute them; and in total systems capable of rapid and effective responses to a variety of possible threats (OTA 1987, p. 3). A more detailed list is given in Table 5.2. Many of the systems to fill these gaps were already under development, and the OTA commented:

> There are still important engineering problems to be solved, and important pieces of equipment may yet fail to materialize. But by and large the issue is not one of starting new programmes to fulfil identified needs, but rather one of keeping the necessary programmes alive, both technically and financially. (OTA 1987, p. 4).

Indeed, for the OTA, provided sufficient finance was available to move from development to production, there was no reason why many of the required systems could not be deployed within the next decade. Aside from the obvious caveat over resources, this does tend towards optimism since certain key systems are encountering major technological problems. A particularly good example of this is the Joint STARS (Surveillance Target Attack Radar System), an airborne radar system designed to locate moving targets and control attacks against them. For some years the development of this system, critical for shorter-range FOFA tasks, has been hampered by problems over its potential vulnerability (since to be effective it would have to fly dangerously close to the FEBA), and over its technology. Reports indicated major cost overruns and delays in the radar such that flight testing had to begin without the radar (Walker 1988, p. 101). Thus by the turn of the decade NATO possessed the technology to undertake effectively and efficiently only some of the tasks in the FOFA mission.

Doubts over technology

The FOFA mission is heavily dependent upon a series of technological advances, some of which are still on the horizon at best. Critics have therefore seen it as yet another example of technological Utopianism and of the West's tendency towards technological overreliance (Canby 1985; Connell 1986) This can

Table 5.2 Technological deficiencies for FOFA tasks (1987)

Deficiency	Corrective	Status of corrective (1987)
1 Lack of ground-launched missiles	MLRS ATACMS	in production Full-scale development
2 Limited night/bad weather flying capabilities	LANTIRN F-15E TORNADO*	Limited procurement In procurement In procurement
3 Little ability to destroy massed armoured formations	CEM (Combined Effects Munitions) and DPICM (Dual Purpose Improved Conventional Munition) Smart anti-armour submunitions TMD (Tactical Munitions Dispenser) NATO Modular Stand-Off Weapon	In procurement In procurement In development In procurement In development
4 Little ability to target rapidly moving combat units	Joint STARS Aquila RPV	Full-scale development Full-scale development
5 Limited cross-corps support	ATACMS	Full-scale development
6 Counter to enemy air defences	Various air defence suppression and avoidance programmes	Various stages of development and production
7 No deep attack capability	B52s/conventionally armed cruise missiles	No development yet

Note: *MLRS/ATACMS might be used instead of aircraft.

Source: OTA 1987, p. 9.

be overstated. Traditional interdiction/strike (IDS), of which FOFA is essentially an elaboration (albeit a sophisticated elaboration), already exists as a NATO capability in the form of aircraft such as the F-111 and Tornado. Moreover the introduction of sophisticated runway denial weapons such as JP 233 provide a quantum leap in OCA capability. Thus some deep-strike capability already exists. Nevertheless, if FOFA is to be fully realized as a doctrine, new and emerging technologies must be exploited. As with most new technologies, therefore, three basic questions must be asked: will it work, what counter-measures are possible and how effective might they be, and how much will it cost?

1 *Will it work*, or more accurately will the technologies work sufficiently well to do the tasks required of them? The history of the development of hi-tec systems is not overly encouraging – Nimrod, DIVAD and Maverick are just three examples of 'state of the art' weapons systems going horribly wrong in development. Moreover tests of these systems can fall well short of battle conditions (Connell 1986). Further, systems which perform well in tests and on exercise may perform disastrously in battle due to unforeseen circumstances (the British Type 42 destroyers in the Falklands for example). In particular the C3I systems FOFA is so reliant on may prove especially vulnerable to friction (from information overload, jammimg, 'bugs' in the software, etc.).[4]

It is insufficient however to write off weapons systems merely because they are high technology and have not acquired the 'battle proven' tag. But more substantial reasons do exist for doubting whether new technology will fully meet FOFA's requirements. Firstly, as Stephen Canby has argued, the complexity of the systems is such that the opportunity for failure is greatly increased. This opportunity for failure exists not just in mechanical terms but with system software and C3I. As Canby has commented: 'The reliability of this complex equipment in a hostile environment is bound to be debatable' (Canby 1985, p. 14). Although this does not mean all complex systems are inherently unreliable (indeed some complex systems have proved extremely reliable), the more complex a system the greater the chance of failure, particularly at the leading edge of technology. Secondly, deep strike is a highly synergistic concept, and many of the systems involved are themselves highly synergistic. The nature of synergism means that dependencies are created, and that the failure of one component may therefore seriously compromise the effective working of the whole. This must be linked to the doubts expressed above arising from the complexity of the technologies involved, and the possibility of the repeated destruction of a key but vulnerable element by enemy forces. Thus a series of linked probabilities is established, and the cumulative chance of failure rises steadily as more links are added to the chain.

In addition, complex and synergistic systems can be poor at adapting to changed or unforeseen circumstances. Preprogramming and preplanning are key elements in controlling complex synergistic systems, which produce system rigidity (Canby 1985, p. 14). The history of warfare however tends to suggest that flexible, highly adaptive structures are much more effective (van Creveld 1985). Thus new technology may actually produce a system which, despite a technological potential for flexibility, is necessarily constrained by rigid pre-planning in order to maintain control.

2 *What counter-measures are possible, and how effective might they be?* Technological advance is not a one-way street, but an interactive process most commonly characterized by measure and counter-measure. One of the most obvious, yet nevertheless common flaws in the arguments of the advocates of new technologies is that they envisage the application of a particular technology onto existing conditions where specific counter-measures have not been fully deployed. The impact of new and emerging technologies however must be gauged in the light not only of probable and possible counter-measures, but also of the impact of the deployment of similar technologies by the opposing side.

In his critique of deep strike, Canby contends that not only are the technologies unlikely to work effectively, but that even when they do work they will be vulnerable to cost-effective counter-measures (Canby 1985, pp. 17–20). The counter-measures identified by Canby fall roughly into two categories. Firstly surveillance and guidance systems may be overcome by using terrain and buildings to mask forces (particularly in assembly areas), by jamming, or by the use of decoys. Chaff, infra-red flares, and corner reflectors on otherwise innocuous vehicles are all cost-effective counter-measures which may swamp surveillance and guidance systems, or at the very least provide a multiplicity of targets for sub-munitions. Secondly, sub-munitions have of necessity small warheads which can cause only limited damage. To destroy their targets they have to hit them, and even if they hit, protective armour, fire suppressors, and other safety features may mean that the vehicles survive. For example, the Soviet development of reactive armour for T 64B and T 80 main battle tanks rendered the vast majority of NATO's ATGMs (temporarily?) ineffective (Zaloga 1987). Similar developments may counter the effectiveness of FOFA sub-munitions. Thus, Canby argues, the weapons are too limited in their effect, and their guidance systems too readily countered.

In addition doubts have been raised over the ability to create choke points, and over the effectiveness of OCA. Superficially the destruction of the 60 or so bridges across the Oder, Vistula and Elbe would appear a major blow to WTO follow-on forces. Moreover, experience from as long ago as Vietnam suggests that the technology for this exists, at least with aircraft-launched weapons, and probably with missiles as well. But Soviet bridging capabilities are such that Jon Connell has suggested that they would be able to replace most of the bridges destroyed by NATO within two hours. Similarly, although 80 per cent of the WTO's air power is based at a mere couple of dozen airfields, the ability to destroy these airfields with conventional munitions alone may still remain outside NATO's grasp (Connell 1986).

These latter arguments however miss an important point: the aim of missions against fixed targets is not so much their irrevocable destruction as disruption. Successful OCA may so disrupt the coordination of an air offensive that its effectiveness is greatly reduced, while the confusion produced by the temporary destruction of bridges, rail centres or other choke points may have similar effects on the timing of a WTO offensive. Interdiction is an important element in disrupting an offensive, and in increasing the complexity of planning and execution. But it does not attempt the unrealistic feat of isolating the FEBA from the strategic rear.

Canby's criticisms are less easily dealt with, but they are nevertheless not wholly convincing. The dynamic of technological change is not limited to measure and counter-measure, but must include responses to counter-measures. Thus counter-measures such as flares, chaff and reactive armour are all vulnerable to further technological developments. What is unclear however is whether such counter-counter-measures would be effective (chaff for example remains an effective counter-measure some 45 years after its introduction), and whether the cost would be acceptable.

3 *How much will FOFA cost?* Accurate prediction of the cost of new weapon technologies is far from easy, particularly given the possibility of large cost overruns for projects at the leading edge of technology, and the often partisan nature of analyses. Thus a wide variety of estimates have been offered for the cost of FOFA. At the lower end of the scale, former US Secretary of Defense Caspar Weinberger rather optimistically claimed that the cost of new technologies for FOFA could be met within existing resource guidelines (Beach 1986, p. 169). In 1982 General

Bernard Rogers estimated implementing FOFA would require a 4 per cent real increase in European defence spending for the period 1983–8 (Rogers 1982), which by 1984 had increased to 7 per cent (Greenwood 1985, p. 78). Other estimates varied from $10 billion to $30 billion (Huxley 1987, p. 184). This needs to be placed within the context of an Alliance where defence budgets are encountering zero or even negative real growth.

Other doubts

In addition to these questions over technology other arguments have emerged in the FOFA debate. One of the major points of criticism concerns the increased emphasis on striking WTO territory. This is arguably unsuitable for a defensive alliance such as NATO. (Dankbaar 1984, p. 146; Windass 1985, pp. 43–4). When taken in conjunction with the emphasis of both AirLand Battle and the NORTHAG concept of operations on seizing the initiative, critics have perceived a dangerous trend towards the offensive in the West's thinking. Although there is a critical difference between the air attack of enemy assets in the rear and the occupation of enemy territory by ground forces, the danger lies in the extent to which FOFA might be perceived as offensive by the WTO and prompt a reactive threat geared to pre-emption which is potentially destabilizing in a crisis. The WTO might perceive the threat of a NATO pre-emptive strike with FOFA weapons as a major threat sufficient to warrant a pre-emptive strike of their own. The value of airfields and C3I centres, and their vulnerability to air strikes, means that the side which strikes first and hardest will gain a significant, perhaps decisive advantage (von Bulow 1986, p. 131). Moreover, the inadequacies of NATO's air defences places a premium on NATO debilitating WTO airforces on the ground, before the latter have the opportunity to reciprocate. This requirement will not have escaped the WTO, who in turn may decide that the best way to avoid repeating the Arab experience of 1967 is to strike first.

Fears have also been expressed that the development of FOFA technologies will act as an invitation to the Soviets to join in a new arms race. If the Soviets attempt to follow NATO in the development of ETs, and if NATO's doctrine requires the Alliance to maintain a technological lead, then the stage would appear set for an accelerated arms race. There was also some hesitancy within NATO since most of the advanced technologies identified for FOFA are of American origin, leading Europeans to fear FOFA as a vehicle for further penetration of European high-technology and defence markets by US companies. From a European perspective,

FOFA's requirements fitted neatly within a series of new American systems under development in the 1980s, systems which had few or no European counterparts. The end result, it was feared, would be a continuation of the 'one-way street': Europe buying US high-technology defence goods, allowing America to dominate advanced defence technology. Since the official adoption of FOFA in 1984 much attention has been paid to this problem, and a greater American awareness of European sensitivities has become apparent. In particular the 1985 Nunn Amendment attempted to encourage the 'two-way street'. However, the feeling persists that the technologies underpinning FOFA, and particularly the more advanced technologies, remain dominated by US companies.

Perhaps the most important criticism levelled at FOFA, however, is that it is in danger of diverting attention and resources away from where the real battle will be taking place: at the FEBA. The defence of the central front does not lie deep in the enemy rear but on the inner German border. Deep strike can disrupt, delay, or even partially destroy enemy follow-on forces, but if the battle is lost at the FEBA, then of what use is this? Given the increased resources required by FOFA and the financial limitations on NATO budgets there is a danger that money is found for FOFA by reducing the effectiveness of forces at the FEBA, particularly in terms of new equipment. Although there might be some room for manoeuvre within budgets, there appears to be a prima-facie case that if more resources are not made available, FOFA can only be funded by money from elsewhere within defence budgets. This would include money otherwise allocated to forces defending the FEBA. In itself this might not be overly worrying provided there was sufficient slack in defence budgets to allow such reallocation. But as money for equipment is likely to be very tight, this sort of slack does not seem to exist. Expensive programmes such as ATACMS may therefore be delayed (particularly in the case of European procurement of this American system), or may incur opportunity costs elsewhere in defence budgets. Some of this problem can be overcome by effective management, while conventional arms control may also ease the problem. The situation may also be helped by the dual use of weapons systems, especially aircraft, for both the close and deep battles. But there are dangers in this latter course in that the platforms might be required for both tasks at the same time, or that attrition from tasks in one mission will degrade the effectiveness of another. American and European F-16 aircraft for example would be in heavy demand in the early days of a conflict for FOFA tasks, for the air superiority battle, and for close support. Simple bean-counting exercises suggest that the combination of limited numbers available and projected high attrition rates will produce a shortfall in capability for at least one of these missions.

FOFA may also be vulnerable to Soviet operational developments. Initial fears concerned a greater emphasis on first-echelon forces, and consequently somewhat less importance being placed on follow-on forces. This might have been accomplished in one of two ways, firstly by attempting to achieve even greater levels of surprise in an attack so that NATO defences would be caught unprepared. First-echelon forces would therefore encounter less opposition, and be able to defeat NATO without the aid of second-echelon forces. Or secondly Chris Donnelly suggested that the Soviets might 'front load' their forces, by placing more units in the first echelon, in effect making the second echelon a reserve force (OTA 1987, pp. 68–9). But neither of these appear convincing at the end of the decade. Developments in arms control, unilateral WTO force reductions, and the changed political climate in Eastern Europe have made the sort of surprise attack required in the first approach politically and militarily inconceivable. And the front loading of forces appears severely constrained by the terrain of the central front. Quite simply there is not the room for front loading without risking confusion, overcrowding, and the creation of tempting massed targets for NATO artillery and air forces.

A variation of this theme is that the Soviets might attempt to overcome FOFA by an emphasis upon pre-emptive attack. If NATO air forces and C3I centres could be destroyed or weakened by such an attack, then the effectiveness of the FOFA mission might be seriously degraded. This of course would also have a major effect on crisis stability.

And finally it is by no means clear how a Soviet shift to defensive defence would affect FOFA. At the very least it would seem to reduce the importance of the FOFA mission, though the degree would be dependent upon the nature of the defensive defence scheme. FOFA may even become irrelevant and anachronistic with some defensive schemes, detracting from security through its pre-emptive potential rather than adding to it.

Conclusion

The 1980s saw major developments in NATO doctrinal thinking, particularly with AirLand Battle, the British Corps Concept and NORTHAG concept of operations, and FOFA. These doctrinal innovations exhibited a number of shared characteristics: a new-found emphasis on the operational level of war; the extension of battle in time and space (deep battle/FOFA); the primacy of seizing the initiative, and the importance of offensive actions at the operational level; and a shift towards manoeuvre warfare. This fitted the requirements of the early–mid-1980s, particularly the perception of an increased and well-defined Soviet threat, and the growing dissatisfaction with early nuclear use. These innovations created a risky but credible doctrine for NATO, a doctrine which presented the possibility of defeating the WTO first-operational echelon and thus creating the sort on shock necessary to stop the war before nuclear weapons were used. But by the turn of the decade this thinking was beginning to appear dated. The reduced Soviet threat, the WTO movement towards defensive defence, and the political changes in Eastern Europe combined to undermine many of the assumptions upon which these doctrines were based. Instead, the offensive, manoeuvre-oriented and deep-strike components have begun to appear threatening and destabilizing in the new age of reduced tensions. The requirement may still exist for a strong NATO defence; but the particular requirements of the early 1980s have so changed that the doctrines created to meet those requirements have been overtaken by events and now appear anachronistic.

Notes

1 A more detailed description of this can be found in McInnes 1988.
2 The phrase 'by stealth' was coined by the House of Commons Defence Committee in their 1985 report on commitments and resources (Third Report from the Defence Committee 1985, p. xli).
3 Reports of Israeli operations in 1982 for example suggest that Israeli infantry preferred to walk beside their APCs rather than ride in them against the relatively poorly equipped PLO (Gabriel 1984, pp. 200–1).
4 Research on nuclear command and control for example suggests that it is highly vulnerable to such effects.

6

Non-offensive defence

A radical alternative to the NATO doctrines outlined above is that of non-offensive defence (NOD, sometimes called non-provocative defence or defensive defence). NOD was largely developed in the wake of the European peace movement of the early 1980s, and finds most of its support in Europe. This is particularly so in West Germany, where the SPD has adopted it as its defence policy (Brauch 1989, pp. 1–2; Dean 1988, p. 62).

NOD is a broad-based approach to security whose underlying theme is the promotion of stability by reducing the fear of attack.

> The principal source of insecurity in Central Europe is the fear of aggression on the part of both Eastern and Western states, based largely on worst case assessments of each others' military capabilities . . . the strategies and force postures of both NATO and the Warsaw Pact are [viewed as] offensive in character and highly unsuitable because they invite pre-emption. (Flanagan, 1988a, p. 110)

NOD therefore identifies the major source of instability as the fear of attack, and consequently advocates the pursuit of purely defensive doctrines and force structures to promote stability in peace and in crisis situations (Buzan 1987a, pp. 276–7; Macintosh 1989, pp. 6–7). NOD is critical of current NATO strategy and doctrine on a number of grounds, but principally that it is destabilizing, provocative and too dependent upon high-technology weapons systems which may not work (Harvey 1988, p. 12; Rogers 1988, p. 21). Doctrines such as FOFA, AirLand Battle and the use of the counter-stroke in the NORTHAG concept of operations are seen as being offensively oriented and therefore destabilizing. The commitment to offensive counter-air operations to gain air superiority, and the development of long-range high-precision weapons are similarly seen as dangerously pre-emptive: a conventional disarming strike against airfields, C3I assets and supply depots is not only possible but might constitute a war-winning move. Once the WTO acquires similar capabilities (some of which they already possess) then the pressure to strike pre-emptively in a crisis might be impossible to deny: victory would come to he who struck first (von Bulow 1986, pp. 130–1; Flanagan 1988a, pp. 110–13).

It is important to note that for the supporters of NOD it is not merely the doctrines of the WTO and NATO which have created this situation but the force structures:

> Western tanks which are sufficient to destroy Eastern tanks upon the West's own territory, and thus repel a WTO invasion are also sufficient successfully to move onto Eastern territory . . . long-range precision strike forces which can destroy and/or hinder the forces of an invader behind his lines *after* he launches his invasion can also be used to destroy and/or hinder the forces of a defender *before* an attack is launched, thus ensuring a successful aggression. (Saperstein 1988, pp. 59–60)

NOD analysts have developed the problem of force structure to encompass the relationship between the military balance and stability (Boserup 1988, pp. 16–18). Thus stability is considered to exist *not* when there is some sort of equivalence in military capabilities, but when the defensive capabilities of both sides outweigh their offensive capabilities.

> Conventional stability exists only when the robust defense capabilities of each side clearly exceed the offense capabilities of the other. To create such a regime of 'mutual defense superiority', the rewards for attack and pre-emption must be systematically reduced, and the structured advantages of the defender must be exploited in order to compensate for the residual advantages of the attacker. (von Muller and Karkoszka 1988, p. 39)

The first key feature of NOD then is the *structural inability* of military forces to undertake offensive actions. Neither the formulation of defensive doctrines nor a rough equivalence in force levels is sufficient to create defensive stability: doctrine can be rapidly changed, and equivalence may be destabilizing if the balance consists of forces which place a high premium on pre-emption. But the structural inability to attack or bombard other states is both stabilizing and reassuring. This structural inability to attack offers a way out of the traditional difficulty of distinguishing between offensive and defensive weapons systems, though devising a credible defensive scheme which is incapable of offensive operations has created some difficulties (Brauch, 1989, p. 17; Buzan 1987a, pp. 277–8; Unterseher 1989, p. 2).

One of the major claims made by NOD analysts is that this explicit defensive orientation allows the traditional superiority of the defence over the offence to be exploited. This belief in defensive superiority is derived from an interpretation of Clausewitz, and is based on a number of factors: that the defender can prepare the ground over which the battle is to be fought and can exploit local knowledge of the land; that an attacker has to move into the open to advance, and is therefore a vulnerable target; that an attacker's logistics would have to stretch over enemy territory and are therefore vulnerable; and the belief that technology is moving to favour the defence, the watershed being the use of precision-guided munitions (PGMs) in the 1973 war in the Middle East (Brauch 1989, p. 17; von Bulow 1986, p. 113; Buzan 1987a, p. 277; von Muller and Karkoszka 1988, p. 39; Windass 1985, pp. 46–7).

A second key feature of NOD is the emphasis upon attrition. Many of the NOD schemes developed in the mid to late 1980s attempted to negate a Soviet *Blitzkreig* by trapping armoured forces in an infantry net, forcing them to conduct a battle of attrition rather than one of manoeuvre. In this way the momentum of an attack would be broken and the prospect of a quick victory denied to the Soviets. Thus von Bulow talks of 'defensive entanglement' and Unterseher of the 'spider and the web' in their respective defensive schemes (vol Bulow 1986; Unterseher 1989). This, though, creates problems with the stated aim of minimizing civilian casualties (Macintosh 1989, p. 7; Saperstein 1988, p. 64). The attrition implicit in such schemes would inevitably involve considerable loss of life, damage to property and societal upheaval. The major consolation though would be that this would be considerably less than if nuclear weapons were used.

A third feature of NOD is the intention to reduce and eventually eliminate both the pressures to pre-empt, and the means to pre-empt. The aim of this is to reduce the advantages and means of attack and therefore to increase stability in peace and in crisis situations. The problem of pre-emption is tackled from two distinct approaches. The first is to remove those weapon systems which possess a pre-emptive capability (particularly missiles and air-launched weapons with long range and high accuracy). If NATO undertook this unilaterally, it would reduce the fear of aggression and/or pre-emption for the WTO. As a bilateral agreement it would greatly reduce the means of attack, as well as going a long way to eliminating reciprocal fears of surprise attack. The second approach is to deny an aggressor targets for pre-emption. This is accomplished by creating large numbers of low-value targets rather than a few high-value targets. In particular the decentralization of air defences, command and control, logistics, and the restructuring of ground units into small packets of forces would deny a potential aggressor lucrative targets for attack. In contrast the current NATO system of large armoured formations, a few key airfields, centralized command and control, and large logistics dumps are seen as plum targets for attack, and therefore an invitation for pre-emption. This 'no target principle' is considered a major factor in contributing to stability (Brauch 1989, p. 4; Moller 1989, p.4; Saperstein 1988, p. 64; Unterseher 1989, p. 2).

A fourth feature of NOD is the attempt to achieve arms-race stability. By creating a defensive defence, the action-reaction phenomenon of the security dilemma is dampened (see Ch. 1). Because of the reduced threat, attack is less likely, and there is less pressure to develop counter-measures. The pressure to continue the development and deployment of new weapons is reduced, and the arms race is relaxed (Buzan 1987a, pp. 281–2; Moller 1989, p. 4; Unterseher 1989, p. 2).

Perhaps not surprisingly given its links with the European peace movement, NOD is in favour of reducing reliance on nuclear weapons. NOD analysts are generally critical of what they perceive as the 'nuclearization' of security policy. They argue that nuclear threats are inherently dangerous, provocative and destabilizing. Such threats fail to reassure or contribute towards the building of trust, while in an age of strategic nuclear parity extended deterrence lacks credibility. At the very least, NOD analysts tend to favour a no first use policy, retaining minimum deterrent arsenal to deter nuclear threats. Most however tend to see this as little more than a step towards global nuclear disarmament (Boserup 1988, p. 18; Brauch 1989, pp. 4 and 21; Buzan 1987a, p. 277; Flanagan 1988a, pp. 111–2; Moller, 1989, p. 6).

Finally NOD is not a means of improving the current security system, but of facilitating the creation of a new security environment. Its priority is on war avoidance by the removal of threats, rather than deterrence by the threat of punishment. It is therefore closely allied with notions of common security, particularly in its emphasis upon the interdependence of security and the destabilizing nature of offensively oriented force structures (von Bulow 1986, p. 113; Buzan 1987a, p. 277; Flanagan 1988a, p. 111; Macintosh 1989, p. 2).

The development of non-offensive defence

NOD schemes can be traced back to the 1950s and the West German Colonel Bogislaw von Bonin. Von Bonin was the chief military planner for the precursor of the Federal Ministry of Defence, the Amt Blank, and therefore wrote as an official of some standing.[1] His scheme was to establish a defensive belt over 50 km deep. This belt was to be manned by 150,000–200,000 light infantry and local militia, using anti-tank weapons and fighting from numerous small, well-camouflaged field fortifications. They would be protected by minefields, and supported by allied mechanized reserves positioned in depth to counter any enemy forces which penetrated the defensive belt. These mobile reserves would be stationed outside West Germany in peacetime, as would all nuclear weapons. When this removal of 'provocative' weapons and forces from West Germany was coupled to the purely defensive border belt, von Bonin claimed that the result was a credible, non-confrontational defence. His critics however claimed he had merely devised a new Maginot Line which would only serve to solidify the division of Germany (Brauch 1989, pp. 3–9; Dean 1988, p. 65; Gates 1987, p. 304).

Although von Bonin briefly reappeared in the mid–1960s (Brauch 1989, pp. 8–9), the next major step in NOD came in the 1970s from a group of civilian analysts mostly working at the Max Planck Institute under the leadership of Carl Friedrich von Weizsacker (though Horst Afheldt was later to become its most prominent spokesman). In 1971 Weizsacker's group published a major study which identified the consequences of a limited nuclear war as being catastrophic. The group therefore advocated that priority be given to policies of war prevention, but argued that nuclear deterrence was unsuitable for this since technology rendered the balance of terror potentially unstable. This study created a minor stir, but it was only with Horst Afheldt's *Defence and Peace* (1976) that a major debate was provoked. Afheldt developed the idea of an area defence force covering all of the Federal Republic with the exception of major population centres (these were excluded to minimize casualties). This defensive network was to consist of thousands of small light infantry groups (*c.*20–30 men each). These *techno-kommandoes* were to be locally based and armed with sophisticated ATGMs. They would be structurally incapable of attack, would offer a multitude of low-value targets, and would halt an attack by sucking armoured forces into an attritional battle conducted across the length and breadth of the Federal Republic (Brauch 1989, pp. 10–14; Dean 1988, p. 69).

Over the years Horst Afheldt has developed his model (particularly with the publication of *Defensive Venteidigung* in 1983) so that it now consists of two defensive nets linked by a communications net. The first defensive net consists of groups of *techno-kommandoes*, each covering 10–15 square km up to a depth of 100 km. The groups stationed near the border would consist of regulars on constant alert to deal with a surprise attack, while those towards the rear of the belt would be mainly reservists mobilized in times of crisis. The second net consists of mobile (armoured) forces and medium-range rockets. These would be based 20–80 km from the border, and are intended to break up major enemy concentrations. As with the original 1976 model, tactical nuclear weapons are considered unnecessary and dangerous, and are therefore to be removed from West Germany (Flanagan 1988a, p. 114; Gates 1987, p. 306).

Afheldt's ideas acquired considerable popularity in the early 1980s with the rise of the European peace movement and the protests over Pershing II and cruise missiles. The debate also broadened out from West Germany, with study groups appearing in Britain and Denmark. In 1984 an important step was made in opening up a dialogue with the Soviet bloc when the East–West Pugwash conference established a study group on NOD. Mainstream political parties also began to display an interest in NOD, particularly the SPD in West Germany. But it was the anti-nuclear movement which dominated the security debate, and NOD was little more than an offshoot in the debate over the stationing of cruise and Pershing II missiles in Europe (Brauch 1989, pp. 4 and 13–16; Harvey 1988, p. 14).

With the signing of the INF treaty and the changing strategic agenda in the late 1980s (particularly the increased interest in conventional arms control and stability), NOD began to move towards the centre of the security debate, albeit still as an alternative to established interests and concerns. NOD schemes proliferated, particularly in West Germany. Amongst the more important of these, Norbert Hannig developed the concept of a 'fire barrier' – an unmanned belt of defences 4 km deep, constantly monitored by electronic sensors which were capable of bringing artillery, mortar and rocket fire down onto any force attempting to penetrate this barrier. Behind the barrier light infantry armed with ATGMs would deal with breakthroughs or *desanty* operations. Major General Jochen Loser, a retired Bundeswehr officer, developed a three tier defence of a 'shield' of Bundeswehr light infantry on the border, a 'sword' of NATO armoured brigades for counter-attacks, and a militia for rear-area security. The shield forces would wear down an attacker, and channel him towards concentrations of fire, possibly using barrier defences as well. The sword forces would then eliminate aggressors. Initially the sword forces would be composed of NATO armoured brigades, but Loser envisaged a gradual transition to light infantry for this role as well. This scheme involved greatly increasing the numbers of conventional forces, particularly from the European members of NATO (including a doubling of Bundeswehr field strength).

Andreas von Bulow similarly argued for a sword and shield form of defence. Von Bulow's shield forces consisted of 200 home defence regiments, each of c. 2000 men (mainly reservists) deployed in a belt 40–60 km deep. These regiments were to be divided into eight motorized companies, each covering an area 5 km by 10 km. The forces would be armed with ATGMs and supported by artillery. The shield would locate and wear down any aggressor, using prepared positions for cover. Stationed behind these shield forces would be a sword of NATO armoured brigades, with further home defence forces providing rear-area security and integrating the necessary support services. As with Loser, von Bulow envisaged an expanded Bundeswehr supported by NATO armoured units.

Finally Albrecht von Muller combined the 'sword and shield' approach with Hannig's fire-barrier concept to create a four-layer defensive scheme. The first layer would consist of a fire belt 5km west of the border to 40–60 km east which would be automated and free of NATO troops. Behind this a 20–50 km layer of light infantry would use hit and run tactics to slow and degrade attacking forces. Those forces which penetrated the second layer would be dealt with by dispersed armoured forces in a manoeuvre zone, and finally a network of semi-mobile territorial defence units would provide rear-area security. In collaboration with Andrzej Karkoszka of the Polish Institute for International Affairs, von Muller also developed some of the ideas for force reductions produced by the Pugwash working group. The von Muller-Karkoszka plan called for a reduction in equipment to equal levels set at 50 per cent of the inventory of the weaker side, with specific limitations on force density and mobility; a ban on ammunition stockpiles within 150 km of either side of the border; a ceiling on strike aircraft and armed helicopters; but no limitations on barrier technology systems (including ATGMs) with ranges under 50 km (Bulletin of the Atomic Scientists 1988, p. 23; von Bulow 1986, pp. 129–43; Dean 1988, pp. 69–75; Flanagan 1988b, pp. 114–5; Gates 1987, p. 306; Macintosh 1989, p. 9).

Most NOD schemes concentrate on the ground war, with only passing reference made to the air war (usually involving the elimination of deep-strike systems and the use of surface to air missiles for air defence). A more detailed analysis of the air war however has been devised by Bjorn Moller of the Centre of Peace and Conflict Research at the University of Copenhagen (see Table 6.1). Moller's proposals cover the whole range of tasks performed by air power. The strike mission is curtailed as destabilizing. Strategic nuclear attack is rejected as flawed and unethical, but minimum forces are kept to maintain strategic stability. Deep strike is rejected as destabilizing and not cost-effective. Battlefield air support is to be undertaken by short-range (and therefore non-offensive) surface to surface missiles, supported by STO(V)L (short take-off and vertical landing) jet aircraft, which could be based at a number of small airfields, therefore reducing the value and increasing the number of targets. For air defence, offensive counter-air missions are abandoned as destabilizing, and greater reliance is placed

Table 6.1 A non-offensive air defence

Criteria	Force structure
Only minimum deterrence counter-value potential	Only few long-range bombers No ALCMs
No long-range, ground-attack capability	No fighter-bombers with AS-weapons
No deep interdiction or OCA capability	No long-range cruise missiles no long-range target acquisition capability
No lucrative targets	Dispersed air bases – STOVL
No long-range or mobile naval aviation	No aircraft carriers
Tactical concentration	Interceptors with AA weapons
Air superiority above own territory	SAMS, interceptors (AA weapons)
Air defence capabilities, incl. defence against helicopters	Low level air defence systems
Close air support capability	Short-range aircraft and helicopters with AS weapons
Strategic reconnaissance	Satellites, airships
Tactical reconnaissance	RPVs, scout helicopters, Sensor arrays, Infantry squads

Notes: AA: Air-to-air   AS: Air-to-surface.
Source: Moller 1989, p. 80.

on ground-based defences (SAMs, etc.) supported by a few fighters (preferably STO(V)L). Strategic airlift is considered potentially destabilizing as it might form the basis for a prompt attack capability. Instead Moller advocates greater emphasis on sealift (though he acknowledges that the strategic airlift capability created by civilian airliners would remain as a residual capability). Tactical airlift is considered important, and Moller advocates the use of transport helicopters because of their comparatively limited ranges. Early warning requirements are reduced by the non-provocative stable NOD system, while tactical surveillance may be accomplished by relatively cheap drones. Finally aircraft carriers are to be phased out because of their offensive potential (Moller 1989, pp. 71–80).

Interest in NOD has not been confined to NATO, but has spread to the WTO. Gorbachev's advocacy of defensive defence, and WTO declarations in Budapest (1986) and Berlin (1987), have indicated a degree of official interest in NOD. A number of East European analysts have produced schemes for NOD, probably the most important of which is that outlined in 1987 by the then Polish leader Wojcieck Jaruzelski. The plan proposed the reduction of nuclear and conventional armaments as well as the strengthening of confidence-building measures. Jaruzelski proposed exchanging lists of systems considered by each side to be the most threatening. These systems would then be gradually withdrawn from a given zone, destroyed, or placed in storage under international control. Both sides would also cooperate in designing doctrines which would be reciprocally recognized as purely defensive (Boserup 1988, p. 19; Harvey 1988, pp. 14–15; Karkoszka 1988; Kokoshin 1988; Macintosh 1989, p. 9).

The above is merely a brief outline of a few of the more important NOD schemes. Although some NOD schemes are not particularly well thought through, others have been developed over a number of years with relatively sophisticated models. One such model which is worth more detailed examination is the 'spider and web' model developed by Lutz Unterseher and the Study Group on Alternative Security Policy (SAS) based in Bonn.

The spider and the web: the SAS model

The SAS has been developing its model for NOD since 1980. Initially the model was purely defensive and concerned air and ground forces alone. As the model developed mobile units were added for counter-attacks, and attention began to be paid to the naval dimension (Forsberg 1988, p. 50).

The SAS model consists of three elements for the ground war:

1. A 50-mile-deep forward infantry zone consisting of 450 battalions in a decentralized 'net' or 'web'. Regular troops would create 150 of these battalions and would be mainly deployed near the border as a hedge against surprise attack. The remaining 300 battalions would each have a skeleton of 25 per cent regulars, the remainder being made up from reservists. Unlike the traditional hierarchical system of military organization, the web is totally decentralized with no fighting command above the level of battalion. Communication is lateral between adjacent battalions rather than vertically to higher commanders. These net battalions would also collect intelligence, creating a highly redundant C3I system.
2. A mobile force consisting of 150 armoured, cavalry (anti-tank forces) and light mechanized infantry battalions. Unlike the von Muller and Loser schemes which placed armoured 'sword' forces behind an infantry 'shield', in the SAS model these mobile forces would largely be located *within* the infantry net (hence the 'spider and web' description). These mobile battalions would be placed in a hierarchical command structure, and would consist of 90 per cent regular troops.
3. A light rearguard of overlapping infantry and mobile forces to protect against *desanty* operations and special forces. The force would be almost entirely reservist, the infantry defending key objectives and mobile forces offering support.

The key to the SAS model is the synergistic manner in which the 'web' infantry and 'spider' mobile battalions interact. The infantry would conduct an attritional battle based on area defence, delaying, splitting up and canalizing an attacker. They would be highly decentralized even within the battalion to provide low-value targets. They would fight from field fortifications (many of which would be rapidly constructed using prefabricated elements) using ATGMs, scatterable mines, mortars and barriers. Small numbers of armoured vehicles, utility helicopters and short-range artillery would also be available. Each infantry group would have a number of hardened sites to fight from, creating too many targets for an enemy to destroy completely, while the range of their weapons would allow them to support other battalions under heavy attack. The net infantry would also provide an important supporting function to the mobile forces, being the prime means of intelligence gathering and of logistical supply. Rather than being dependent on a long logistics tail, mobile forces would be able to live off the net infantry. Decentralized supply dumps would offer numerous low-value targets for enemy attack rather than a few key targets which might encourage pre-emption. A dug-in communications network would also be based on the net infantry, providing a high degree of system redundancy.

The mobile 'spider' forces would be used to block, contain or counter-attack massed enemy formations, ultimately destroying them. Their mobility would allow them a degree of flexibility and the ability to concentrate at key points, but their dependence on the static net infantry for logistics would deprive them of any offensive capabilities. Mobile forces could also be used to reinforce sectors depleted through heavy fighting (what Unterseher calls 'repairing the meshes'). The mix of mobile forces would be determined by terrain and mission. In combination with the net infantry, the SAS intend the mobile formations to create a rapidly changing problem structure for an attacker. An aggressor would have his forces delayed and degraded by the infantry 'web', would be subject to sudden fierce attacks from mobile forces, but would have no major targets to concentrate his forces against. His momentum would therefore be slowed and his firepower dissipated.

For air defence the SAS model relies heavily on the low-target profile of the spider and web ground forces to reduce the effectiveness of enemy air attacks. The defender's offensive counter-air capabilities (and deep strike/interdiction) would be relinquished. Instead air defence would rely on a two tier-system of SAMs and light STOL fighters. SAMs would operate in a string of clustered positions along the border, with a few in the rear to protect key installations (e.g. airbases receiving transatlantic reserves, ports, etc.). These would be supplemented by hand-held SAMs deployed with the net infantry. The STOL fighters, $c.$ 400–500 in total, would act as a flexible support to the SAMs, covering the spaces between clusters. STOL capability would allow them to operate from dispersed airfields offering low-target profiles. Finally $c.$ 200–300 V/STOL fighters might be used for close air support, again operating from dispersed airfields to reduce the vulnerability of the force and discourage pre-emption.

Finally the SAS model provides a three-tier defence of the Baltic coast and its exits into the North Sea:

1. A system of mobile land-based anti-ship missiles moving at random between hardened and/or camouflaged positions, $c.$ 20 batteries in all.
2. A full complement of mine warfare vessels, kept at current strength but constantly modernized.

3 A flexible, mobile force of fast patrol boats and helicopters, operating from dispersed bases and armed with anti-ship missiles. The force would consist of perhaps 30–40 medium helicopters and 40–50 patrol boats.

A number of features of this naval scheme are worth commenting upon. Firstly it repeats the pattern of the ground war in having an area defence force of anti-ship missiles (a 'web') backed up by a mobile firefighting force ('spider'). Secondly, with the exception of the anti-ship helicopters, there are no naval aviation forces, nor are there amphibious forces. This is because both are considered to possess some offensive potential. Thirdly, assets are dispersed to offer a low-target profile. And finally the scheme is closely integrated into the defence of the Baltic coastline to further reduce its offensive potential, and to maximize cost-effectiveness (Grin and Unterseher n.d.; Grin and Unterseher 1988; Unterseher 1989).

Characteristics of non-offensive defence

NOD schemes tend to display a number of shared characteristics, the most evident of which is the emphasis on area defence. The SAS, von Bulow, von Muller, Loser and Afheldt models all place considerable importance on the defence of territory by large numbers of dispersed infantry. This offers a low target profile, but also forces an aggressor into an attritional battle, disrupting momentum and dissipating strength (von Bulow 1986, pp. 148–9; Grin and Unterseher n.d., p. 3; Moller 1989, pp. 7–8; Saperstein 1988, p. 67; Windass 1985, p. 45). Linked to this is an emphasis on exploiting the defensive potential of terrain, and the use of man-made barriers to canalize forces and to provide defensive cover (Brauch 1989, p. 12; Gates 1987, p.302; Saperstein 1988, p. 66). The result is a reactive defence, with little or no assertive capability. This is in line with the principle of non-provocation, but allows the initiative to pass to an aggressor. It is also in danger of offering a predictable pattern of defence with little operational flexibility.

A second common characteristic of NOD schemes is the assumption that technology is increasingly favouring the defensive and, linked to this, the widespread use of PGMs dispersed throughout the infantry to destroy enemy tanks and aircraft:

> We will be able to equip the simple infantry man on the battlefield with relatively inexpensive arms that within seconds can shoot

down sophisticated equipment or destroy heavy armor worth millions. This technology will also make it possible to render the adversary blind and directionless in a matter of minutes (von Bulow, 1986, p. 113).

New technologies enable infantry to destroy the principal weapons of armoured assault, the tank and aircraft. New surveillance aids are creating a transparent battlefield, robbing attacking forces of tactical and strategic surprise. In combination with new target acquisition capabilities, this improved battlefield surveillance has also rendered large vehicles on the move (such as tanks) vulnerable to attack from concealed defensive positions. Finally the improved firepower offered by ATGMs and scatterable mines allows infantry to exploit this vulnerability. In Jonathan Dean's words, 'Mobility of firepower has replaced mobility of troops' (Dean 1988, p. 70). These technologies are central to NOD. They enable NOD analysts to create defensive schemes which appear credible in the face of an armoured assault, but which are also ostensibly non-provocative: the combination of static infantry and relatively short-range firepower offers little or no offensive capability (von Bulow 1986, p. 127; Dean 1988, pp. 66 and 70; Flanagan 1988a, p. 112; Gates 1987, p. 303; Herolf 1988, pp. 42–4; Saperstein 1988, p. 62).

Implicit in this is a major assumption about the relationship between mobility and firepower. NOD analysts tend to assume that the firepower of (operationally) static forces can offset the operational mobility (or to be more accurate, manoeuvre) of an armoured aggressor (Dean 1988, p. 70; Gates 1987, pp. 301–5; Windass 1985, pp. 49–50). The rationale for this is based largely upon the defensive potential of technology.[2] As technology by its very nature may change, NOD schemes may need the protection of an arms control regime to prohibit or limit the development of new technologies.

A further characteristic of NOD is the use made of reservists in (generally) manpower-intensive defences. This is particularly so with those schemes using infantry for area defence. Large numbers of regulars are eschewed for a variety of reasons: cost; diminishing numbers of young (male) adults, particularly in the Federal Republic; and the potentially provocative nature of large regular armies (albeit predominately infantry). Territorially based reservists could also exploit local knowledge. They might also be highly motivated since they would be defending their own homes and villages. Finally the highly developed road infrastructure in the Federal Republic would facilitate the call-up of reservists

(Brauch 1989, pp. 23–4; von Bulow 1986, p. 148; Dean 1988, p.76; Saperstein 1988, pp. 68–9; Windass 1985, p. 50).

The change in emphasis away from the existing layer-cake structure of armoured corps provided by a variety of NATO nations to a force of locally based reservists raises questions over the role of the NATO allies in the defence of West Germany. Most NOD schemes, implicitly or explicitly, envisage a reduced allied presence in Germany. Those schemes which retain some armoured and air elements (e.g. the SAS 'spider and web' defence) imply a continued but reduced presence (Unterseher 1989, p. 10). Others such as Afheldt, Loser and Hannig foresee a much reduced presence, and even the eventual exclusion of the NATO allies from the defence of West Germany (Dean 1988, p. 78).

The system of locally based reservists also reinforces the principle of decentralization which characterizes NOD. Decentralization, particularly in C3I but also in other fields such as logistics, creates two important effects for NOD. Firstly it reduces the offensive potential of forces still further – decentralization of command may have little effect on area defence operations but acts as a severe restriction on offensive capability. Secondly it reduces the incentive for surprise attack by offering a multitude of low-value targets and by creating a highly redundant command system. In contrast, traditional hierarchical command systems are vulnerable to decapitation and therefore encourage pre-emptive attack.[3]

Finally NOD is characterized by the assumption that a Soviet assault would be conducted along the lines of a *Blitzkrieg*, with the most important weapons being the tank and the aircraft. Those models which pay attention to Soviet artillery strength tend to claim that the dispersed nature of area defence offers few worthwhile targets for an artillery barrage. Little attention tends to be paid to assaults by dismounted infantry, and *desanty* operations are discussed by reference to rear-area security troops (usually militia, with perhaps a skeleton of regulars and a few thinly spread armoured battalions).

In summary then, NOD is based upon the following underlying principles to promote stability:

1 The structural inability to undertake offensive operations.
2 An emphasis upon attrition rather than *Blitzkrieg*.
3 The reduction of pre-emptive pressures by the removal of weapons systems with a pre-emptive capability, and by the 'no targets principle'.
4 The expectation of arms-race stability.
5 A reduced reliance on nuclear weapons.

The defensive schemes which have resulted from these principles tend to demonstrate the following characteristics:

1 An emphasis upon area defence.
2 The assumption that technology favours the defensive.
3 The use of firepower to counter mobility.
4 An extensive system of reservists.
5 Reduced alliance contributions.
6 Extensive decentralization.
7 The assumption of a Soviet *Blitzkrieg* method of attack, emphasizing tanks and aircraft.

Criticisms of non-offensive defence

Not surprisingly NOD has been subjected to a barrage of criticism. Political, economic and technological problems have been identified with particular defensive schemes, and with NOD in general. But perhaps the most severe criticisms have focused upon the military dimensions of NOD.

The first and most basic point made by critics is to challenge the assumption that defence is stronger than attack. Indeed modern conventional wars (particularly the Middle East wars of 1967, 1973 and 1982) have tended to suggest that the reverse might be the case. The case for defensive superiority is based upon two arguments: that local knowledge and preparation of terrain may be exploited; and that an attacker must move into the open which, with new technology, renders him vulnerable to attack. Although local knowledge may be important, the success of past invasions tends to suggest that it is not a decisive factor in battle. Preparation of the battlefield may also be limited by a variety of factors. Peacetime preparation may be constrained by environmental concerns. Preparation in a crisis may be destabilizing in encouraging attack before defences are completed. And preparation in war may be of limited use – sufficient engineer resources may not be available, while the lack of time may limit the amount of preparation possible. To some extent these problems may be overstated. NOD analysts have pointed out that barriers such as woods or canals may be constructed in peacetime which are environmentally friendly, and that prefabricated defences might be quickly established in war. These mitigate but do not solve the problem. Preplaced barriers are a set problem which can be planned against; prefabricated fortifications will still need sufficient engineers to install them, and there is no guarantee that these engineers will be available (most NOD schemes pay little attention to engineer requirements), while the prefabricated nature of such fortifications may lack the strength to withstand a modern artillery barrage (Gates 1987, p. 314). Terrain may therefore favour the defence, but the degree to which it does so varies and is unlikely to be decisive.

The second reason for assuming defensive superiority is intrinsically linked to technology. Whereas a defender may be concealed, an attacker must reveal himself and move into the open to advance. In so doing he renders himself vulnerable to attack, particularly given modern weapons and surveillance and targeting aids. Thus defence has an important edge over offence. This raises a whole series of questions concerning technology and the means of attack. The first point is that NOD analysts tend to ignore or play down the ability of modern firepower to suppress defences. Infantry equipped with ATGMs may be unable to fire their weapons simply due to the weight of enemy artillery fire. Even the dispersed nature of infantry defences will be of little use since, given the limited range of ATGMs, artillery need only suppress a relatively small area across which an advance is planned.

The second technological problem is the reliance on PGMs and the claim that these weapons have shifted the balance of firepower in favour of the defence: 'in the race between armour and the armour-penetrating missiles, the missile is gaining the advantage. As the cost of tanks soars, so the cost of destroying them falls' (Windass 1985, p. 51). But PGMs, and particularly ATGMs are no panacea. PGMs tend to be vulnerable to counter-measures, either those directed at the operator, or aids to confuse 'smart' missiles (electronic counter-measures, flares to decoy infra-red seekers, etc.). PGMs also work poorly in bad weather, and some also at night (Dean 1988, p. 71; Gates 1987, pp. 313–14). Most serious however are the doubts which emerged in the late 1980s over the capabilities of the ATGM. Several serious problems were identified with current (second)-generation ATGMs, which would only be partially solved by the third-generation systems under development. These problems covered a variety of areas. The size and weight of current ATGMs (c. 50 kg) limits the number which can be carried by infantry. If range and warhead size are to be increased, then the prospects for reducing weight and size are limited. An infantry platoon might be limited to perhaps a dozen ATGMs, less if SAMs are also carried, and even fewer if no transport is available.[4] Accuracy is poor: in some peacetime tests only 10 per cent of ATGMs have hit their target.[5] Even if the missile hits its target, there is no guarantee that it will destroy it. Soviet improvements in tank armour (particularly the deployment

NON-OFFENSIVE DEFENCE

of explosive reactive armour, ERA, on all of the tanks in the Western Group of Forces), and possible improvements in fire suppression and damage control have greatly reduced the lethality of NATO's ATGMs: the new British man-portable LAW 80 has been revealed to be obsolete, the widely used Milan is ineffective against Soviet tanks with ERA, and the US Army's Dragon ATGM has a kill probability of just 6 per cent. Attempts to overcome ERA have yet to display significant success. Milan 2, with a larger warhead and an extended probe to overcome ERA, was reported as still being ineffective by the US Army/Marine Corps in October 1987; TOW 2B has been delayed due to development problems; and the European Trigat will not be available until 1997, and will be far from cheap (RUSI 1989b; Schemmer 1989).

The implications of this are clear: a platoon heavily equipped with ATGMs would be lucky to destroy even a handful of Soviet tanks with today's technology, while the cost of third-generation ATGMs may prohibit widespread deployment. But more importantly it reveals the dynamic nature of technological change. Relying on technology to give the defence an advantage can only be a temporary phenomenon. There is no guarantee that non-offensive defensive technologies will remain a credible means of defence.

The structural inability to undertake offensive operations – a key feature of NOD – creates a second set of problems. With no offensive capability, critics have questioned how territory lost to an enemy might be regained (Gates 1987, p. 309). Although some of the more sophisticated NOD models (such as the SAS model) do have some mobile forces, it is clear that interest lies more in their ability to conduct operations against enemy forces moving forward than in set-piece counter-attacks to regain lost ground. The SAS model in particular would have difficulties in regaining lost ground in that the mobile forces are dependent upon static 'web' forces for C3I and logistics. Thus when they move out of the web into enemy-held territory (as would be required in a counter-attack) they would lose this support. It is also far from clear whether the web could support a concentration of mobile units sufficient to launch a counter-attack. Thus the SAS model's structural inability to attack refers to set-piece counter-attacks as well as to major offensives.

The generally static nature of NOD schemes also provides a set problem for attackers to plan against, and can offer little flexibility for defensive forces. Those schemes which include mobile elements would appear to have a greater degree of flexibility, but this may be limited by the small size of these mobile forces (usually battalions) and by the limited support services available to them.

This lack of flexibility is most apparent in the scenario of a successful Soviet breakthrough. NOD analysts tend to assume that area defences will dilute an attacker's strength such that a breakthrough would be easily dealt with by mobile forces:

> The object of a line of prepared all-round defence areas on the frontier is not only to prevent penetration by an attacking power. It is to force the aggressor to concentrate his forces on a narrow front to punch a gap, use up fuel and ammunitions and delay and tire its troops. The mobile forces which penetrated it would then fight at a disadvantage. Their supplies would be in jeopardy and their retreat cut off. (Windass 1985, p. 49).

This appears unduly optimistic. Given the pattern of Soviet offensive doctrine, what would probably happen is that the first attacking waves would secure the breakthrough allowing the second echelon or OMG to exploit it (see Ch. 4). This second echelon/OMG would be a strong fresh force, not one which had fought a bloody attritional battle and therefore vulnerable to mobile battalions deployed in depth.

One may also question the degree of attrition imposed upon an attacker by an area defence scheme. To use Afheldt's model of groups of 20–30 *techno kommandoes* covering 10–15 square km through to a depth of 100 km, a Soviet Army attack might concentrate an entire division on a 10–15 km front, its flanks being covered by another division to tie down defenders on the edge of the breakthrough sector. A further division would remain in reserve. Thus over 600 tanks (and several hundred more infantry combat vehicles) could face perhaps 100 groups of *techno kommandoes* armed with ATGMs. Assuming each group fired 10 ATGMs before being destroyed, that 25 per cent of these hit a tank, and a kill probability for these of 25 per cent, only one in 10 Soviet tanks might be destroyed. And this excludes the possibility of chemical weapons being used to further degrade defences.

Finally the idea that Soviet lines of supply would be in jeopardy and that a breakthrough force would be in danger of being cut off seems illusory. The forces to do this would be overrun. Even if they were still alive they would probably lack the will or the missiles to engage in telling attacks.

The lack of flexibility in NOD schemes can also be seen in the assumption of a single form of attack, namely a massed armoured attack. But by presenting an inflexible defence to counter this single form of attack, NOD schemes encourage the development of alternative means of attack. Thus the Soviets may develop new operational concepts based on dismounted infantry, or may place an even greater emphasis on *desanty* operations to bypass a line of defences and capture key psychological targets (such as cities) to erode the defenders' will to resist (Gates 1987, p. 310).[6]

Interestingly most NOD analyses pay little attention to the problem of defending cities, despite their high-target profile. This may be due to a reluctance to consider the damage to people and property that such a defence would entail. But given the increasing urbanization of the Federal Republic, fighting in built-up areas (FIBUA), would seem to be unavoidable. Although this may assist defending forces in that armoured offensives have generally been slowed in urban environments, it also creates problems. In particular most ATGMs are useless in urban environments since they require some distance for the operator to gain control of the weapon and for sufficient acceleration (perhaps 500 m).

The extensive use of reservists may also pose problems. As David Gates notes, although light infantry may be very effective in certain circumstances, it is a task for élite troops not reservists. The tactical ability and the weapons skills required are considerable, and therefore unsuited to reservists with minimal annual training. Gates also notes that the psychological effects of modern firepower would impose strains which reservists might be unable to manage

> Confronting charging armoured divisions is not a job for the squeamish, half-hearted or inadequately trained . . . Reservists often do possess admirable qualities, notably enthusiasm. They might also be prepared to fight especially stubbornly in defence of their own neighbourhoods. Such strengths alone, however, will not suffice when it comes to engaging hostile armour in classical light infantry style. (Gates 1987, p. 312)

A final military problem is that of sustainability: keeping forces in the field fighting. NOD schemes tend to decentralize logistics to maintain low-target profiles. Moreover, schemes such as the SAS's 'spider and web' model envisage armoured forces living off the infantry web to reduce its logistics tail. The result is that infantry battalions, companies or even platoons would have to maintain sufficient supplies to allow them to fight for several days unsupported. Given the likely daily expenditure in terms of weapons and fuel, the amounts required for this would be staggering.[7] In all likelihood infantry on breakthrough sectors would quickly use up their supply of ATGMs and find that the decentralized logistics system is unable to resupply them quickly enough before they are overrun.

Aside from these purely military problems a number of more political difficulties can be identified. Although most NOD schemes reduce the capability of NATO forces to engage in offensive actions, they do not remove it (Saperstein 1988, p. 63). The SAS model for example contains the possibility that infantry may be concentrated and support an armoured advance. This may not be easy, particularly given the constraints imposed by decentralized logistics, but it may still be possible. Nor does removing all armour constitute a structural inability to attack: the German spring offensive of 1918 achieved impressive rates of advance based on light-infantry tactics (Griffith 1981, pp. 79–83). Some 'offensive' capability, though, might be desirable to protect interests outside national territory. This might involve naval forces for the protection of shipping lines, or rapidly mobile forces for out-of-area operations. Some capacity for relieving West Berlin might also be required. All of these contingencies sit uneasily with structurally defensive schemes of defence.

Critics have also questioned the impact of NOD on deterrence. Deterrence by punishment would clearly be replaced with deterrence by denial. The question then is whether the Soviets might be persuaded of the strength of this defence, and might not be tempted to try and wear NATO down. If the Soviets were committed to an attack, they would face the prospect of a long haul at worst, and a quick victory at best. Would this be sufficient to deter? Might they not consider the risk worth taking since, even if things went wrong, they would probably retain some minimal gains (Flanagan 1988b, pp. 47–8). Chapter 1 suggested that the failure to win may create sufficient pressures as to deter the Soviets from attacking if victory was uncertain. But it also suggested that conventional deterrence would be better served by the prospect of a decisive WTO defeat, rather than a protracted attritional struggle as is offered by NOD.

The extensive use of reservists and the creation of defensive barriers could lead to an even greater militarization of the Federal Republic. Given the current level of protest over low-flying aircraft and military exercises in the Federal Republic, it seems unlikely that further militarization would be a popular option, let alone the psychological impact of building a defensive barrier in the West when the barriers to the East are crumbling.

NOD would also have a major effect upon the NATO alliance. Most NOD schemes propose a reduced alliance presence, and some an eventual removal of all non-German troops from the Federal Republic. This could have a major effect upon the cohesion of the Alliance. Although it might be seen as an advantage by some in freeing NATO from the structural rigidity of the cold war

(Booth 1988), it might also be a destabilizing element in times of crisis when Alliance cohesion might serve to bolster deterrence.

Finally there is an economic dimension to NOD. Most NOD schemes attempt to reduce the cost of defence through a smaller regular army, and the use of cheap weapons such as PGMs rather than multi-million-pound tanks and aircraft. But these savings may prove elusive. Building defensive barriers and physically shaping the battlefield will require major investment in civil and military engineering (Buzan 1987a, p. 285), while the cost of distributing sufficient numbers of modern PGMs amongst dispersed infantry may prove exorbitant. And this cost will not be shared with other NATO allies as at present. Thus NOD may prove more expensive for West Germany than the current force structure on the central front.

Conclusion

NOD attempts to deal with some very real problems of NATO strategy in a radical and innovative manner. The schemes devised so far, however, appear to lack military credibility and raise a number of political and economic problems. For many of these schemes military credibility would be enhanced if they were implemented bilaterally rather than unilaterally (one of the major advantages of the Jaruzelski plan), but even then some problems would remain. But as more sophisticated models are devised, and as the strategic agenda changes, NOD may be an approach to European security whose time is coming.

Notes

1. Though his defensive schemes appeared to have led to his removal from his position in the Amt Blank and his subsequent ostracization (Brauch 1989, p. 7).
2. It is also based in part upon the use of terrain to conceal forces. But this again assumes a level of technology whereby concealed firepower is more potent than mobile firepower.
3. Paul Bracken has examined this phenomenon with regard to nuclear command and control. Bracken concludes that there is considerable structural instability in a system of hierarchical command and control with vertical integration of warning and alerts. Bracken also noted that the highly decentralized communications system created by the Bell telephone company offered a very redundant communications net, but once the system moved to a few centralized microwave

relay stations it lost much of its structural redundancy (Bracken 1983). NOD attempts to create a system which exploits these principles.
4 Current West German mechanized infantry are equipped with just three Milan ATGMs per platoon (Isby and Kamps 1985, p. 182)
5 The poor accuracy of current systems is largely due to the guidance method which requires the launcher/operator to guide the missile to the target. When coupled to a long flight time (perhaps 20 seconds for 4000 metres) there is considerable opportunity to bring the operator under fire, or for the tank to undertake evasive manoeuvre. Third-generation ATGMs with 'fire and forget' guidance systems should erase this problem.
6 Although NOD emphasizes low target profiles, this can only apply to military targets. Large economic and political targets would still remain, and their capture might have profound effects upon the will to resist.
7 An M1 tank division would require 600,000 gallons of fuel alone each day. The degree to which the support tail could be reduced (a key feature of the SAS model since this limits the offensive capabilities of armoured forces) should not be exaggerated. The technical expertise and repair shops required to keep tanks running for example could not be easily decentralized to area defence infantry.

Conclusion

The world is changing, and for NATO it may have changed decisively. For the past 40 years the central front has occupied a position of primacy in NATO strategy and policy making. The reason for this was the perceived Soviet threat poised on the borders of West Germany. As that threat receded in the late 1980s, and particularly with the profound changes in the non-Soviet WTO states, so the central front is being transformed into the theatre for new approaches to European security.

In the early 1980s NATO was faced with the problem of increased unease over its strategy of nuclear reliance. Concern was expressed across a range of interested parties, from NATO's senior military commander, General Bernard Rogers, to the populist protestors on the peace movement. NATO's response was to attempt to raise the nuclear threshold, and a number of conventional doctrines were developed which seemed to assist in this process. NATO's confidence in its conventional capabilities were not necessarily misplaced: the geography and structure of forces on the central front did not weigh decisively in favour of a WTO offensive, nor did the WTO possess an unquestioned superiority in coventional forces. In this context the new NATO doctrines emphasizing deep strike, manoeuvre and seizing the initiative, though not without their problems, did offer some prospect of defeating initial WTO echelons.

By the late 1980s–early 1990s, though, the problem for NATO was shifting away from one of a massive Soviet threat to one of constructing a new, more stable system of European security. The Soviet Union's proclaimed shift to a purely defensive doctrine had merely been the harbinger of this change. By the end of the decade the changes in Eastern Europe had almost totally eroded the WTO's credibility as an offensive military alliance (at least for the foreseeable future). Moreover the CFE negotiations offered the prospect of a European conventional balance in which NATO would no longer be outnumbered by WTO forces. When combined with NATO's technological superiority and the growing likelihood that East European governments would resist a Soviet offensive move, the credibility of a Soviet conventional threat was fast receding.

The difficulty facing NATO was how to respond to these changes. The doctrines developed in the 1980s to oppose a Soviet *Blitzkrieg*-style offensive had not only begun to look hopelessly dated, but were increasingly seen as obstructing the movement towards a new, more stable European security system. The emphasis on manoeuvre, deep strike and seizing the initiative appeared provocative and unnecessarily offensive in outlook. Similarly the very premise of NATO strategy – of a competitive zero-sum relationship with a largely homogenous Soviet bloc – was becoming rapidly obsolete. NATO strategy was a product of 'old thinking'; what was required was a new approach aimed at constructing a more cooperative relationship based on reducing tensions and instabilities rather than one based on threats.

The combination of common security and non-offensive defence (NOD) may offer NATO a way forward into the changed condition of the 1990s. Certainly common security's emphasis on cooperation for mutual security appears better suited to the 1990s than the continuation of a competitive, confrontational strategy. NOD is not without its problems (though its military credibility may be somewhat greater against the reduced Soviet offensive capabilities of the 1990s than against a Soviet *Blitzkrieg*-style offensive of the mid-1980s). Work remains to be done on NOD schemes, and on developing an agenda for common security. But given the changes of the past few years, the strategic agenda and priorities on which NATO strategy and doctrine are currently based are in danger of obsolescence.

Bibliography

Afheldt, Horst (1988), 'New policies, old fears', *Bulletin of the Atomic Scientists*, September, pp. 24–8.
Allison, Roy (1989), *Soviet Military Doctrine: New Thinking on Nuclear and Non-nuclear Strategy*, paper presented at the 1989 Ministry of Defence/University of Birmingham Regional Seminar, Centre for Soviet and East European Studies, University of Birmingham.
Arnold, Major C. (1977), 'Current Soviet tactical doctrine', *Military Review*, July, pp. 16–24.
Bagnall, Gen. Sir Nigel (1984), 'Concepts of land/air operations in the central region I', *RUSI Journal*, vol. 129, no. 3, pp. 59–62.
Bagnall, Gen. Sir Nigel (1986), evidence before the House of Commons Select Committee on Defence, Second Report of the Defence Committee Session 1985–6, *Statement on the Defence Estimates 1986*, HC 399 (London: HMSO).
Ball, Desmond (1981), *Can Nuclear War be controlled?*, Adelphi Paper No. 169 (London:IISS).
Barnaby, Frank (ed.) (1978), *Tactical Nuclear Weapons: European Perspectives* (London: SIPRI/Taylor & Francis).
Barnaby, Frank (1987), *The Automated Battlefield: New Technology in Modern Warfare* (Oxford: Oxford University Press).
Baylis, J. (1988), 'NATO strategy: the case for a new strategic concept', *International Affairs*, vol. 64, no. 1, pp. 43–59.
Beach, General Sir Hugh (1986), 'On improving NATO strategy', in Andrew J. Pierre (ed.), *The Conventional Defense of Europe: New Technologies and New Strategies* (New York: Council on Foreign Relations), pp. 152–85.
Bellamy, C. (1987), *The Future of Land Warfare* (London: Croom Helm).
Bellany, I. and Huxley, T. (eds) (1987), *New Conventional Weapons and Western Defence* (London: Frank Cass).
Betts, Richard (1977), *Surprise Attack: Lessons for Defence Planning* (Washington DC: Brookings).
Biddle, S. (1988), 'The European conventional balance: a reinterpretation of the debate', *Survival*, vol. 30, no. 2, pp. 99–121.
Blackaby, Frank (1984), 'No first use of nuclear weapons – an overview', in Frank Blackaby, Josef Goldblat and Svenne Lodgaard (eds), *No First Use* (London: SIPRI/Taylor & Francis), pp. 3–26.
Bluth, Christoph (1989), 'The evolution of Soviet military doctrine', *Survival*, vol. 30 no. 2, pp. 149–61.

Booth, Ken (1988), *Steps Towards Stable Peace in Europe*, International Politics Research Paper No.4 (Aberystwyth: Department of International Politics, University of Aberystwyth).

Booth, Ken (1989), 'Alternative defence', in Ken Booth and John Baylis, *Britain, NATO and Nuclear Weapons: Alternative Defence versus Alliance Reform* (London: Macmillan), pp. 3–236.

Boserup, Anders (1988), 'A way to undermine hostility', *Bulletin of the Atomic Scientists*, September, pp. 16–19.

Bracken, Paul (1976), 'Urban sprawl and NATO defence', *Survival*, vol. 18, no. 6, pp. 254–60.

Bracken, P. (1983), *The Command and Control of Nuclear Forces* (New Haven, Conn., and London: Yale University Press).

Brauch, Hans Gunter (1989), 'West German approaches to alternative defense', paper given at the joint International Studies Association/British International Studies Association annual conference, London, March–April.

Brinkley, Colonel William A, (1986), 'Across the FLOT', *Military Review*, September, pp. 30–41.

Bulletin of the Atomic Scientists (1988), 'A menu of European defense plans', *Bulletin of the Atomic Scientists*, September, p. 23.

von Bulow, Andreas (1986), 'Defensive entanglement: an alternative strategy for NATO', in Andrew J. Pierre (ed.), *The Conventional Defense of Europe: New Technologies and New Strategies* (New York: Council on Foreign Relations), pp. 112–57.

Bundy, McGeorge, Kennan, George F., McNamara, Robert S and Smith, Gerald (1982), 'Nuclear weapons and the Atlantic Alliance', *Foreign Affairs*, vol. 60, no. 4, pp. 753–68.

Burton, Major C. J. (1986), 'Thoughts on a new look for 1st British Corps', *British Army Review*, no. 84, pp. 44–6.

Buzan, Barry (1987a), *An Introduction to Strategic Studies: Military Technology and International Relations* (London: Macmillan).

Buzan, Barry (1987b), 'Common security, non-provocative defence, and the future of Western Europe', *Review of International Studies*, vol. 13, no. 4, pp. 265–79.

Canby, Steven L. (1985), 'New conventional force technology and the NATO–Warsaw Pact balance: Part I', in *New Technology and Western Security Policy: Part II*, Adelphi Paper No. 198 (London: IISS), pp. 7–20.

Canby, Steven L. (1989), 'The quest for technological superiority – a misunderstanding of war?', in *The Changing Strategic Landscape: Part III*, Adelphi Paper No. 237 (London: IISS), pp. 26–40.

Carlton, David and Levine, Herbert M. (eds) (1988), *The Cold War Debated* (New York: McGraw-Hill).

Chalmers, Malcolm and Unterseher, Lutz (1988), 'Is there a tank gap? Comparing NATO and Warsaw Pact tank fleets', *International Security*, vol. 13, no. 1, pp. 5–49.

Cockburn, Andrew, (1983), *The Threat: Inside the Soviet Military Machine* (London: Hutchinson).

BIBLIOGRAPHY

Cohen, E. (1988), 'Toward better net assessment: rethinking the European conventional balance', *International Security*, vol. 13, no. 1, pp. 50–89.

Committee on the Present Danger (1978), *Is America Becoming Number 2? Current Trends in the US–Soviet Military Balance* (Washington, DC: Committee on the Present Danger).

Committee on the Present Danger (1982), *Has America Become Number Two? The US–Soviet Military Balance and American Defense Policies and Programs* (Washington, DC: Committee on the Present Danger).

Connell, Jon (1986), *The New Maginot Line* (London: Secker & Warburg.)

Coox, Alvin D. (1985), *Nomonhan: Japan against Russia, 1939*, 2 vols (Stanford, Calif.: Stanford University).

Cordesman, Anthony H. (1988), *NATO's Central Region Forces: Capabilities, Challenges, Concepts* (London: Jane's).

van Creveld, Martin (1985), *Command in War* (Cambridge, Mass.: Harvard University Press).

Dankbaar, Ben A. (1984), 'Alternative defense policies and the peace movement' *Journal of Peace Research*, vol. 21, no. 2, pp. 141–53.

Dean, Jonathan (1987), *Watershed in Europe: Dismantling the East–West Military Confrontation* (Toronto: Lexington).

Dean, Jonathan (1988), 'Alternative defence: answer to NATO's central front problems?', *International Affairs*, vol. 64, no. 1, pp. 61–82.

Defence Attaché (1982), 'A one-sided result in the air', *Defence Attaché*, 1982, no. 4, p. 35.

DeLauer, Richard D. (1986), 'Emerging technologies and their impact on the conventional deterrent', in Andrew J. Pierre (ed.), *The Conventional Defense of Europe: New Technologies and New Strategies* (New York: Council on Foreign Relations), pp. 40–70.

Donnelly, Christopher N. (1977), 'Soviet techniques for combat in built-up areas', *Military Review*, November, pp. 37–48.

Donnelly, Christopher N. (1978), 'Tactical problems facing the Soviet army: recent debates in the Soviet military press', *International Defense Review*, vol. 11, no. 9, pp. 1405–12.

Donnelly, Christopher N. (1983), 'The Soviet operational manoeuvre group: a new challenge for NATO', *Military Review*, March, pp. 43–60.

Donnelly, Christopher N. (1985), *Heirs of Clausewitz: Change and Continuity in the Soviet War Machine* (London: IEDSS).

Donnelly, Christopher N. (1988), *Red Banner: The Soviet Military System in Peace and War* (London: Jane's).

Drea, Edward J. (1981), *Nomonhan: Japanese–Soviet Tactical Combat, 1939* (Fort Leavenworth, Kans.: Combat Studies Institute).

Dziak, John J., (1981), *Soviet Perceptions of Military Doctrine and Military Power: The Interaction of Theory and Practice* (New York: Crane, Russak).

Dzirkals, Lilita I. (1976), *Military Operations in Built-up Areas: Essays on some Past, Present and Future Aspects* (Santa Monica: RAND).

Epstein, Joshua M. (1984), *Measuring Military Power: The Soviet Air Threat to Europe*. (Princeton, NJ: Princeton University Press).
Epstein, Joshua M. (1986), *The Calculus of Conventional War: Dynamic Analysis without Lanchester Theory* (Washington, DC: Brookings).
Epstein, J. (1987), *The 1988 Defense Budget* (Washington, DC: Brookings).
Epstein, J. (1988), 'Dynamic analysis and the conventional balance in Europe', *International Security*, vol. 12, no. 4, pp. 154-65.
Erickson, John (1975), *The Road to Stalingrad* (London: Weidenfeld & Nicolson).
Erickson, John (1977), 'Soviet ground forces and the conventional mode of operations', *Military Review*, January, pp. 49-56.
Erickson, John (1985), *The Road to Berlin*, (London: Grafton).
Erickson, John, Hansen, Lynn, and Schneider, William (1986), *Soviet Ground Forces: An Operational Assessment* (Boulder, Colo.: Westview).
ESECS (1983), *Strengthening Conventional Deterrence in Europe: Proposals for the 1980s* (London: Macmillan).
Fallows, James (1981), 'America's high-tec weaponry', *Atlantic Monthly*, May, pp. 21-33.
Faringdon, H. (1986), *Confrontation: The Strategic Geography of NATO and the Warsaw Pact* (London: Routledge & Kegan Paul).
Farndale, Gen. Sir Martin (1985), 'Counter stroke: future requirements', *RUSI Journal*, vol. 130, no. 4, pp. 6-9.
Flanagan, Stephen J. (1988a), *NATO's Conventional Forces: Options for the Central Region* (London: Macmillan).
Flanagan, Stephen J. (1988b), 'Non-offensive defence is overrated', *Bulletin of the Atomic Scientists*, September, pp. 46-8.
FM 100-5 (1982), *Operations* (Washington, DC: HQ US Army).
FM 100-5 (1986), *Operations* (Washington, DC: HQ US Army).
Forsberg, Randall (1988), 'Toward a nonagressive world', *Bulletin of the Atomic Scientists*, September, pp. 49-54.
Freedman, L. (1986), *The Price of Peace: Living with the Nuclear Dilemma* (London: Firethorn Press).
Friedburg, Aaron L. (1987), 'The assessment of military power: a review essay', *International Security*, vol. 12, no. 3, pp. 190-202.
Friedman, N. (1988), *The US Maritime Strategy* (London: Jane's).
Gabriel, Richard A. (1984), *Operation Peace for Galilee: The Israeli-PLO War in Lebanon* (New York: Hill & Wang).
Gates, D. (1987), 'Area defence concepts: the West German debate', *Survival*, vol. 29, no. 4, pp. 301-317.
Glantz, Lt Col. David M. (1983), 'Soviet operational formation for battle: a perspective', *Military Review*, February, pp. 2-12.
Goure, Daniel (1987), 'The impact of an INF agreement on Soviet nuclear strategy and forces in Europe', in W. Thomas Wander (ed.), *Nuclear and Conventional Forces in Europe: Implications for Arms Control and Security* (Washington, DC: American Association for the Advancement of Science), pp. 145-167.
Gray, Colin S., (1976), 'Across the nuclear divide: strategic studies past and present', *International Security*, vol. 2, no 1, pp. 24-46.

Greenwood, D. (1985), 'Economic implications: finding the resources for an effective conventional defence', in S. Windass (ed.), *Avoiding Nuclear War: Common Security as a Strategy for the Defence of the West* (London: Brassey's).

Griffith, Paddy (1981), *Forward into Battle: Fighting Tactics from Waterloo to Vietnam* (Chichester: Anthony Bird).

Griffith, Paddy, and Dinter, Elmar (1983), *Not Over By Christmas: NATO's Central Front in World War III* (Chichester: Anthony Bird).

Grin, John, and Unterseher, Lutz (1988), 'The Spiderweb defense', Bulletin of the Atomic Scientists, September, pp. 28–30.

Grin, John, and Unterseher, Lutz (no date), 'Make the other dance to one's tune: the military rationale of the SAS defense concept (Bonn: SAS, unpublished paper).

Gunsburg, Jeffrey A. (1979), *Divided and Conquered: The French High Command and the Defeat of the West, 1940* (Westport, Conn.: Greenwood Press).

'Halberdier' (1983), 'Counterstroke: an option for the defence', *British Army Review*, no. 73, pp. 30–2.

Hamilton, Andrew (1985), 'Redressing the conventional balance: NATO's reserve military manpower', *International Security*, vol. 10, no. 1, pp. 111–36.

Hamilton, Hon. Archie (1989), 'Conventional arms control: an agenda for the 1990s', *Bulletin of the Council for Arms Control*, no. 47, pp. 3–4.

Hamilton, Nigel (1981), *Monty: the Making of a General, 1887–1942* (London: Hamish Hamilton).

Hanne, W. (1983), *AirLand Battle and the Operational Maneuver Group* (Carlisle Barracks, Pa: Strategic Studies Institute, US Army War College).

Harvey, Hal (1988), 'Defense without aggression', *Bulletin of the Atomic Scientists*, September, pp. 12–15.

Hellstrom, M. and Rothschild, E. (1985), 'Report on the discussions in working group I: the concept of common security', in R. Vayrynan (ed.), *Policies for Common Security* (London: SIPRI/ Taylor & Francis).

Herken, Gregg (1985), *Counsels of War* (New York: Knopf).

Herolf, Gunilla (1988), 'New technology favours defense', *Bulletin of the Atomic Scientists*, September, pp. 42–4.

Herring, Eric (1988), *Strategic Concepts and Nuclear Threats: Testing Schelling and Morgan*, International Politics Research Paper No. 5. (Aberystwyth: Department of International Politics, University of Aberystwyth).

Herspring, Dale R. (1986), 'Marshal Akhromeyev and the future of the Soviet armed forces', *Survival*, vol. 28, no. 6, pp. 524–35.

Herspring, Dale R. (1989), 'The Soviet military and change', *Survival*, vol. 31, no. 4, pp. 321–38.

Hoffman, S. (1985), 'Thoughts on the concept of common security', in R. Vayrynan (ed.), *Policies for Common Security* (London: SIPRI/ Taylor & Francis).

Holden, Gerard (1989), *'New Thinking' and Defensive Defence: The Foreign and Domestic Policy Contexts of Gorbachev's UN Initiative*, Peace Studies Briefing No. 37 (Bradford: Department of Peace Studies, University of Bradford).

Holmes, Richard (1986), *Acts of War: The Behaviour of Men in Battle* (New York: Free Press).

Holmes, K. (1988), 'Measuring the conventional balance in Europe', *International Security*, vol. 12, no. 4, pp. 166–73.

Homer-Dixon, Thomas F. (1987), 'A common misapplication of the Lanchester square law: a research note', *International Security*, vol. 12, no. 1, pp. 135–9.

Hooper, Wing Commander R. W. (1989), 'Mikhail Gorbachev's economic reconstruction and Soviet defense policy', *RUSI Journal*, vol. 134, no. 2, pp. 15–22.

Hubatshek, Gerhard (1988), 'Radical plans for W. German Army', *Jane's Defence Weekly*, 26 March, p. 574.

Huntington, Samuel P. (1984), 'Conventional deterrence and conventional retaliation in Europe', *International Security*, vol. 8, no. 3, pp. 32–56.

Huxley, Tim. (1987), 'Emerging technology: no conventional wisdom', in Ian Bellamy and Tim Huxley (eds), *New Conventional Weapons and Western Defence* (London: Frank Cass), pp. 176–91.

IDDS (1989), *Cutting Conventional Forces I: An Analysis of the Official Mandate, Statistics and Proposals in the NATO-WTO Talks on Reducing Conventional Forces in Europe* (Brookline, Mass.: IDDS).

International Institute for Strategic Studies (1989), *The Military Balance 1989–90* (London: IISS).

Isby, David C. (1988), *Weapons and Tactics of the Soviet Army* (London: Jane's).

Isby, David C., and Kamps, Charles Jr. (1985), *Armies of NATO's Central Front* (London: Jane's).

Isnard, Jacques (1989), 'Major reshuffle ahead for French forces', *Jane's Defence Weekly*, 12 August, p. 240.

Jervis, R. (1978), 'Cooperation under the security dilemma', *World Politics*, vol. 30, no. 2, pp. 167–214.

Jones, Archer (1978), 'The new FM 100–5: a view from the ivory tower', *Military Review*, February, pp. 27–36.

Kaiser, Karl, Leber, Georg, Mertes, Allois and Schulze, Franz-Joseph (1982), 'Nuclear weapons and the preservation of peace: a German response to no first use', *Foreign Affairs*, vol. 60, no. 5, pp. 1157–70.

Karber, Phillip A. (1976a), 'Dynamic doctrine for dynamic defense', *Armed Forces Journal International*, October, pp. 28–9.

Karber, Phillip A. (1976b), 'Soviet lessons of the Middle East War', *Army Research and Development News*, vol. 17, no. 6, p. 13.

Karber, Phillip A. (1979), 'The impact of new conventional technologies on military doctrine and organization in the Warsaw Pact', in Christoph Bertram (ed.), *New Conventional Weapons and East-West*

BIBLIOGRAPHY

Security (London: Macmillan), pp. 29–37.

Karkoszka, Andrzej (1988), 'Merits of the Jaruzelski plan', *Bulletin of the Atomic Scientists*, September, pp. 32–4.

Kaufmann, William W. (1983), 'Nonnuclear deterrence', and 'The arithmetic of force planning', in John J. Steinbrunner and Leon V. Sigal (eds), *Alliance Security and the No-First-Use Question* (Washington, D.C.: Brookings), pp. 22–42 and 208–216.

Kokoshin, Andrei (1988), 'Restructure forces, enhance security', *Bulletin of the Atomic Scientists*, September, pp. 35–8.

Korbonski, Andrzej (1982), 'The Warsaw Treaty after the twenty-five years: an entangling alliance or empty shell?', in Robert W. Clawson and Lawrence S. Kaplan (eds), *The Warsaw Pact: Political Purpose and Military Means* (Wilmington, Del.: Scholarly Resources Inc.), pp. 3–26.

Krass, A. (1985), 'The death of deterrence', in R. Vayrynan (ed.), *Policies for Common Security* (London: SIPRI/Taylor & Francis).

Lanchester, F. W. (1916), *Aircraft in Warfare: the Dawn of the Fourth Arm* (London: Constable).

Lebow, R. (1987), 'Deterrence failure revisited', *International Security*, vol. 12, no. 1, pp. 197–213.

Lepingwell, John W. R. (1987), 'The laws of combat? Lanchester re-examined', *International Security*, vol. 12, no. 1, pp. 89–134.

Lider, Julian (1986), *Origins and Development of West German Military Thought*, 2 vols (Aldershot: Gower).

Lind, William S. (1977), 'FM 100–5, Operations: some doctrinal questions for the United States' Army', *Military Review*, March, pp. 54–65.

Lok, Joris Janssen (1989), 'Changing WP threat in Europe', *Jane's Defence Weekly*, 2 December, p. 1220.

van Loon, Henry (1989), 'Shrinking pool of reservists getting NATO's attention', *Armed Forces Journal International*, March, p. 70.

Luttwak, Edward N. (1982), 'Why we need more "waste, fraud and mismanagement" in the Pentagon', *Survival*, vol. 24, no. 3, pp. 117–30.

MccGwire, Michael (1987), *Military Objectives in Soviet Foreign Policy* (Washington, DC: Brookings).

McInnes, Colin (1988), 'BAOR in the 1980s: changes in doctrine and organisation', *Defense Analysis*, vol. 4, no. 4, pp. 377–94.

Macintosh, James (1989), *Non-Offensive Defence Regimes*, Occasional Paper No. 4 (Manitoba, Winnipeg: Department of Political Studies, University of Manitoba).

Mackenzie, Major General J. J. G. (1989), 'The counter-offensive', paper presented at UK Ministry of Defence/King's College London conference on Britain and the Central Region, July.

Mackenzie, Major General J. J. G., and Reid, Brian Holden (eds) (1989), *The British Army and the Operational Level of War* (London: Tri-Service Press).

Maddock, Rowland (1988), *The Efficiency of the Soviet Defence Economy: A Non-Quantitative Analysis*, International Politics Research Papers

No.2 (Aberystwyth: Department of International Politics, University of Aberystwyth).
Martin, L. W. (1985), *Before the Day After* (London: Newnes).
Mason, Air Vice-Marshal R. A. (ed.) (1986), *War in the Third Dimension: Essays in Contemporary Air Power* (London: Brassey's).
Mearsheimer, J. (1982), 'Why the Soviets can't win quickly in central Europe', *International Security*, vol. 7, no. 1, pp. 3–39.
Mearsheimer, J. (1983), *Conventional Deterrence* (Ithaca, NY: Cornell University Press).
Mearsheimer, J. (1988), 'Numbers, strategy and the European balance', *International Security*, vol. 12, no. 4, pp. 174–85.
Meyer, Stephen M. (1988), 'The sources and prospects of Gorbachev's new political thinking on security', *International Security*, vol. 13, no. 2, pp. 124–163.
Moller, Bjorn (1989), 'Air power and non-offensive defence: a preliminary analysis', paper given at the joint International Studies Association/British International Studies Association annual conference, London, March–April.
Montgomery, Field Marshal Viscount (1958), *Memoirs* (London: Collins).
von Muller, Albrecht, and Karkoszka, Andrzej (1988), 'An East–West negotiating proposal', *Bulletin of the Atomic Scientists*, September, pp. 39–41.
NATO (1988), *Conventional Forces in Europe: the Facts* (Brussels: NATO Press Service).
NATO's NORTHAG Concept: A Critique (1987), BASIC Report 005 (London: British American Security Information Council).
Niepold, Gerd (1987), *Battle For White Russia: The Destruction of Army Group Centre, June 1944*, trans. Richard Simpkin (London: Brassey's).
Office of Technology Assessment (OTA, 1987), *New Technology for NATO: Implementing Follow-On Forces Attack* (Washington, DC: US GPO).
Orme, John (1987), 'Deterrence failures: a second look', *International Security*, vol. 11, no. 4, pp. 96–124.
Palme, Olaf (1982), *Common Security: A Programme for Disarmament*, The Report of the Independent Commission on Disarmament and Security Issues under the Chairmanship of Olaf Palme (London: Pan).
Pay, J. (1988), 'The battlefield since 1945', in C. McInnes and G. Sheffield, (eds), *Warfare in the Twentieth Century: Theory and Practice* (London: Unwin Hyman), pp. 213–35.
Petersen, Phillip A., and Hines, John G. (1983), 'The conventional offensive in Soviet theatre strategy', *Orbis*, vol. 27, no. 3, pp. 695–739.
Phillips, R. Hyland, and Sands, Jeffrey I. (1988), 'Reasonable sufficiency and Soviet conventional defense: a research note', *International Security*, vol. 13, no. 2, pp. 164–78.
Pierre, Andrew J. (1986), 'Enhancing conventional defence: a question of priorities', in A. Pierre (ed.), *The Conventional Defense of Europe: New Technologies and New Strategies* (New York: Council on Foreign

Relations), pp. 9–39.
Posen, B. (1984), 'Measuring the European conventional balance: coping with complexity in threat assessment', *International Security*, vol. 9, no. 3, pp. 47–88.
Posen, B. (1988), 'Is NATO decisively outnumbered?', *International Security*, vol. 12, no. 4, pp. 186–202.
Ramsey, Paul (1968), *The Just War: Force and Political Responsibility* (New York: Scribner).
Richardson, Gen. W. (1986), 'FM 100–5: the AirLand Battle in 1986', *Military Review*, March, pp. 4–11.
Rogers, Gen. B. (1982), 'The Atlantic Alliance: prescriptions for a difficult decade ahead', *Foreign Affairs*, vol. 60, no. 5, pp. 1145–56.
Rogers, Gen. B. (1983), 'Strike deep: a new concept for NATO', *Military Technology*, 1983, no. 5, pp. 38–50.
Rogers, Paul (1988), 'The nuclear connection', *Bulletin of the Atomic Scientists*, September, pp. 20–3.
Romjue, J. (1984), *From Active Defense to AirLand Battle: The Development of Army Doctrine 1973–82*, TRADOC Historical Monographs Series (Washington, DC: US GPO).
RUSI (1989a), 'The Warsaw Pact: a change of direction?', *RUSI Newsbrief*, vol. 9, no. 3, pp. 17–19.
RUSI (1989b), 'Are anti-tank weapons obsolete?', *RUSI Newsbrief*, vol. 9, no. 10, pp. 79–80.
Saperstein, Alvin M. (1988), 'Primer on non-provocative defense', *Arms Control*, vol. 9, no. 1, pp. 59–75.
Schemmer, Benjamin F. (1989), 'Army, Sec Def's office at loggerheads over anti-armour', *Armed Forces Journal International*, May, pp. 53–60.
Schulte, Heinz (1988), 'W. German army may lose up to 7 brigades', *Jane's Defence Weekly*, 26 November, p. 1327.
Scott, Harriet Fast, and Scott, William F. (1988), *Soviet Military Doctrine: Context, Formulation and Dissemination* (Boulder, Colo.: Westview).
Sigal, Leon V. (1983), 'No first use and NATO's nuclear posture', in John D. Steinbrunner and Leon V. Sigal (eds), *Alliance Security: NATO and the No First Use Question* (Washington, DC: Brookings), pp. 12–15.
Simpkin, Richard (1984), *Red Armour: An Examination of the Soviet Mobile Force Concept* (London: Brassey's).
Simpkin, Richard (1987), *Deep Battle: The Brainchild of Marshal Tukhachevskii* (London: Brassey's).
Snyder, G. (1961), *Deterrence and Defense* (Princeton, NJ: Princeton University Press).
Snyder, Jack (1987), 'The Gorbachev revolution: a waning of Soviet expansionism?', *International Security*, vol. 12, no. 3, pp. 93–131.
Starry, Gen. Donn A. (1978), 'A tactical evolution – FM 100–5', *Military Review*, August, pp. 2–11.
Starry, Gen. Donn A. (1981), 'Extending the battlefield', *Military Review*, March, pp. 31–50.

Starry, Gen. Donn A. (1983), 'To change an army', *Military Review*, March, pp. 20–27.
Statement on the Defence Estimates 1986, vol. 1 (1986) (London: HMSO).
Statement on the Defence Estimates 1987, vol. 1 (1987) (London: HMSO).
Statement on the Defence Estimates 1988, vol. 1 (1988) (London: HMSO).
Suvorov, Viktor (1981), *The Liberators: Inside the Soviet Army* (London: Hamish Hamilton).
Swan, Capt. Guy C. III (1986), 'Countering the daring thrust', *Military Review*, September, pp. 42–53.
Syrett, David (1977), 'Blitzkrieg, PGMs and Central Europe', *Military Review*, July.
Towell, Pat.(1984), 'Nunn loses round on burden sharing', *Congressional Quarterly Weekly Report*, vol. 42, no. 25, pp. 1480–1.
Third Report from the Defence Committee (1985), *Defence Commitments and Resources and the Defence Estimates 1985–6*, vol. 1, HC 37–I, (London: HMSO).
Thomson, Dr James A. (1989), 'An unfavourable situation: NATO and the conventional balance', in *The Changing Strategic Landscape: Part III*, Adelphi Paper No. 236 (London: IISS).
TRADOC (1976), 'TRADOC's reply', *Armed Forces Journal International*, October, p. 27.
TRADOC (1981), *AirLand Battle and Corps Operations – 1986*, Pam 525-5 (Fort Monroe, Va.: TRADOC).
Unterseher, Lutz (1989), *The Spider and the Web: the Case for a Pragmatic Defence Alternative* (Bonn: SAS).
Vayrynan, R. (1985), 'Introduction: towards a strategy of common security', in R. Vayrynan (ed.), *Policies for Common Security* (London: SIPRI/Taylor & Francis).
Vigor, Peter H. (1983), *Soviet Blitzkrieg Theory* (London: Macmillan).
Walker, Karen (1988), 'Setback for Joint STARS programme', *Jane's Defence Weekly*, 23 January, p. 101.
Waltz, Kenneth N. (1979), *Theory of International Politics* (Reading, Mass.: Addison-Wesley).
Walzer, Michael (1977), *Just and Unjust Wars: A Moral Argument with Historical Illustrations* (New York: Basic Books).
Warner, Edward L. III (1989), 'New thinking and old realities in Soviet defence policy', *Survival*, vol. 31, no. 1, pp. 13–33.
Watkins, Admiral James D. (1986), 'The Maritime Strategy', *US Naval Institute Proceedings*, special issue, January, pp. 2–17.
Wheeler, Nicholas J., and Booth, Ken (1987), 'Beyond the security dilemma: technology, strategy and international security', in Carl G. Jacobsen (ed.), *The Uncertain Course: New Weapons, Strategies and Mind-sets* (London: SIPRI/Oxford University Press).
Windass, Stan (1985), 'Essentials of defensive deterrence', in Stan Windass (ed.), *Avoiding Nuclear War: Common Security as a Strategy for the Defence of the West* (London: Brassey's) pp. 43–61.
WTO (1989), *Statement by the Committee of the Ministries of Defence of the Warsaw Treaty Member States: Correlation of the Relative Numerical*

BIBLIOGRAPHY

Strength of the Armed Forces and Armaments of the Warsaw Treaty Organization and the North Atlantic Treaty Organization in Europe and Adjacent Sea Areas (Berlin: Panovama DDR).

Zaloga, Steven J. (1987), 'Soviet reactive tank armour update', *Jane's Defence Weekly*, 1 August, p. 163.

Index

Active Defense 117–21, 123
adaptive dynamic model 81
Afghanistan, Soviet involvement in 10, 54
Afheldt, Horst 167–8, 174–7, 180
AirLand Battle 108, 116, 121–34, 161–2, 163
   evolution of 121–4
   debate over 129–34
air power 78–9, 98–100, 133, 143–4, 145, 169–71, 173
   offensive counter-air 153–4, 158
   see also tactical air power
Akhromeyev, Marshal 103–4
alternative defence: *see* common security, non-offensive defence, Soviet Union: new thinking
area defence xix, 174
armoured division equivalent (ADE) 73
arms control xviii, 9, 26
   see also CFE, SALT
ATGM (anti-tank guided munition) – *see* PGM
attrition-FEBA expansion model 81

Bagnall, General Sir Nigel 134–9, 148
   see also Corps Concept, NORTHAG concept of operations
Barbarossa, Operation 88
Blitzkrieg 12, 17, 25, 96, 98, 186
Bonin, Col. Bogislaw von 167
Brezhnev, Leonid 96
   Brezhnev doctrine 38
British army 36, 45
   see also Bagnall, Corps Concept, Farndale, NORTHAG concept of operations
Bulow, Andreas von 169, 174–7
burden-sharing 34–5

central front xix, 185–6
   military structure 31-2, 44–57
   geography 39–44
   urban sprawl 43, 102, 181

C3I (command, control, communications and intelligence) 69–70, 87, 102, 131, 144–5, 156, 161, 172
CFE (Conventional Forces in Europe talks) 59, 60, 66–8, 114, 142, 185
chemical weapons 122, 128, 133
common security 21–9
conventional balance – *see* military balance
confidence building measures (CBMs) 26–7
conventional defence xix, 8–12, 116ff.
conventional deterrence 14, 17–20
Corps Concept 116, 134–9, 141–9, 161–2, 163
   see also NORTHAG concept of operations
crisis stability 15, 100
cruise missiles 16, 35, 168
Czechoslovakia 51, 54, 56

deep battle 122, 126–7, 132–3
   see also FOFA
deep operations (Soviet) – see OMG
defensive defence 108, 109, 111–13, 171
   see also NOD
deterrence – *see* conventional deterrence, flexible response, nuclear deterrence
disarmament – *see* nuclear disarmament

East Germany 37, 51, 54
Eastern Europe xviii, xix, 37, 38–9, 185–6
   see also Czechoslovakia, East Germany, Hungary, Poland
echeloning 50, 122, 149–50
   see also Soviet Union: military doctrine
Epstein, Joshua M. 81
escalation 2–6, 8, 14, 16, 97
ET (emerging technology) 149, 153–9

Farndale, General Sir Martin 140
fire-barrier defence 168, 174–7

199

firepower 88–9, 92, 98–9, 118, 120, 124, 175
flexible response 1–8, 14
FM 100–5 – *see* Active Defense and AirLand Battle
FOFA (follow-on forces attack) 108, 116, 149–62, 163
forward defence 36, 97, 135
France 34
　position in NATO 37
　military forces on the central front 47–8

Germany – *see* East Germany, West Germany
Gorbachev, Mikhail xvii, 104ff., 171
　speech to the United Nations, December 1988 9, 58, 109, 113
　see also Soviet Union: new thinking
Great Patriotic War 86–91

Hannig, Norbert – *see* fire barrier defence
Hungary 52

INF (intermediate range nuclear forces) 7, 168
　see also cruise; Pershing II

Jaruzelski, General Wojcieck 171
Just war – *see* nuclear weapons: morality

Kruschev, Nikita 92–5, 97

Lanchester, F. W., laws of combat 79–81
logistics 69–70, 172–3, 181
　see also sustainability
Loser, Major-General Jochen 168, 172, 174–7

Maginot Line 36, 135, 142–3
manoeuvre 36, 71, 89–90, 92, 120, 124, 130–2, 136, 142–6, 165, 175, 186
　see also Blitzkrieg
military balance 9–10, 59–83, 141–2
　force levels in Europe 44–57, 62–8
　force: space ratios 82
　see also reserves
mines 144
mobile group – *see* OMG
mobilisation – *see* reserves
Moller, Bjorn 169–71
Muller, Albrecht von 169, 172, 174–7

NATO 31–7, 185–6
　unity of 16

resource constraints 9, 10, 35–6, 69, 158–9, 160
US-European relations 33–5, 160
US commitment to NATO xviii, 3
German unification 36–7
offensive operations 125, 129–30, 145–6
　see also central front, flexible response, forward defence, NATO strategy
NATO strategy xviii–xix, 1–21, 116ff., 125, 185–6
　European attitudes to 2–5
　see also deterrence, flexible response, forward defence
no first use 14–21, 166
NOD (non-offensive defence) xix, 27, 112, 163–84, 186
non-provocative defence – *see* NOD
NORTHAG (northern army group) concept of operations 139–49, 161–2, 163
no-target principle 166
nuclear deterrence xviii, 1–21, 22–3, 166, 182
　raising the nuclear threshold 8–12
　minimum deterrence 13–21
　see also flexible response, INF, NATO strategy, no first use, nuclear weapons
nuclear disarmament 23, 27, 110–11, 166
nuclear weapons 15–16, 99, 122, 166
　morality 13
　legal restrictions on use 13–14
　see also cruise missiles, INF, Pershing II

OCA (offensive counter-air) – *see* air power
Ogarkov, Marshal 103–4
OMG (Operational Manoeuvre Group) 100–2, 135
　mobile group 90
operational level of war 91, 127–8

Palme Commission 21
　see also common security
permanently operating factors 87–91
Pershing II 16, 35, 168
PGMs (precision guided munitions) 98, 117, 119, 167–9, 170–1, 174–5, 178–9, 180
Poland 51–2, 54, 56

INDEX

Reagan, Ronald 34
  US defence build-up under xvii
Realism 21–2
reasonable sufficiency 108–11
REFORGER (reinforcement of forces in Germany) 48, 76
reinforcements – *see* reserves
reserves 47–8, 54–5, 56, 75–8, 147
  see also REFORGER
Rogers, General Bernard 8, 150, 185

SALT (Strategic Arms Limitation Talks) xvii
second cold war xvii–xviii
security dilemma 23–5, 105, 166
Soviet threat xvii–xviii, 85–6, 105, 113–14, 185
Soviet Union xvii, 37, 85–115, 143–4
  military doctrine 17, 85–115, 118, 121
  nuclear strategy and nuclear war 91, 92–7, 103, 105, 110–11
  conventional war 92, 96–104
  relations with the WTO 38–9, 48–50
  'revolution in military affairs' 92–5
  new political thinking xvii–xviii, 105–8
  economic problems 105
  see also Akhromeyev, air power, Barbarossa, Brezhnev, defensive defence, Gorbachev, Great Patriotic War, Kruschev, Ogarkov, permanently operating factors, reasonable sufficiency, Stalin
spider and web defence 171–7
Stalin, Joseph 87–92
Starry, General Donn A. 122–4

surprise 71, 77–8, 88, 94, 100, 125, 143
sustainability 9, 131–2, 147–8

tactical air power 10, 78–9, 89, 99–100
  see also air power
TRADOC (Training and Doctrine Command) 117–34, 150
TVD (theatre of military operations) 49, 104

United States
  forces in Europe 3, 45, 47–8, 62–8, 116
  commitment to NATO xviii, 3, 4–5, 33–5
  army doctrine 117–34
  see also Active Defense, AirLand Battle, burden-sharing
Unterseher, Lutz – *see* spider and web defence

Vietnam war 10, 117

Weizsacker, Carl Friedrich von 167
West Germany 36–7, 139–40, 163
  see also central front
WTO (Warsaw Treaty Organisation 37–9, 59–83, 171
  political structure 38–9, 48
  military organisation 48–57
  readiness of forces 54–5, 75–6, 78
  reliability 38–9, 57, 83, 102
  morale and training 61, 62, 102
  standardisation of equipment 61
  1987 Berlin meeting 171
  see also Soviet Union